100 THINGS
MISSOURI FANS
SHOULD KNOW & DO
BEFORE THEY DIE

Dave Matter

TRIUMPH
BOOKS

Library of Congress Cataloging-in-Publication Data

Names: Matter, Dave, author.
Title: 100 things Missouri fans should know & do before they die / Dave
    Matter ; foreword by Brock Olivo.
Other titles: One hundred things Missouri fans should know and do before they
    die
Description: Chicago, Illinois : Triumph Books, 2018. | Series: 100
    things...fans should know
Identifiers: LCCN 2018004262 | ISBN 9781629371825 (paperback)
Subjects: LCSH: University of Missouri—Sports—Miscellanea. | BISAC: SPORTS
    & RECREATION / General. | TRAVEL / United States / Midwest / West North
    Central (IA, KS, MN, MO, ND, NE, SD).
Classification: LCC GV691.U5644 M37 2018 | DDC 796.04/30977829—dc23
LC record available at https://lccn.loc.gov/2018004262

This book is available in quantity at special discounts for your group or organization. For further information, contact:

Triumph Books LLC
814 North Franklin Street
Chicago, Illinois 60610
(312) 337-0747
www.triumphbooks.com

Printed in U.S.A.
ISBN: 978-1-62937-182-5
Design by Patricia Frey
Photos courtesy of AP Images

To Molly, Jackson, Connor, and Will—my home team.

Contents

Foreword

Our Family

"Brock, would you be willing to write the foreword?" *Answer him! Say something. Tell him how honored you are.* Needless to say, it was an honor and a great surprise to be asked to write this foreword. To be culled from the long list of decorated football alumni who also call themselves Missouri Tigers is very humbling. It's important that the reader understands that any number of us could be writing this because what *really* makes playing for Mizzou special is more than meets the eye, and I'd be remiss if I didn't share it with you.

It's not the Rock M or Truman the Tiger, not the 125 years of tradition or the history of great coaches and All-American players, not the decal on our helmets or the 70,000 strong in attendance on Saturdays. It's not even the players on our sideline. Rather, it's when you take all of the aforementioned things and add them up, time and again. They always equal the same thing: *family.* That's what makes playing here so special. And what is the fundamental building block of a good, strong family? It's *love.* Our Mizzou family is no exception; and our love manifests itself in the locker room, the weight room, the training room, the Total Person Program, and beyond.

Why am I talking about family and love in the foreword of a book about a Division I football program? Because when you dig down to the core of what's behind the saying "the time of my life," it's love, and love exists in the game of football. Examples include encouragement from teammates; the stoic, tough love from a coach; and the adoring love from fans. Most of us weren't aware of how remarkable that love was, even though we were living it intensely on a daily basis. Some of us keep it alive every day; others are indifferent to those memories…or so we think. Then we find ourselves in a restaurant 600 miles away from Columbia and we see Mizzou on TV, or we're at a bowl party and the Tigers are on, or we're at the coffee machine at work and people are talking about the Missouri Tigers…*our* Missouri Tigers. That's when we flash back to our days spent schlepping across campus with sore legs and hips, bruised and scabbed up from head to toe with the pressure of academia, the media, family, friends, girlfriends, coaches, and our self-pride. As we think about those times, we realize we've never felt so alive and so driven and so fraternal with another group of people in our lives. It's at that moment that we remember why we chose to become Tigers. No one cares if we were a starter or the last guy off the bench—all that counts is that we were there.

That's why any one of my fellow alumni could be here helping Dave tell our story with the same passion and the same love, and I know most of us would end up saying the same things. We have a certain amount of Tigers DNA inside of us by the time we take our helmets off after that last game. For some of us, it may lie there, dormant for months, years, maybe even decades, before we tap back into it. But we feel it there, and when we need it, we can harness it anytime, anywhere. For me, some of those moments have been: hugging a former teammate I haven't seen in 20 years, or holding his son in my arms while I bragged to him about how good his daddy was. Shaking the hands of the players from back in the 1940s and '50s who built the foundation of the program. Going on vacation to Italy with Corby Jones almost two decades after we took our last snap together, and watching my five-year-old daughter, Sofia, look at him as if he were a god. Crowding around the TV with other Tigers faithful to cheer on former Tigers who are playing in the NFL. Rallying around Dave Rowe when he was diagnosed with cancer and watching him return to the field. That DNA, that lifeblood, is being able to tell my children someday that I played for Larry Smith, the coach *Sports Illustrated* called "the man you would most want your son to play for." It's breaking down all barriers of race, religion, age, class, and any other excuse for dividing us. It's about being part of something much bigger than any individual or accolade, and it goes beyond the painted lines on Faurot Field. It's about *us*.

Our Field

When I hung up the phone with Dave that evening he called to ask me to write this foreword, I looked at my wife, Federica, and she knew it was an emotional moment for me. Even though she was raised in Italy, where American football is played but widely considered a barbaric and superfluous hobby, she understood why I needed a Kleenex right then and there. I would have one more opportunity to talk about Mizzou football, and she knew how much it meant to me.

She has yet to attend a game at Faurot Field, but even she knows how special that place is to the roughly 3,000 men who have had the privilege of wearing the Black and Gold. Faurot is our present-day gladiator's arena. It's where the culmination of more than a century of tradition is celebrated in a unified *roar* from some of the most fervent fans in college football. "M-I-Z!" "Z-O-U!" The last time I heard that chant as a Missouri Tiger was on November 15, 1997, and I still get goose bumps as I write about it now. There are few places in the world that can get a Tigers fan's blood pumping like Faurot Field on a Saturday afternoon in the fall. As a player, it's even more surreal when you feel it down on the field. And I mean *feel* instead of *hear*.

It takes the right chemistry (time of day, time of year, opponent, weather, rankings) to feel Faurot at its best, and when that happens, it's nothing short of awesome. Bob Stanley, who was a pillar in our football program for many years as the head equipment manager, recently recounted a story to me about our home field. He told me that when the No. 1–ranked Nebraska Cornhuskers came to Columbia on November 8, 1997, to play an unranked 6–3 Tigers team, he left the locker room for the field a little sooner than usual because there was something extraordinary about the vibe in the air. As Bob made his way to the MU sideline, he was greeted by longtime fan and supporter Fred DeMarco, who had taken his usual post near the Mizzou bench. Bob noticed Fred's eyes were a little glassy and he asked him if he was all right. Fred told him how for the first time in more than a decade, the Missouri Tigers mattered and they were finally in a game that mattered. That meant our fans mattered, our concession stand workers mattered, our maintenance crew mattered. *We mattered!* Fred had a feeling there would be something different about that night, and he was right. The proverbial corner was about to be turned.

Knowing those two guys the way I do, I can imagine their conversation, and now *my* eyes are glassy. And I can recall what my teammates and I were doing in that moment, in the calm before the storm, in our locker room underneath the growing crowd above us. Deep down, with a quiet confidence, we were preparing to validate Fred DeMarco's premonition. Minutes later, we came bursting out of those doors and we did just that. The electricity Faurot Field produced that Saturday night was the stuff we had dreamed about as kids, growing up as Tigers fans, hoping maybe one day *we* could be the catalyst for renewing the excitement of years past.

Our Voice

There was a sophomore journalism major in the stands that November evening in 1997 who mattered as well—Dave Matter— and no one is more qualified to write a book about Missouri athletics than him. He's familiar with the sounds and smells of our stadium. He's met the greats from the glory days of the 1960s, '70s, and '80s, and the stars who have put Mizzou on the map again since Larry Smith and then Gary Pinkel took the reins as successive head coaches. If names such as Paul Christman, Pete Woods, Eric

Wright, and Phil Bradley aren't familiar to neo–Mizzou fans, they will be now. Dave knows the fabric of a Missouri Tiger, and he has followed the ebb and flow of Ol' Mizzou over the years. He was there for the lopsided losses, the near-upsets and, finally, a reason to write about what makes us fall in love with college football over and over again in our country: the Cinderella story. Every generation of college football has its dynasties and its doormats. The paradigmatic shifts in football (to steal a phrase from a Thomas Kuhn book) are what keep people craving the next great underdog story. Mizzou football has been born again on different occasions over the past century, and Dave will walk Tigers fans through the winding halls of our heartbreaks, our triumphs, and our traditions, as *one of us*.

—Brock Olivo
Missouri Tiger, 1994–97

Acknowledgments

One person who will never get to read this book helped make it possible. In 1998 I was halfway to a journalism degree at Mizzou and landed a dream job for an aspiring sportswriter in need of beer money. (Mom and Dad, beer is what we called books at Mizzou. Trust me.) *Columbia Daily Tribune* sports editor Kent Heitholt gave me a chance to write about sports, and unlike the countless other Mizzou J-school students scurrying around campus covering the Tigers, I got paid—not much but enough to stock up on all those books. Two years later, Kent promoted me to full-time, to cover the MU football program. I was 22 and in no way worthy of the gig, but I am eternally grateful. Kent was taken from us a year later but will never be forgotten.

Since then I've worked for editors who in their own unique ways supported my work, turned me loose on the beat, and pushed me toward a higher standard: Joe Walljasper at the *Tribune* and Roger Hensley, Cameron Hollway, and Mike Smith at the *Post-Dispatch*.

This project required numerous fresh interviews and many hours spent foraging the archives of the *Post-Dispatch* and *Columbia Tribune*. Several former Mizzou athletes, coaches, and broadcasters were especially gracious with their time, notably Norm Stewart, Jon Sundvold, Gary Link, Tom Dore, Kim English, Ed Blaine, Corby Jones, Craig Heimburger, Nip Weisenfels, Roger Wehrli, Howard Richards, Phil Bradley, Pete Woods, and Mike Kelly. A special thanks, too, to Gary Pinkel, who was gracious enough to have me as his tag-team partner for his 2017 autobiography, *The 100-Yard Journey*.

T.J. Moe, one of the great go-to quotes in my time on the beat, pitched in with his own chapter about Mizzou's epic 2010 win over Oklahoma. And, of course, there's Brock Olivo. To no surprise, the former running back poured his heart into a beautiful foreword with vivid detail and raw emotion. I contend it's the best writing in the book.

Nobody deserves more gratitude for making this project possible than the person who sacrifices most for my career. Molly Matter could write her own book on how to survive being married to a beat writer. With incredible will and patience, she guts through the road trips, the missed holidays, the interrupted dinners, the ever-present iPhone, the tweets, the texts, and the endless deadlines. I could never repay her love, support, and stiff upper lip when all hell breaks loose on the beat in the middle of date night. For our twin boys, Connor and Jackson, your spirit, curiosity, and creativity zap me with inspiration and energy on a daily basis. Just make sure to consult me before becoming journalists. The same goes for our youngest, Will Matter, who came along while I was working on this project in 2016. Mom and Dad, thank you for leaving me the *Post-Dispatch* sports page to devour every morning and supporting my dream to see my byline there someday.

Introduction

In early 2015, the folks at Triumph Books contacted me about writing this book.

My first thought: *Do we need to torment Mizzou faithful with another 80,000 words on their star-crossed athletics history?*

To be fair, Mizzou fans have endured lifetimes of anguish since the school started keeping score in football in 1890 and in basketball 16 years later. There was the Fifth Down, along with its evil siblings the Flea Kicker, Bert Coan, 4.9 seconds, and Norfolk State. And they're all chronicled within these pages. I promise, it's not intended as an exercise in sports masochism, but these are the moments that make up the Mizzou fan DNA. If your heart is black and gold, it's covered with a layer of scar tissue from breaking so many times.

But for every black cloud that's hovered over Boone County, there are powerful bursts of light peeking from behind, often overpowering the darkness. Brilliant athletes, colorful coaches, unmistakable characters, and moments of glory that gave Mizzou diehards goose bumps, captured their hearts, and filled their memory banks for eternity. You want proof of the human spirit's resiliency? Consider the Mizzou football fans who rode on Woody's Wagon, sat through the Norman Conquest, let Shevin Wiggins and Matt Davison crush their souls, and still came back each and every fall believing this would be the season the sleeping giant opened his eyes, climbed out of bed, and thundered his way to a championship.

Maybe this is the year, right?

Over the course of writing this book, I covered what might be remembered as the most tumultuous 12 months Mizzou athletics has ever seen. Longtime athletics director Mike Alden stepped down. The men's basketball team had its worst season in 48 years. The football team's starting quarterback was suspended not once, not twice, but three times . . . and then kicked off the team for good. Football players joined a campus protest and staged a boycott of all team activities. Gary Pinkel, the school's stoic leader in football victories, was diagnosed with cancer and retired from coaching. The basketball program imposed sanctions for NCAA violations. Bill Self and the Kansas state legislature annexed the city of Columbia and changed Mizzou's colors to pink and purple.

OK, the last one didn't happen, but you'd believe it, right?

It's time for another layer of scar tissue, folks, but in these pages you'll read about far more than Mizzou misery. Legendary coaches and players, historic games, triumphant moments, unique traditions. They all make up the last century-plus of Mizzou football and men's basketball. National championships? Not a one, but it's been a thrill ride from one decade to the next.

My favorite interview through the course of this project came on a summer afternoon with former Mizzou hoops player and forever Mizzou diehard Gary Link, the team's longtime radio analyst. Link told a great story about the 1982 NCAA tournament. He was 10 years out of college and running his family's construction business in St. Louis. Norm Stewart brought one of his most talented teams to the Midwest regional in St. Louis. The Tigers had an easy path to the program's first Final Four. Link came to the game by himself. He climbed the stairs at the Checkerdome and watched the Tigers lose to Houston, two rounds short of the Final Four. He wept.

He said, "I thought, *Man, if this team can't get there . . .*"

More than 30 years later, when you saw Linker courtside on game day—he was the one wildly flapping his hands as he set the scene on the radio—you wouldn't find a bigger believer that something good was right around the corner. His Tigers always had a chance, up until the final buzzer. He saw the rays of gold behind every black cloud.

"Oh my gosh, absolutely," he said. "We're down eight with two minutes to go; I believe we can get three stops and win the game."

Are Mizzou fans cursed? Nahhh. They're just patient and loyal and hopeful . . . and voracious readers. Enjoy.

The Jut-Jawed Thin Man from Mountain Grove

In 1995 Don Faurot's heart gave out, but for parts of eight decades, it belonged to Mizzou. Faurot wasn't the University of Missouri's first football coach. He doesn't have the most wins or the greatest winning percentage in team history. But his legacy transcends that of any coach who came before or after.

The pride of Mountain Grove, Missouri, Faurot built Missouri football into a championship program in the 1930s and '40s, but a win-loss record could never solely capture his contributions to the state's flagship school—and the game of football. Not that Faurot's was too shabby at 101–79–10 over 19 seasons.

Faurot was one of the sport's great innovators, a visionary who gave life to an offensive philosophy that later won countless games for other coaches for generations. He was a longtime administrator with a keen business sense and acquired knack for hiring coaches. He was, if nothing else, a Mizzou lifer, a man tethered to his football program, his athletics department, and his school that he helped nurture for decades. And by all accounts, Faurot led with unmatched grace and class.

Upon Faurot's retirement from coaching after the 1956 season, the *New York Times* suggested that the name of the split T be changed to the Faurot T as an homage to its "originator and strategist." But despite the Gray Lady's hopes, the nickname for Faurot's offensive creation never stuck. Others adopted the option-based system and took it to greater heights on the national scale, but those who knew Faurot best could fully appreciate his mark on college football at large, not just at Mizzou.

"To this day, if someone was capable of doing this, if they gave me 22 players, no assistant coaches, no telephone, just 22 players and to play another coach with 22 players of equal ability, the one coach I would fear the most was Don Faurot," Hall of Fame Mizzou coach Dan Devine told the *Columbia Daily Tribune* when Faurot died in 1995. "He could coach every position."

Faurot's family moved around to different parts of Missouri during his childhood and for a while lived in Columbia. Faurot, who lost parts of two fingers on his right hand during a farming accident as a young man, would find his way to Rollins Field to watch the Tigers practice during his time in Columbia. The Faurots later moved back to Mountain Grove, which didn't have a high school football team, but Don wound up back at Mizzou for college, where he played baseball and basketball, ran track, and eventually joined the football team, lettering in 1923–24.

After college, Faurot got into coaching and spent nine years at Kirksville Teachers College, a school later known as Northeast Missouri State and then Truman State. Faurot won 63 games in nine years there, including a 26–6 takedown of Missouri in 1933 in Columbia.

Faurot had turned down an offer to join Missouri's staff as an assistant after the 1931 season, but in 1935, he returned to his alma mater to revive a program that had collapsed under the failed Frank Carideo regime. Three weeks and three wins into his first season, Faurot had eclipsed Carideo's victory total from the previous three seasons. The Tigers improved immediately on Faurot's watch but didn't really take off until quarterback Paul Christman's arrival in 1938. The centerpiece to Faurot's offense, Christman was Missouri's first national star, leading the Tigers to the 1939 Big Six Conference title. Christman finished among the Heisman Trophy's top five vote-getters in both 1939 and 1940. Faurot always credited Christman for turning around a program that hadn't won a conference championship since 1927.

But Faurot figured out how to sustain the Tigers' success after Christman, who would remain the school's most prolific passer for nearly 30 years after his departure. Without a capable passer on the roster and loads of running backs, Faurot figured his best chance to attack defenses was on the ground. For years he'd used the single-wing offense popularized by Pop Warner. That wouldn't work without a skilled passer. In pro football, George Halas's Chicago Bears were punishing opponents with the T-formation. In the college ranks, Clark Shaughnessy mastered the system at Stanford. In 1940 Halas and Shaughnessy rode the T to championships in the NFL and college football, respectively. The T quickly became the most popular offense at both levels of the sport.

But not at Missouri. Faurot didn't like the T-formation's heavy use of motion. He wanted more space between his linemen to create running lanes for his fleet of backs. And unlike in most other offenses, Faurot's ball carriers would include the quarterback. With wider splits between the linemen—a foot between the center and guards, two feet between the guards and tackles, and cavernous three-foot gaps between the tackles and ends—the quarterback in Faurot's split T would take the snap and have three options on most plays: hand off to a halfback for a quick-hitting plunge up the middle, keep the ball on a sprint down the line and around the corner, or pitch to a trailing tailback who could run around a convoy of blockers or throw downfield to a streaking end. Over time, the split T would evolve into the wishbone, veer, and triple-option attacks that ruled generations of college football.

Defenses had few answers for Faurot's invention as the Tigers led the nation in rushing in 1941 and Tigers running back Bob Steuber led the nation in yards per carry. With Steuber, Harry Ice, and Faurot's endless collection of runners dashing behind star blockers Darold Jenkins and Mike Fitzgerald, Faurot's system was born as the Tigers won consecutive Big Six championships.

Faurot left Missouri during World War II, after the 1942 season, and the split T went with him. While serving as the head coach at Iowa Pre-Flight School during the war, Faurot taught the split T to his assistant coaches, Jim Tatum and Bud Wilkinson. They took the system with them to their subsequent coaching stops, most notably at Maryland and Oklahoma, respectively. Unlike Faurot, both would win national championships running his offense.

But Faurot had already secured his legacy at Missouri by then. He returned to coach the Tigers from 1946 to 1956, though he never won another league title. Faurot resumed his post as athletics director when he returned from the war, a challenge perhaps greater than coaching the Tigers. As AD, Faurot was forced to tackle enormous debt in the athletics department, as much as $500,000 in the early years of his administration. To pay off the debt, Faurot scheduled nonconference road games that paid handsomely, including nine games at Ohio State from 1939 to 1949. The Tigers won just one of those contests, but they helped clear the books and boost a budget that grew from $70,000 in 1935 to $1.7 million when Faurot retired as AD in 1967.

As AD, Faurot handpicked some coaches who would go down as all-time greats at Mizzou: football's Dan Devine, baseball's John "Hi" Simmons, basketball's Sparky Stalcup, and track's Tom Botts. Simmons and Botts both delivered national championships to Mizzou. And like Faurot, Devine and Simmons have athletic facilities named in their honor.

In 1972 the playing surface at Memorial Stadium was named in Faurot's honor and a statue of his likeness was erected outside the north concourse, with the following epitaph, written by *St. Louis Post-Dispatch* icon and Mizzou historian Bob Broeg:

> Here stands the symbol of Ol' Mizzou, famed "Thin Man" from Mountain Grove, a boy who helped build this stadium and a football coach who filled it with victories

and fresh hopes. Faurot overcame boyhood mishap that cost him the first two fingers at the middle joint. Gutty, jut-jawed guy lettered in baseball at Missouri, captained the basketball team and punted as a 148-pound linebacker for top-rated 1924 Tigers.

Mastered in agriculture, but never left football. He head-coached Kirksville Teachers nine spectacular seasons and returned in 1935 to Missouri, which was embarrassed in defeat and debt.

Don quickly solved both with vigorous home-state recruiting and manfully over-scheduled on the road for bigger receipts. Winning built bowl teams and a need to super-structure the stadium, now Faurot Field.

Old coach's greatest gridiron accomplishment in 19 seasons was his creation of a unique Split-T formation that featured celebrated quarterback option.

Although widely sought, intensely loyal, Coach Faurot never left MU until someone up there wanted another Boy Scout.

Into his 10th decade, Faurot still parked his lawn chair at the Mizzou practice fields in the early 1990s to watch the Tigers go through drills. He never missed a home game and occasionally exercised with the players while maintaining an office at the team facility, across the street from the field that bore his name.

Faurot, inducted into the College Football Hall of Fame in 1961, died in 1995 from congestive heart failure. The patriarch of Mizzou football and a trendsetter for the game at large, Faurot forever changed the school and the sport.

His statue remains a touchstone from Mizzou's past, a meeting place for fans before games—not unlike its bronze peer to the east, Busch Stadium's crouched slugger, Stan Musial—and marks the entrance for every visitor from near and far to the House That Don Built.

"It's hard to imagine one individual who had more of an impact on the University of Missouri and intercollegiate athletics than Don Faurot," Mizzou AD Joe Castiglione once said. "What he did transcends time, and it is something that will virtually last forever."

2 The Storm from Shelbyville

Coach Norm Stewart sat over a bowl of soup on a fall afternoon in 2015 and pondered the question: *A hundred years from now, how should I be remembered?*

It had been 16 years since Stewart coached his last game at Missouri. With 731 wins on his record and eight conference championships, nothing mattered much beyond the chowder under his nose and his weekend plans with his wife, Virginia.

"Hell, nobody here's going to remember anybody 100 years from now," he said. "You know? I don't worry about that."

Stormin' Norm could still bring the thunder.

"My wife and I both…she worked and still does—we worked hard."

That's why Stewart, a bit slower but still sharp into his eighties, didn't apologize for spending his winters in Palm Springs or for his family's lavish vacations to Europe or China or Africa. If a friend needled Stewart for his postretirement lifestyle, the coach jabbed back. Stewart said, "I tell him, 'Hey, you son of a bitch, for five years I lived in a stucco house. To get it cool, we had to run water over the top of the roof. My wife raised children and about went crazy because she was confined to our house. You pay your way.'"

For 32 years along the Mizzou sideline, Stewart paid his way with wins, championships and, many nights, peerless coaching as he presided over his alma mater's greatest teams and greatest players. Taking over a program that had badly decayed after his playing days in the 1950s, Stewart guided the Tigers to 634 wins in 32 seasons, eight Big 8 regular-season titles, and six tournament championships. He took 16 teams to the NCAA tournament and produced 29 players drafted by the NBA.

Only a couple goals went unaccomplished during Stewart's celebrated career: the Tigers never reached a Final Four on his watch, let alone won a national championship. As of 2018, there were 21 head coaches who had won 700 Division I games. Only three others failed to make a Final Four.

If that shortcoming bothered Stewart as he reached his eighties, he didn't show it. He said:

> This is the woulda, coulda, shoulda deal, but had we won in '76—[when] we had a good chance to win the national championship—or had we won in '80, I always thought once we knocked down one pin, it would be like winning the Big 8. Once we did that once, then we won eight of them.
>
> Once you do something, and your organization is sound and you've got a good base, you can repeat those things and stay up there. But obviously we never figured out how to win that national championship. I've never been disappointed about that because I had such great players. They were really good. They could play and they understood the game. But more importantly, there are 15 of them that live in [Columbia]. I always told them, "If you're going to live in the town where you played, you better be more than a damn player. You better know how to conduct yourself."

Because where you were from always meant just as much to Stewart as where you were going.

Born in Leonard, Missouri, Stewart grew up in nearby Shelbyville, the youngest of four siblings. His father, Kenneth, worked for Standard Oil. The family was closer to poor than rich. Stewart prefers "disadvantaged." "But we always had a nice home," he said. "I couldn't have asked for a better childhood."

At Shelbyville High, Stewart played basketball for the school's superintendent, C.J. Kessler, the man who convinced Stewart to stay out of trouble and redirect his energy to the basketball court. It paid off with All-State honors and interest from college programs. Kessler tried talking close friend and Indiana coach Branch McCracken into signing Stewart, but the Hoosiers balked. Instead, McCracken suggested Kessler send his star player to Sparky Stalcup at Missouri. "Branch told him to send me to Missouri," Stewart said, "so I came to Missouri."

As simple as that. From 1953 to 1956, Stewart scored more points than all but one player in team history. He also pitched for the baseball team during its 1954 national championship season. Or, as Stewart wrote in his memoir, "I was a thrower on a team that had a great pitching staff."

After a few games with the NBA's St. Louis Hawks, Stewart returned to Missouri to help Stalcup coach the basketball team, which led to a head-coaching offer at Iowa State Teacher's College, later known as Northern Iowa. There in Cedar Falls, Iowa, Stewart won 97 games in six years. "I was happy there," he said.

The program at his alma mater, though, had started to crumble under the disastrous Bob Vanatta regime, including consecutive three-win seasons in 1966 and '67. Missouri athletics director Don Faurot reached out to Stewart about interviewing for the job, but so did an influential politician, Morris E. Osborn, the former Missouri speaker of the house...who was from Shelbyville.

"Morris was a very elegant speaker," Stewart recalled. "In those days, there were speakers and there were talkers. Morris was a speaker. He'd say, 'Norm, this job, I think, would be good for you.' I had a crew cut at the time. When he finished he said, 'Norman, have you let your hair grow out yet?' I said, 'No, Morris, but I could.' He said, 'I think that would be an excellent idea.' The butch haircut was not to his liking."

But the young coach was. At 32, Stewart took over the Missouri program, and after a 10–16 debut season, the Tigers soon pounced on the Big 8 behind stars of the 1970s John Brown, Al Eberhard, and Willie Smith.

On offense, the Tigers ran Stewart's variation of the triple post or triangle offense popularized by Tex Winter at Kansas State. It was a disciplined offense that wasn't easy to learn.

"Most of Coach Stewart's teams, when they were good, they were usually junior and senior teams because by then they understood all the nuances of that offense," said former guard Jon Sundvold, who played more games for Stewart (128 from 1979 to 1983) than any player during his 32 seasons. "It was the junior-senior teams that knew how to take advantage of defenses that tried to stop certain things on that offense."

On defense, Stewart's system was an unyielding brand of man-to-man. "We would never switch," said former player Gary Link, who played for Stewart from 1971 to 1974. "We'd go over the top of everything."

Stewart demanded toughness, and his best teams reflected his personality. They didn't flinch in the most hostile settings, and embraced chances to play on the Big 8's biggest stages. Not every high school star was mentally equipped to play for the taskmaster.

How did Stewart motivate his players? "Out of fear," Link said. "To be real honest, you didn't want to let your teammates down and you didn't want to let him down. He was hard. We all had our fathers. He was never a father figure. We looked at him as a coach.

That's what he was supposed to be. He was very demanding, but he never asked you to do something you couldn't do."

Link continued, "He had different sets of rules for different players. He'd make it very clear at the beginning of the year: 'John Brown and Al Eberhard, they're our two best players. If anyone has any problem with that, deal with me. I'm the coach. I expect more from them, too.'"

Stewart's best players, his most loyal players, thrived in that environment. "I loved it," Link said. "Nothing was left to chance. You knew right where you stood. He's Shelbyville, Missouri. What you see is what you get."

"One thing I probably admired most about him was he never took a day off," Sundvold recalled. "There was never a day where he didn't give you something to challenge you to get better, no matter if you were the last player on the team or the All-American. I never felt like I had a day off until I graduated and turned in my stuff. He was always coaching."

Stewart was at his best on the road, whether sparring with Oklahoma's Billy Tubbs at Lloyd Noble Center or absorbing chants of "Sit down, Norm" at Kansas's Allen Fieldhouse. "When you were a junior or senior and went to Allen Fieldhouse, it was like a day off," said Sundvold, whose class won back-to-back games in Lawrence in 1982 and '83. "It didn't matter what the students were going to yell at me, because at least I'm not at practice with the old guy. He liked that. He liked having tough, ornery kids on the road. We were his guys."

"Back then, [it wasn't] like it is now, where guys have headphones on [during warmups] and everyone knows each other," Link said. "There were rivalries. When you played KU or Oklahoma, if he'd catch you looking down at the other team before the game, he'd tell you, 'You want to play for us or for them?'"

Stewart's psychological ploys became part of his legend. At the 1972 Volunteer Classic in Knoxville, Tennessee, Stewart didn't like the pregame NBA-style introductions, so before the championship game against host Tennessee, he told his five starters to scatter to different corners of the arena so the spotlight operator couldn't find them. "The fans started booing and going crazy before the game even started," Link said. "Coach told us, 'We've got them right where we want them.' We won the damn tournament and they never invited us back."

Stewart's success continued into the 1980s with four straight Big 8 titles, led by Sundvold, Steve Stipanovich, and Ricky Frazier. The Tigers began to reinvent their style in the late 1980s with prolific scorers Derrick Chievous, Doug Smith, Anthony Peeler, and assistant coach Rich Daly's convoy of Detroit imports. More Big 8 championships and NCAA tournament heartbreak ensued. Stewart's teams won the league's regular-season crown in 1987, 1990, and 1994 but never got closer to the biggest prize than the Elite Eight.

In a 21-month span, two major developments forever shaped Stewart's career. On February 9, 1989, Stewart collapsed on a flight to Oklahoma, forcing an emergency landing in Oklahoma City. He was initially diagnosed with ulcers, but in Columbia, doctors discovered colon cancer. "I remember telling Virginia, 'Don't spend the insurance money yet,'" Stewart later wrote. He underwent surgery to remove a tumor and missed the rest of the season while Daly coached the Tigers to the Big 8 tournament title and a couple wins in the NCAA tournament.

Stewart returned for the following season, but another form of adversity struck the program: an NCAA investigation into recruiting violations. In 1990 the Tigers replaced four starters but climbed to No. 1 in the national polls and enjoyed one of the best regular seasons in team history. But after another quick NCAA tournament exit—this time to Northern Iowa, of all teams—the NCAA finally dropped the hammer in the fall of 1990 after a two-year investigation. The sentence: two years probation, a postseason ban for 1991, and recruiting restrictions.

But Stewart endured, leading the Tigers back to the NCAA tournament from 1992 to 1995, including an eighth Big 8 regular-season crown in 1994 with a 14–0 run through conference play.

As the Big 8 became the Big 12 in 1996, Stewart's program began to sputter, missing the NCAA tournament for three straight years for the first time since 1973 to 1975. They returned to the bracket in 1999, but after another first-round loss, Stewart stepped down on April 1. He was 64 and the seventh-winningest coach in major college basketball history.

Athletics director Mike Alden had been on the job less than a year, and many wondered if Stewart's decision to retire was his own. At the time, Stewart insisted nobody was pushing him out. Not Alden. Not boosters. Not campus administration. "I was sad," said Link, who worked in the athletics department. "To me, it didn't feel like he went out on his own terms. I don't know that. But I guess I wish he would've had one more really good year. Five years earlier we were 28–4…. It very well could have been his call, but just knowing how competitive he is and all the successes he had with all the great teams he had…"

Those competitive instincts were still there at 80. Back to that soup bowl in 2015. I asked him, "When you stepped down, did you think you could still coach?"

"I could have still coached, yeah," he said. "I could have coached 10 years later. But growing up the way I did, I couldn't see myself achieving much more. And I guess I didn't have the drive."

Stewart paused and thought about that last statement. Didn't have the drive? Hell, no. That wasn't true. "I can't say that," he amended. "I'm still competitive as hell. And it bothers me a little bit. I have to remind myself that I can still say stupid things. I just felt like it was the time to [retire]. So I did it. And I haven't looked back. Now, I can evaluate it. I could have made some adjustments and probably stayed, but I didn't. So you go on."

In retirement, Stewart made it clear to his bosses he'd be willing to help the basketball program, including his replacement, 32-year-old Duke assistant Quin Snyder. "I tried to get Quin to show there was a passing of the torch," Stewart said. "They didn't want anything to do with me. I said, 'Hey, that's fine with me.' And it wasn't just Quin. But I said, 'Hey, I don't have a problem with that. Shit, I'm busy. I've got a lot of things to do.'"

For years, Stewart kept his distance from the program—he spent one season as a TV analyst on local broadcasts—but resurfaced more often after MU ousted the Snyder regime. In 2014 Mizzou delighted Stewart when Alden hired his longtime assistant Kim Anderson as head coach.

Stewart remained heavily involved with Coaches vs. Cancer—the organization he founded in 1993—which by 2016 had raised nearly $100 million to support the American Cancer Society. In 2014 the Virginia and Norman Stewart Cancer Center opened at Columbia's Boone Hospital. Stewart's devotion to the cause is every bit a part of his legacy as any victory on the court, all of which the sport celebrated in 2007 when Stewart was inducted into the National Collegiate Basketball Hall of Fame.

In 2017 dozens of former players gathered around Stewart outside Mizzou Arena for the unveiling of Stewart's bronze statue, a tribute to the school's greatest living coach and, Stewart hoped, a touchstone to honor the program for years to come. After the unveiling ceremony, Stewart said, "I've been out of [coaching] 18, 19 years, and people might not know who that is, but I hope people bring their children, I hope they bring their grandchildren, I hope they bring their friends and they come by; and [that] the players that were there, the student assistants and doctors and trainers, all bring their friends and point to that [statue] and say, 'I helped put that there.' Because they did. They're the ones who put it there. And I'm so proud that it's me."

Six of the seven All-Americans Stewart coached at Mizzou surrounded him for the day's ceremony, including Doug Smith, who gave an emotional speech about his coach's influence and battle with cancer. "He taught us things father figures do," Smith said. "Not knowing my father growing up, [Coach Stewart] was a tremendous person in my life, and I owe everything to him today. I'm a person of few words, but I will share a little bit. We knew if there was anyone who could make it back, it was Coach. His tenacity, his grit, his determination, and all those things he had within himself, he put in us. That's what made it easy for us to go on the floor and play. We owe everything to you."

Smith added, "When I travel across the country, since I'm a big guy, people say, 'Did you play college basketball?' I say, 'Yeah, I played a little bit.' 'Where did you play?' 'University of Missouri.' 'Enough said. You played for Norm.' No matter where you go, Norm Stewart is Missouri basketball. It's synonymous. There's only one name."

3 Devine Intervention

Ed Blaine can't remember who the Tigers were playing or what happened on the field that day, but he can't forget the trajectory of Dan Devine's clipboard. It whizzed over the head of his teammates and smashed into the lockers behind them. "Had that hit a player in the neck, it probably would have killed him," said Blaine, an All-American offensive lineman for Mizzou in the early 1960s. "He was facing away from us. He would pace up and down to give us that final inspiration. He walked away from us and spun around and didn't even look."

Blaine wasn't in the clipboard's line of fire—not on that day, at least. "But the guys who were had to drop to the floor," Blaine said. "It banged off the locker. We were like, *Man, talk about motivation.*"

Devine's fits of rage were always under control to the point they were calculated tirades, Blaine decided years later. With his bursts of emotion—whether during a pregame speech before the biggest game of the season or after a training camp drill that didn't match his demands for perfection—Devine could instill fear like no man Blaine had ever met. "He'd get in my face screaming and had this look in his eye that he was dead serious," Blaine said. "He [made] such an impression on the players. That's why we were so successful…. He had such a powerful personality. Now, looking back, I can't believe he was angry. But he displayed anger in a way that was convincing. You were afraid. You were literally trembling."

Small in stature, Devine was a titan in football. He coached on the game's biggest stage in the NFL and enjoyed his single greatest achievement with a national championship at Notre Dame. But his strongest legacy in coaching football is forever tied to his time at Mizzou, the program's glory years in the 1960s. From 1958 to 1970, before teams watered down schedules with games against directional schools from inferior conferences, Devine won more than 70 percent of his games at Missouri, going 92–38–7 with two Big 8 championships, five second-place finishes, and six bowl appearances. The Tigers could have played in more bowls under Devine but turned down invitations in 1961, '66, and '67.

In the 1960s, Missouri never lost more than three games in a single season. No other team from a major conference could say the same. Under Devine, who served as athletics director from 1967 to 1970, the Tigers scheduled with courage, playing nonconference games against the likes of Penn State, Michigan, SMU, Minnesota, Arkansas, UCLA, and Notre Dame.

Until Gary Pinkel came along at the turn of the millennium, Devine stood as the program's undisputed most successful coach. When he left Columbia for the Green Bay Packers after the 1970 season, Devine was eight wins short of Don Faurot's school record—in six fewer seasons coaching the team. Pinkel would win more games but in a different context, and captured division titles that didn't exist in the 1960s. But Devine triumphed where his predecessors fell short.

It was Faurot who convinced Devine to coach the Tigers, luring the 33-year-old away from Arizona State, where he'd won 27 games in three seasons. Daniel John Devine, born in Wisconsin but later reared in Minnesota by his aunt and uncle, agreed to succeed Frank Broyles after the 1957 season, when Broyles left for the head coaching job at Arkansas. Devine had his initial doubts about Mizzou but believed in Faurot, the legendary coach then serving as MU's AD. MU offered Devine a five-year contract with a $15,000 salary. "The money was good, the program was more established and in a bigger and more well-known conference," he wrote in his memoir, *Simply Devine*. "Trying to win there would be another challenge, and that idea had always appealed to me."

Devine's 13 seasons at Missouri were loaded with signature moments, but a defining scene came in the locker room at Oklahoma in the penultimate week of his debut season, in 1958. The Tigers lost 39–0 to the sixth-ranked Sooners, their fourth defeat of the season. Devine wasn't sure what to tell the players after the carnage, so he jumped on the training table and made a promise: in two years, when the Tigers would return to Norman, they'd beat the Sooners and dedicate the game to those seniors standing before him.

First, though, the Tigers needed a change. After a 21–20 loss to Colorado in 1959, Devine and trusted defensive coach Al Onofrio redesigned the defense, a midseason tactical change that affected the program for the next decade. Hoping for more heat on the quarterback, Onofrio adopted a six-man line and unleashed edge rushers Russ Sloan and Danny LaRose to attack the backfield. The Tigers won their final three regular-season games, including shutouts of Air Force and Kansas State, before losing to Georgia in the Orange Bowl.

Expectations soared in 1960. The Tigers won their first season opener in 13 years and ripped off nine straight wins, including, as promised, a victory at Oklahoma. Norris Stevenson, the program's first African-American scholarship player, had runs of 65 and 76 yards in the 41–19 throttling, after which the Tigers were greeted to a parade around campus when the team returned to Columbia. For the first time in team history, Missouri was voted the No. 1 team in the national poll with one regular-season game left, against Kansas. A throng of media came to Columbia that week to get a look at the country's top-ranked team.

Years later, Devine wrote, "I learned a lot that week, lessons which I remembered and applied for years into the future. I realized it was the head coach's job to handle the distractions, and I didn't get it done." Neither did his team, as Kansas stunned Mizzou 23–7 to win the Big 8 title—temporarily. It was later discovered that Kansas had used an ineligible player, halfback Bert Coan, and was stripped of the victory and conference title. That came as little consolation to the Tigers, who fell out of the national championship picture. Mizzou closed the season with an Orange Bowl win over Navy.

The 1960 team stood as Devine's greatest until 1969, when the Tigers won the Big 8 and finished 9–2 with another Orange Bowl appearance, a loss to Penn State. During the decade of dominance, Devine developed a constellation of all-time great players: LaRose, who earned Heisman Trophy votes in 1960; tailback-turned–defensive back Johnny Roland; spine-rattling linebackers Gus Otto

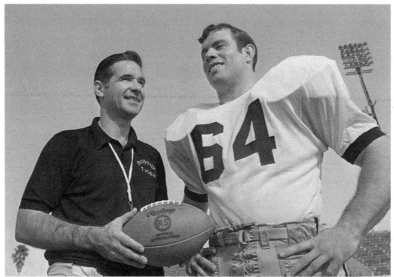

Missouri coach Dan Devine and team captain Carl Garber take a break from preparations for the 1968 Gator Bowl.

and Andy Russell; dominant offensive linemen such as Francis Peay, Russ Washington, and Mike Carroll; dazzling defensive back and return specialist Roger Wehrli; and offensive stars Gary Lane, Joe Moore, Terry McMillan, and Mel Gray, among others.

Among his many lasting contributions was Devine's treatment of the team's first minority players. Broyles recruited Stevenson from St. Louis and running back Mel West from Jefferson City, but it was under Devine's watch that the program embraced racial integration. Devine's early years at MU included several instances of restaurants and hotels refusing to serve his black players. The first time a restaurant turned away black players was in 1958, in College Station, Texas. Devine told the entire team to get back on the bus. He later wrote, "I was shocked that this kind of prejudice was still taking place. I broke down and cried, believing that I had let my team down. I prided myself on preparation.... I vowed to never again let something like this happen to my team."

That meticulous approach and sense of loyalty endeared Devine to his players. "His strong point was his motivation," Wehrli said. "He got us ready for every game. We never went into a game that we weren't completely prepared [for] psychologically."

"His strong suit wasn't X's and O's," added Roland, who later coached for Devine with the Packers and at Notre Dame. "It was discipline. Fear. Intimidation…. Dan's fiery Irish personality generally showed up. But it really didn't have to when I was [at Missouri], because we knew what our jobs were. We knew we didn't want to disappoint our coach."

After the 1970 season—at 5–6, Devine's only losing record in 22 seasons as a college coach—he couldn't resist the overtures from the NFL. Devine had grown weary of recruiting but was torn when the Green Bay Packers offered him their head coaching position. He finally relented.

But Devine didn't have the same level of success in the pros and returned to the college game in 1975, coaching Notre Dame to six winning seasons and winning 76 percent of his games and the national championship in 1977. After coaching, he returned to Arizona to spend time with his wife, Jo, who had been diagnosed with multiple sclerosis. In 1992 Devine found his way back to Missouri to help restore a fledgling athletics department. Serving his second term as AD—the first time around, Devine was the man responsible for hiring legendary basketball coach Norm Stewart— Devine helped launch fund-raising that led to multiple facility renovations.

Two years after he lost his beloved Jo, Devine died in 2002 at the age of 77 after suffering complications from heart surgery. His long coaching career had multiple milestones but made its greatest impact in one place. "Devine made Missouri," Blaine said. "If you ask, 'What was Devine's greatest success?' It was taking the University of Missouri from being an ordinary team to being great."

4 We Do What We Do

Two of Gary Pinkel's college teammates at Kent State—Jack Lambert, the Hall of Fame linebacker, and Nick Saban, the collector of national championship rings—reached stardom early in their careers. Over time, the man in the visor caught up.

Becoming the career wins leader in Missouri football history didn't come easily for Pinkel, who was hired after the 2000 season at a place known as a coaching graveyard. Some fans had Pinkel's burial plot picked out during losing seasons in 2004 and 2012, but his survival instincts took over both times and the program returned to its steady pace.

The son of George and Gay Pinkel, the coach grew up in Akron, Ohio, the middle sibling between sister Kathy and brother Greg, both of whom suffered from hereditary spastic paraplegia, a neurological disorder that left them both with physical disabilities. Pinkel was spared the disease and went on to become a star football player. "That was just emotionally very difficult for me personally," he said. "I felt like the chosen one."

Inspired by his siblings, Pinkel earned All-America honors at Kent State, where he played tight end and met his mentor, Coach Don James. Pinkel would later coach under James at Kent State, then again at the University of Washington, where he eventually became offensive coordinator for the nationally acclaimed Huskies. That led to his first head coaching job at Toledo, where from 1991 to 2000 Pinkel won more games (73) than any previous Rockets head coach.

On November 30, 2000, he was introduced as the new head coach at Missouri, the fourth man to accept that title since 1984. He'd won more games at Toledo than Mizzou's last three head coaches combined. MU also considered Florida State offensive coordinator Mark Richt, who instead became the head coach at Georgia; Wisconsin defensive coordinator Kevin Cosgrove; Western Michigan coach Gary Darnell; and TCU coach Dennis Franchione.

"I remember when I took [the job], Nick Saban was on the phone saying, 'What are you doing?'" Pinkel said. The Tigers had just two winning seasons in the 17 years before Pinkel arrived. After the team's first winter workout, Pinkel entered his coaches' locker room and found his entire staff, most of them transplants from Toledo, hunched over in disbelief. The rebuilding job was bigger than they expected.

"They've got their elbows on their knees and their faces in their hands," Pinkel said. "All of them do. There's 13 guys sitting there like this. I said, 'Hey, guys, there's a reason we're here. OK?'"

Pinkel didn't have instant success at Mizzou—his first two teams went 9–14—but the breakthrough came in 2003, an 8–5 season led by breathtaking quarterback Brad Smith, a player Pinkel's staff recruited at Toledo and convinced to follow them to Mizzou. After a setback season in 2004—multiple second-half meltdowns led to a 5–6 record—Pinkel gave his offensive staff the OK to adopt a no-huddle spread offense, borrowing concepts from Urban Meyer's offense at Utah. (Coincidentally, it was Meyer who buzzkilled Pinkel's debut game at Mizzou in 2001, coaching Bowling Green to a 20–13 upset on Faurot Field.)

Smith thrived in the spread, got the Tigers back to a bowl game in 2005—the team's second trip in three years to Shreveport, Louisiana, for the Independence Bowl—then handed the keys to quarterback Chase Daniel, perhaps the most important player Pinkel recruited to Mizzou. Pinkel's Tigers won 30 games with Daniel at the controls of the offense, and Pinkel earned AP Big 12 Coach of the Year honors in 2007.

A few trends emerged during Pinkel's first decade at Mizzou: staff continuity paid off as the Tigers developed recruiting relationships around Missouri and beyond the state border in Texas and later Florida and Georgia. Gradually, Pinkel's staff got younger through turnover—when the 2015 season began, only four of his original nine assistants were still on the staff—but his core philosophies, first shaped by his mentor, James, stayed intact. He would allow assistants to tweak the offense and defense from season to season. Over time, he'd let down his guard and grow closer to players. But the seeds of his program—talent evaluation, player discipline, off-season development—took root and never changed. Some found his unyielding nature too stubborn. Pinkel swore by his methods because…they worked. "We do what we do," he said countless times every season.

Pinkel also developed a sturdy lineage of franchise quarterbacks, including three straight who all reached the NFL in Smith, Daniel, and Blaine Gabbert. From there, James Franklin and Maty Mauk both guided the Tigers to double-digit-win seasons.

Pinkel's time at Mizzou wasn't without heartache and adversity. In 2005 redshirt freshman linebacker Aaron O'Neal passed out and died during an off-season workout. Pinkel was arrested for drunk driving during the 2011 season, resulting in a one-game suspension and costing him more than $300,000 in salary and contract incentives. In 2015 came the cancer diagnosis that eventually ended his coaching career.

Through it all, though, Pinkel persevered. Mizzou's 41–31 win over Oklahoma State in the 2014 Cotton Bowl punctuated a 12–2 season and made Pinkel the program's career-wins leader, eclipsing Don Faurot with victory No. 102. In the locker room at A&T Stadium, Pinkel broke into a dance as his players surrounded him and chanted, "Geee Peeeeeee! Geee Peeeeeeee! Yeah!" "This isn't about me," Pinkel later said, his hair soaked in Gatorade. "Don Faurot, who he is, things he stood for, I'm honored."

In Alden's last week as AD in 2015, he extended Pinkel's contract through 2021 and made him the sixth-highest-paid coach in the SEC with a salary of $4.02 million.

The good times wouldn't last. Missouri's offense stalled in 2015, ranking among the worst in all of college football as the Tigers won just five games. Late in the season, Pinkel's African-American players staged a boycott of all team activities to support a campus protest demanding the ouster of university system president Tim Wolfe. An otherwise forgettable season suddenly generated international headlines.

In time, Wolfe resigned, the protest ended, and the Tigers resumed practice—but not before another bombshell rocked the program. On November 13, the day before the Tigers would play Brigham Young in Kansas City, Pinkel announced he planned to retire at season's end. Earlier that spring he had been diagnosed with a form of non-Hodgkin's lymphoma. He wanted to spend his remaining healthy years away from the stress and grind of coaching. The next day, the Tigers played their best game of the season, rallied to beat BYU, then celebrated with Pinkel on the field at Arrowhead Stadium, resuming the dance party that had broken out in Dallas two years earlier.

The final chapter of the Pinkel years was more bitter than sweet—the Tigers lost to Tennessee in his last home game and then the next week at Arkansas, Pinkel's final college game—but over 15 years, he made his mark, thriving at a place where promising careers had come to die.

"He resurrected Missouri football from the depths of the ocean to the peak of the mountaintop," former wideout T.J. Moe said. "We're going to look back at this time like we do the 1960s. It is his doing. Coaches have left. Players have left. He's been the mainstay during this time."

5 Southern Comfort

The Mizzou Student Center didn't magically relocate on November 6, 2011. Nope, the building's coordinates were the same as always: 38.94 degrees north latitude, 92.33 degrees west longitude. Unofficially, that's smack-dab in the middle of campus, the middle of Columbia, the middle of Missouri, the middle of America.

Up until that afternoon—a surreal scene to any longtime Missourian, campus employee, or follower of Tigers athletics—Mizzou meant Midwest, not Southeast. But with the official decree from Mike Slive, a stranger to these parts seen only on TV, the geography changed. Missouri was now officially part of the South, as in the Southeastern Conference. Missouri's identity, muddled for years during the Civil War—*Are we Northerners? Are we Southerners?*—was now clear, at least in terms of college athletics. We're SEC, y'all. "Welcome to your new home," Slive, the SEC commissioner, told a packed house that day, announcing Missouri's official acceptance into its new conference.

"We were that first university west of the Mississippi River, setting the pace for a nation as it developed," said Missouri chancellor Brady Deaton, sharing the stage with his counterpart from Florida, Bernie Machen. "Now we are taking a step with one of the fastest-growing regions in the country in one of the most promising, illustrious athletic conferences in our country today, the Southeastern Conference."

Missouri's decision was more than a year in the making and started with rumblings in 2010 that the school was itching to leave a growingly unstable Big 12. The conference's unequal revenue-sharing system and the newly launched Longhorn Network,

Texas's joint venture with ESPN, were the root causes of discontent around the league.

In 2010 Nebraska hightailed it for the Big Ten, and Colorado fled for the Pac-10. By 2011 the remaining Big 12 members banded together and vowed to work out their issues—until Texas A&M planned its getaway, prompting further speculation that the Big 12, then at nine members, was about to crumble.

"I don't think OU is going to be a wallflower when all is said and done," Oklahoma president David Boren said in September 2011, a phrase that Missouri's decision-makers would cite as the point of no return. "Up until that point," Deaton said in 2012, "we were working ourselves to death to make sure the Big 12 survived."

It would, but not with Mizzou. As Texas A&M became the SEC's 13th member, MU began discussions with the league about becoming No. 14. "We were looking for long-term stability as a university—who we were associated with, who we were going to develop long-term partnerships with, who we could have financial security [with] in our planning," Deaton said.

Not everyone at Mizzou was on board initially. Leaving the Big 12 would sever more than a century of association with the original members of the Missouri Valley Intercollegiate Athletic Association, a group of schools that formed in 1907 and evolved into the Big 6, Big 8, and Big 12. In the SEC, Missouri could expect greater revenue from more lucrative TV deals—the SEC Network launched in 2014—and greater national exposure in the country's preeminent football conference.

But the casualty of realignment was clear: Mizzou fans would say good-bye to rivalries that spanned generations, especially the Border War with Kansas. Instead, the Tigers would enter the SEC Eastern Division and hope to form new traditions with the likes of Georgia, Florida, and Tennessee. Missouri insisted the divorce costs would pay off.

Coincidentally, by the summer of 2015, all four people who had stood on the stage to celebrate Mizzou's SEC arrival had left the offices they held that day. Deaton and athletics director Mike Alden stepped down at Mizzou. Same for Machen at Florida and Slive, the SEC commissioner. The decision, though, will outlive them all. In his final week as Mizzou's AD in 2015, Alden called the impact of MU's move to the SEC "immeasurable." "I think that'll be something I'm very proud to be associated with," he said, "because I think it's been great for Mizzou, it's been great for our university, and it's been great for the SEC."

6 Memorial Stadium and Faurot Field

Memorial Stadium and Faurot Field have hosted Heisman Trophy winners and Hall of Fame coaches, national championship teams, and Missouri legends. And the biggest rock 'n' roll band in the world.

On September 18, 1994, the Rolling Stones played a two-hour, 23-song concert for more than 45,000 people on the home field of the Missouri football program—an epic concert that was especially valuable to Mizzou football. Why? Proceeds from the concert raised more than $100,000 to help MU rip up the hated Omniturf playing surface and replace it with natural Kentucky bluegrass. When Missouri installed the new sod a year after the concert, football coach Larry Smith kiddingly thanked Stones frontman Mick Jagger.

The natural grass addition is just one of many facelifts the stadium has undergone since construction crews first broke ground in December 1925 as part of a major campus overhaul. Paired with the new Memorial Union building on campus, the $300,000 stadium was dedicated to the memory of 112 MU graduates and students who were killed in World War I. Carved out of a natural valley between two bluffs south of campus, the new stadium replaced Rollins Field, where the Tigers had played since 1911.

In 1926 Missouri opened Memorial Stadium, with tickets to home games costing $2.50. (Fans had to splurge $3 for tickets to the homecoming game against Kansas.) Athletics director Chester Brewer wrote in the September 1926 edition of the *Missouri Alumnus*:

> The new Memorial Stadium will have approximately 30,000 seats ready for this fall. In addition to this splendid seating capacity it is one of the most unique and unusual structures of its kind in the country, since it is built in a natural amphitheatre. The two sides rest on the hillsides. The south end is left open with a view down the valley. It is one of the most picturesque and conveniently arranged stadiums in the country. The approaches to the stadium are all at the top which gives a unique plan for handling a crowd quickly and conveniently. The stadium will be supplied with 32 entrance gates, which it is believed will enable a crowd of 30,000 to enter without confusion, and which will permit emptying of the stadium within 10 minutes after the close of the game. Another unique feature of the plan is the curved sides, which makes all of the seats on the sides of the field almost equally good.

A week of rain tarnished the grand opening of the new stadium, set for October 2. With less than half the stadium full, Missouri and Tulane both failed to score—"a mudpie tie," as Bob Broeg wrote of that historic waterlogged day.

The next season, the horseshoe-shaped stadium added its signature feature: freshman students took leftover rocks from the stadium construction and shaped them into a massive *M*, 90 feet wide by 95 feet tall. Over time, a tradition was born as freshman students coated the rocks with white paint every August.

In 1949 Memorial Stadium had its first expansion, adding 5,000 seats to the west stands and a press box with room for 50 writers and eight radio booths. In 1965 another 3,595 seats were added, this time in the southeast corner, pushing capacity beyond 44,000.

In 1972, 16 years after Don Faurot had coached his final game at Mizzou, the school named the playing surface in his honor.

In 1978 the south end zone was enclosed, adding another 10,000 seats. Two years later, the stadium saw its largest crowd pass through the gates as 75,298 watched Joe Paterno's Penn State Nittany Lions upset the Tigers 29–21.

In 1985 the stadium became home to one of the worst ideas the university ever hatched. No, not Woody Widenhofer, who that year began a forgettable four-year run as head coach. Less wind flowed through the stadium after the south end zone was closed in 1978, leading to the spread of fungus on the natural grass. MU's solution was Omniturf, a slippery artificial surface first popularized by the University of Oregon. In 1985 Mizzou became the last school in the Big 8 to go artificial—and quickly became home to the league's least popular playing surface. In 1992 the other Big 8 coaches released a joint statement, calling the Omniturf field "a detriment to the home and visiting teams" that "takes away from the integrity of the game."

In 1995 Missouri tore up the hated surface—the Tigers won only 20 of 61 games on the sand-filled turf—and on hand to lay the final piece of real sod to replace the Omniturf was the field's namesake. It was only appropriate that Faurot took part in the ceremony. As an MU player in 1926, Faurot had helped lay sod for the stadium's original field. "It looks awful good now, " Faurot said in August 1995, looking out at the new, natural surface.

Largest Home Crowds through 2017

75,298, vs. Penn State, October 4, 1980
75,136, vs. Texas, September 29, 1979
74,575, vs. Nebraska, November 3, 1979
73,655, vs. Alabama, September 16, 1978
72,348, vs. Nebraska, October 15, 1983
72,333, vs. Colorado, October 18, 1980
72,001, vs. Nebraska, October 24, 1981
71,291, vs. Oklahoma, November 17, 1979
71,168, vs. Georgia, October 11, 2014
71,168, vs. Arkansas, November 28, 2014

Three years earlier, under a set of portable lights, Mizzou had hosted its first night game, a 6–0 loss to Colorado in wet and frigid weather. In 1996 the stadium added permanent lights for night games.

MU continued to spend millions of dollars in stadium upgrades throughout the 1990s and 2000s, including the 2003 installation of FieldTurf, a more forgiving artificial surface. A new video board went up in 2009. In 2014 the stadium opened a new tower on the east side, part of a $45 million renovation that included upper deck seating, luxury suites, and an expanded north concourse.

Seating capacity fluctuated throughout the 1990s and 2000s. In 1995 stadium capacity was reduced to 68,349, then increased to 71,004 in 2009. It was increased again in 2014 as part of the east side additions, to 71,168—more than double the original capacity of the picturesque amphitheater conceived almost a century earlier.

In 2016 new athletics director Jim Sterk unveiled plans for an extension to the south side of the stadium, a vision first conceived by former coach Gary Pinkel. The project would include a new team facility attached to the renovated south end zone structure and is set to open in 2019.

7 Armageddon at Arrowhead

Arrowhead Stadium became Chase Daniel's new home field in 2013 when he signed a free-agent contract with the Chiefs, but no matchup on the Kansas City field could eclipse what he experienced on November 24, 2007. The epic showdown of all showdowns, between archrivals Missouri and Kansas, was unlike any of the 115 Border War games that had preceded that chilly autumn night. Far more than bragging rights were at stake—championships were on the line.

"That's honestly one of my fondest memories, without a doubt: the Armageddon at Arrowhead," Daniel said eight years later. "Winner gets No. 1 in the nation and goes on to play Oklahoma in the Big 12 Championship Game."

The day before Missouri and Kansas would meet on neutral ground in Kansas City, Arkansas upended No. 1–ranked LSU in triple overtime, meaning the winner at Arrowhead between No. 2 Kansas and No. 3 Missouri would surge to the top of the polls and face the Sooners a week later in San Antonio for the league championship. For either team, Missouri or Kansas, back-to-back wins in Kansas City and Texas would clinch a spot in the BCS National Championship Game. Yes, Missouri and Kansas both controlled their own destinies for the national title. Both programs were arguably having their finest seasons simultaneously.

For more than a century, Missouri-Kansas had been a regional rivalry—two state schools in bordering states immersed in history predating the Civil War. The rivalry transcended sports and campus life but rarely, if ever, did the annual matchup attract national attention for football reasons. Most years the Tigers and Jayhawks met in the regular-season finale. Prior to 2007, the two rivals had accepted bowl invitations only five times in the same season. They had only met twice before when both were nationally ranked and never when both were in the top 10.

This game would be *the* game across all of college football. Not Auburn-Alabama. Not Florida–Florida State. Not Oklahoma–Oklahoma State. No, Missouri-Kansas, a national afterthought during most seasons, was the most important game in the country. The Tigers held up their end of the bargain to make it one of the most memorable games either team had ever played.

For Daniel, another incentive hung in the balance: a strong performance could send him to New York for the Heisman Trophy presentation two weeks later. Missouri coaches were sure to showcase their franchise quarterback. As author Mark Godich revealed in his 2013 book *Tigers vs. Jayhawks: From the Civil War to the Battle for No. 1*, Mizzou offensive coaches Dave Christensen and David Yost gave the players a one-page sheet the night before the game, printed on gold paper with black ink. "Go into tomorrow night's game," the page read, "as the most confident, focused, disciplined, ass-kickin' physical team on the field. The Missouri offense will attack Kansas each and every play. Our big playmakers will show Kansas and a national audience what we are all about."

They did. In front of the second-biggest crowd ever to see a game at Arrowhead, Missouri gained control early, taking a 14–0 lead into halftime on a pair of Daniel TD passes. The Tigers would never trail. With two minutes left, Kansas got within six points, but Missouri captain Lorenzo Williams plucked the Jayhawks' final feather, sacking KU quarterback Todd Reesing in the end zone with 12 seconds left to clinch the 36–28 victory. With a clump of Arrowhead turf stuck in his face mask as he walked off the field, Reesing provided one of the game's lasting images. The photo of Sod Reesing—as he will forever be known by Mizzou faithful—hangs in sports bars across Columbia.

Daniel was at his finest, throwing for 361 yards. He completed 40 of his 49 passes. "I'm sure we just sent him to New York," Kansas cornerback Aqib Talib said after the game. "He made good decisions all night and didn't try to force anything. He's got my vote."

"This guy is special," Missouri coach Gary Pinkel said. "I've seen this for a year and a half, but America got to see tonight how special he is."

For the Tigers, the buzz of the epic victory lasted a week, until Oklahoma spoiled the championship dreams in the Big 12 title game. The memories, though, will last a lifetime. "It's pretty amazing to go back and rewatch the game and just see what we were able to do on that big of a stage," Daniel said in 2015. "I'm not going to lie. It still gives me butterflies to this day when I think about it."

8 Eight Big 8 Crowns

In 32 seasons, Norm Stewart never hoisted a national championship trophy. He never reached a Final Four. But when it came to Big 8 conference championships, Stewart had more hardware than Lowe's.

Under Stewart's reign, the Tigers averaged a Big 8 regular-season title every four years. Stewart, who took over his alma mater's program in 1967–68, captured league titles in three different decades, including four in a row from 1980 to 1983. He also finished second six times and third five times.

Stewart's teams historically crapped out in the NCAA tournament—one-and-done eight times in 16 appearances—and some have theorized that Stewart's maniacal emphasis on the league title left Mizzou depleted for the final stretch in March. After winning the marathon, the Tigers couldn't gather their second wind for the sprint. "He put so much pressure on winning the conference," former player Gary Link said. "We never, ever talked about anything more than winning the conference."

Stewart's Tigers managed that part as well as anyone.

1975–76—Big 8 Record: 12–2

The first title came in 1976, Stewart's ninth season on the Mizzou bench. Led by senior All-American Willie Smith and junior stars Kim Anderson and Jim Kennedy, the Tigers clinched the regular-season title with a 35-point thumping of Colorado, MU's first regular-season conference championship since tying for the 1940 title.

"We'd had clubs that came close, that should have been there," Stewart wrote in his memoir, "but this club was the first one for me. For that reason, it was a very special team."

1979–80—Big 8 Record: 11–3

The Tigers clinched their first of four consecutive Big 8 titles behind a cast of stars: Ricky Frazier, Larry Drew, Steve Stipanovich, and Jon Sundvold. But it was a reserve who helped clinch the championship as Mark Dressler stepped in for injured forward Curtis Berry and scored a career-high 18 points in a 12-point win over Oklahoma.

1980–81—Big 8 Record: 10–4

For the first time since 1921, the Tigers captured consecutive undisputed conference titles. With Frazier's game-winning jumper over Kansas State, Missouri became just the fourth school to win back-to-back outright titles since the Big 7 became the Big 8. Against K-State's zone defense, Stewart opted to hold the ball for nearly seven minutes before he unleashed Frazier to attack the basket.

"I felt comfortable," Stewart said after the game. "I thought we'd get a free throw or a layup or [we'd] knock in that last-second shot."

1981–82—Big 8 Record: 12–2

The Tigers had reached No. 1 in the national polls but dropped to No. 4 by the time they visited Oklahoma on February 18 with a chance to win a third-straight Big 8 title. Behind Sundvold's 18 points, the Tigers held off the Sooners and gave Stewart a fourth championship in seven years. They doubled their fortune with a Big 8 tournament title three weeks later in Kansas City.

1982–83—Big 8 Record: 12–2

Sundvold's 18-foot jumper beat the buzzer and Kansas State to capture a fourth-consecutive Big 8 crown. Only 18 teams had previously won four straight outright regular-season titles. Not since Kansas from 1931 to 1934 had another team in Mizzou's league captured four straight championships.

Sundvold and Stipanovich fell short of climbing to college basketball's highest peak, but winning four consecutive conference titles is among the greatest achievements in Mizzou athletics history.

Reflecting on the four-peat, Sundvold said:

It's such a challenge because every team is different. There's four different squads with some common players, but they're all different. The hard part of winning a conference championship, as fans are finding out every year, is the fact that you're playing teams that know you and you know them. You're playing in hostile environments. It's a two-and-a-half-month deal that you have to be good every night and have a toughness to do it.

We won three in a row, had two All-Americans back for our senior year, and weren't picked to win the Big 8. Oklahoma was picked to win our senior year. It's a fight to try to win those games. If you look backward now, it's hard to win at a place like Missouri. Winning four in a row was unheard of, but it was a challenge—a fun challenge.

1986–87—Big 8 Record: 11–3

After winning four straight Big 8 titles, the Tigers went just 20–22 the next three seasons in league play. But a year before anyone expected Stewart's team to contend for another crown, the Tigers stunned the conference with another title. Mizzou finished the regular season with six straight wins and edged Kansas and Oklahoma for the Big 8 championship with a win over Iowa State in the home finale, in front of a record crowd at the Hearnes Center.

"This is the first time I've seen these fans like this," Cyclones coach Johnny Orr said after the game. "The fans are usually lousy here. I guess when you're a contender, they come out and support you. Usually they're nothing. There's always a lot of empty seats."

Stewart didn't have a single senior on the roster, but a nucleus of Derrick Chievous, Nathan Buntin, Lynn Hardy, and Mike Sandbothe, and a collection of role players, stormed the Big 8 by surprise. "Everybody was thinking about next year; all the fans and everybody were thinking about next year," Hardy said. "We were thinking about this year."

1989–90—Big 8 Record: 12–2

The Tigers wore the No. 1 ranking in eight games on their way to Stewart's seventh Big 8 crown and sixth in 11 years. Led by Doug Smith and Anthony Peeler, Mizzou beat Kansas State in the home finale to break away from Kansas and Oklahoma in the league standings.

"I told the players that it's a tradition here," Stewart said. "When you're picked to win and you can come through and win, I think that's extra special. And this is a special ballclub. They've been tremendous, and easy on the old coach."

1993–94—Big 8 Record: 14–0

The first Big 8 team to sweep conference play since Kansas in 1971, the Tigers won the league by four games over Oklahoma State, the biggest margin for Stewart's eight Big 8 champions. When the Tigers clinched the league title with a home win over Oklahoma, they broke protocol and didn't bother cutting down the Hearnes Center nets. "Ain't no celebration going on here until we get the NCAA," senior guard Melvin Booker said. "It'll be a great celebration then."

Like the other eight Big 8 titles, there was no party to follow, as the Tigers fell to Arizona in the NCAA regional finals.

9 Pitchin' Paul: Football's Dizzy Dean

The most celebrated player in the first half-century of Missouri football almost didn't make it to campus. Paul Christman, the brilliant quarterback from St. Louis who'd hold Mizzou's passing records for nearly four decades, wore Black and Gold as a freshman in 1936...at Purdue.

Buried on the Boilermakers depth chart, Christman was unhappy from the start. Friends from back home urged him to enroll at Missouri, but it was too late to join Don Faurot's roster that fall. Faurot wisely added Christman to the team in 1937. The program was never the same.

Christman was a three-time All–Big 6 quarterback for Faurot, guiding the Tigers to 20 wins from 1938 to 1940. He was twice named an All-American and finished among the top five for the Heisman Trophy in 1939 (third) and 1940 (fifth). He was, quite simply, Mizzou's first national superstar.

Christman, who died suddenly of a heart attack at 51 in 1970, can probably thank New York sportswriter Bill Corum for his bright national profile. In 1939 Corum, a native of Boonville, Missouri, convinced fellow Gotham scribe Grantland Rice, the preeminent sportswriter of his time, to cover Mizzou's game at Yankee Stadium against New York University. More than 30,000 were on hand to see Christman's Tigers win 20–7. By season's end, the Tigers were Big 6 conference champions and earned their first Orange Bowl invitation, and Christman was one of the country's biggest stars.

"Football's Dizzy Dean, the ebullient Paul Christman of Missouri, pitched a gorgeous game at the Yankee Stadium yesterday," the *New York Times* wrote of his breakthrough performance. "The big blond junior neglected to take his press notices into the fray with him but he did not need them…. This was a one-man show if there ever was one, a personal triumph for Christman, who did everything required of him and did it superbly…and just to make certain that he had his finger in every pie, he also held the ball on the two point conversion."

By then, Christman had already earned superstar status locally. Faurot gave Christman the freedom to call his own plays, and the 6'1" signal caller brought a sense of levity to the field. "He'd come into the huddle, see that the team was tense and he'd loosen 'em up with something crazy," teammate Bud Orf told Bob Broeg in *Ol' Mizzou: A Century of Tiger Football*. "Like, 'Hey, Bud, your zipper is open.'"

Christman's cool demeanor wasn't limited to the huddle. In one of his favorite stories about the Mizzou star, Broeg wrote

Christman poses for a portait in 1939.

that on the morning of November 4, 1939, as he typed away at his Associated Press office tucked away in the *Columbia Daily Tribune*'s newsroom, Christman popped in after a team breakfast and whispered to the young reporter, "I'll give you a scoop, kid. I'll pass those bums out of the stadium by the half." Those bums from Nebraska were ranked No. 10 and unbeaten. Sure enough, Christman threw three touchdowns in the first half alone as the Tigers won 27–13.

In 1939 Christman ranked among the nation's leaders in passing and led all quarterbacks in Heisman voting, trailing only

Iowa halfback Nile Kinnick, the winner that year, and Michigan halfback Tom Harmon.

As a senior in 1940, Christman played with a sore hamstring suffered during baseball season but still produced another prolific All-American season and finished with a win over Kansas, MU's third-straight takedown of the Jayhawks under Christman's direction. Pitchin' Paul finished his Mizzou career with 1,047 rushing yards and another 2,989 through the air—a school record that stood until 1976.

In the pros, Christman led the Chicago Cardinals to the 1947 NFL championship as part of the Million Dollar Backfield, which also featured Charley Trippi. Christman went on to become one of the top TV analysts in pro football, most famously working in the booth alongside Curt Gowdy.

Christman was voted into the National Football Foundation and College Football Hall of Fame in 1956 and was part of the first induction class of Mizzou's Athletics Hall of Fame in 1990. His No. 44 jersey was among the first three Mizzou retired.

Christman died young in 1970, three days before his 52nd birthday, suffering a fatal heart attack at his home in Lake Forest, Illinois. "I think he knew he was going to die," his wife, Inez Bevelacqua, told the *Post-Dispatch* 20 years later. "Every Sunday for about six weeks, we'd go for a drive. And he'd say, 'If anything ever happens to me, marry for love, someone who'll love you like I did.'"

10 Chase Daniel: The Franchise

Chase Daniel didn't bother writing a speech for the 2007 Heisman Trophy presentation. Missouri's junior quarterback knew he was a long shot for the most prestigious award in college sports, but that wasn't going to ruin his weekend in New York City. "For the most part, I'm just glad to be here," he said, surrounded by his family and coaches. "I'm here. I'm one of the top four players in the nation. Even if I have a horrible season next season for some reason—knock on wood—I can say I've been here at the Heisman Trophy presentation." He added, "I'd be nervous if I felt like I was going to win, but I knew I had no chance. Coming in fourth is fine with me. It's awesome."

There was no shame in finishing fourth the year Florida quarterback Tim Tebow became the first sophomore to take home the trophy. Arkansas running back Darren McFadden took second, followed by Hawaii quarterback Colt Brennan. Daniel earned 25 first-place votes and finished a distant fourth.

But there's no doubt where he ranks among Mizzou's finest quarterbacks. When he finished his college career a year later with a victory in the Alamo Bowl, the Southlake, Texas, native had seized almost every major passing record in school history: single-season yardage (4,335), career yardage (12,515), single-season touchdown passes (39), and career touchdown passes (101). He owned MU's passing-efficiency records for a single game (273.4), for a season (159.4), and for a career (148.9). The competition wasn't close, even among successors Blaine Gabbert and James Franklin. Daniel also set every Mizzou mark for total offense.

Gaudy statistics only partially told the story of Daniel's Mizzou career. Born to run the no-huddle spread offense the Tigers installed before the 2005 season—conveniently, the year he arrived after guiding Carroll High School to the Texas state championship—Daniel might have saved Gary Pinkel's coaching regime and undoubtedly took the program to uncharted heights. Daniel grew up idolizing the Texas Longhorns, but when the home-state power slow-played his recruitment, he fell in love with another team. Missouri was the first school to offer Daniel a scholarship.

As a freshman in 2005, he replaced woozy senior Brad Smith against Iowa State and rallied the Tigers to a 27–24 overtime win, a game that might have salvaged the season and ensured Pinkel another year on the job. Taking over the starting job the next fall, Daniel led MU to an 8–6 record. In 2007 the Tigers won a team-record 12 games and captured their first of two consecutive Big 12 North Division titles. With an epic 36–28 win over No. 2 Kansas at Arrowhead Stadium, Daniel gave the nation a name and face to associate with the Tigers' rise to national prominence, throwing for 361 yards in the game that vaulted Mizzou to No. 1 in the national polls and punched Daniel's ticket to New York for the Heisman ceremony.

Daniel, named the 2007 Big 12 Male Athlete of the Year, became just the second Mizzou player to finish in the top five of the Heisman voting. (Quarterback Paul Christman was third and fifth in 1939 and 1940, respectively.)

As a senior, Daniel threw for more yards, touchdowns, and interceptions, but losses to Oklahoma State, Texas, and Kansas—plus a 41-point debacle against Oklahoma in the Big 12 title game—stripped some luster from an otherwise brilliant season and career. His legacy, though, is unshakable. Daniel was the centerpiece to the program's rise.

On February 13, 2015, in the midst of a profitable NFL career as a backup in New Orleans, Philadelphia, and Kansas City, Daniel was voted into the University of Missouri Intercollegiate Athletics Hall of Fame, along with his two favorite targets: All-American tight end Chase Coffman and All-American receiver Jeremy Maclin. That night, both former teammates testified to their QB's greatness. "The best I've ever seen," Coffman said. "He was able to push you when you needed it. He had the faith in you that you needed."

"He's the kind of guy you want on your team as a quarterback, as a person, as a human being," Maclin added. "The way he approached the game. When you do that and do that day in and day out, everyone respects that. That's the top thing you want. He definitely had control of what we had going on."

11 A Rivalry Born from War

Larry Smith grew up in Ohio. When he became Missouri's head football coach in 1994, he'd coached in his home state, Michigan, New Orleans, Los Angeles, and Arizona. He was a foreigner to the Show-Me State and a newcomer to the Missouri-Kansas Border War. It didn't take long for Smith to catch on.

The night before his 1997 team played the Jayhawks in Lawrence, Kansas, Smith gathered his players for a meeting at their hotel. "I've got something for 'em," Smith told his team.

"We didn't know what he was talking about," offensive lineman Craig Heimburger said. "Was he talking about a secret play or something?" No, not this time. Smith wanted the Tigers to stoke the century-old rivalry when they arrived at KU's Memorial Stadium. "We're going to jog on the field and chant, 'Our house! Our house!,'" Heimburger remembered Smith ordering his players.

"We knew we were the better football team," quarterback Corby Jones recalled. "So we walked out onto their field and chanted, 'Our house! Our house! Our house!'" How did that go over? "That didn't bode well for us," Jones said, laughing. "That was pretty frowned upon."

It was not a good day for the Tigers at Kansas. But the pregame bravado, an edict commanded by the Tigers' ornery head coach, a Border War newcomer quickly bathed in the rivalry's passion, spoke to the rivalry's magnitude, its bitterness, its cold-blooded nature.

"Coach Smith hated Kansas," Jones said. "Anything to diminish them and anything to make them feel or look small, that's what he would do. We were all for it—until I went out there and played the worst game of my career. But that's a different story."

Unlike other college rivalries, Missouri-Kansas—or lowercase *kansas*, as ardent Tigers fans insist—began long before sports mattered at either university. The Border War was born from actual war—real bloodshed, real death, real hate.

Quick refresher: the Kansas-Nebraska Act of 1854 cleared the way for the Kansas territory to become a state. Pro-slavery sympathizers from the South wanted the new state to allow slavery. Abolitionists from the North and East wanted to keep slavery out of Kansas. Violence erupted in 1856 as pro-slavery raiders from Missouri sieged Lawrence, destroying several prominent buildings. Abolitionist John Brown retaliated, killing five pro-slavery men. More raids and battles broke out between Jayhawkers, the anti-slavery fighters from Kansas, and their rival Bushwhackers, the pro-slavery fighters from Missouri.

In 1861, with the Civil War under way, a former schoolteacher named William Quantrill formed a band of pro-slavery guerillas and mounted raids on Union supporters in both states. On August 21, 1863, Quantrill's marauders attacked Lawrence and burnt the city to the ground, killing 180 citizens. Quantrill and his defenders insisted the massacre was revenge for Jayhawker attacks in Missouri, but the Union response was fierce: General Order No. 11 forced the evacuation of four western Missouri counties to prevent the support of violent Bushwhackers. In 1864 the Battle of Westport in Kansas City saw Union armies defeat Confederate forces in one of the Civil War's biggest battles west of the Mississippi River. Less than a year later, the Confederacy surrendered—but the Border War raged for more than a century between the state's flagship schools, separated by 167 miles and generations of hate.

The football teams at the University of Missouri and the University of Kansas met for the first time on Halloween 1891, a 22–10 victory for the Jayhawks in Kansas City, where the annual clash would be played every year until it moved to St. Joseph in 1907. Four years later, the Tigers and Jayhawks met for the first time in Columbia. The game was a dud—the rivals tied 3–3—but Missouri coach Chester Brewer made it famous for another reason, urging former players to "come home" to Rollins Field for the final game of the season. The crowd numbered 9,000. As far as Missouri partisans are concerned, the tradition of homecoming was born.

"Old students and graduates began to assemble at Columbia the middle of the week, and on Friday night the biggest mass meeting ever held at MU took place in the auditorium," the 1912 edition of the *Savitar* wrote. "A few Kansas rooters appeared Saturday morning, but the streets were swarming with Tiger supporters."

The game made its Lawrence debut in 1913 and would alternate campuses until a two-year stay in Kansas City in 1944 and 1945.

Rarely did the rivals meet in nationally relevant games—the 1960 and 2007 editions were prime exceptions—but the rivalry's stakes mattered every season.

Missouri tight end Andrew Jones captured the mutually shared sentiments before the 2008 meeting. "How horrible would that be to go into the off-season knowing that we lost to Kansas?" he said. "That would put the whole state down."

Unlike the football edition, the basketball Border War commanded a national stage many times, mostly during Norm Stewart's watch as the Tigers' head coach. The schools first met on the hardwood on back-to-back March days in 1907, when Axel Isadore Anderson's Tigers swept KU. Anderson would become more accomplished as a physician in Kansas City. His Kansas counterpart would leave another legacy. Dr. James Naismith merely invented the sport.

How good was the rivalry's quality of basketball during the 1970s, '80s, and '90s? During Stewart's 32 seasons on the Mizzou bench, the rival teams combined for 19 regular-season Big 8 championships.

Nobody embraced the rivalry like Stewart, who was recruited out of Shelbyville, Missouri, to play for the Jayhawks by legendary Kansas coach Phog Allen. He chose the other side of the Border War. "Kansas won the national championship in '52 when I graduated high school, and Doc Allen was always great to me," Stewart said. "But when you come here, it's a rivalry. It's like Shelbyville vs. Monroe City. You just try to beat them."

And when they did, Stewart's Tigers enjoyed the moment—in due time. After a big win in Lawrence in 1973, Stewart gave his team strict instructions as the seconds ticked off the clock. "Coach said, 'Shake their hands and let's get out of here,'" former player Gary Link recalled. "We got on the bus, and as soon as we rolled out of Lawrence, Coach turned around and said, 'You just kicked their ass in their building. Go ahead and enjoy it for a while.' We had a wild time on the bus—until we got to Kansas City."

For Stewart's best teams, there was nothing like the annual trip west to Allen Fieldhouse, where students would line up outside the arena on a walkway hours before the game. "Normally, we'd pull up the in the back of the arena, but Norm would stop so we could walk right down the sidewalk by the student body," former All-American guard Jon Sundvold recalled. "His chest was out, his head was high. He'd lead the pack and say, 'Here we go.' We'd walk right through the student body. You could imagine the things said to us. But Norm loved that. He thought it was the greatest thing in the world. He thought if you're not ready to play now, folks, you might as well go home."

After Stewart retired in 1999, the rivalry endured. Former Mizzou guard Kim English remembered Kansas fans spitting on him and his teammates when he walked out of the tunnel at Allen Fieldhouse in 2009. "My sophomore year, there was about a 90-year-old man in the tunnel wearing suspenders and no shirt," English said. "He yelled at me and Marcus [Denmon], and with this drawl, he said, 'Missour-ah, you're going to burn just like you burnt down our town. *Just like you burnt down our town!*' His family had to pull him away from us."

A rivalry founded in wartime lasted more than a century but couldn't survive conference realignment. The Tigers and Jayhawks met for the final time in regular-season play during the 2011–12 academic year, Mizzou's final season in the Big 12 before leaving for the SEC. MU hoped to rekindle the rivalry in nonconference play—not just in football and basketball but in all varsity sports— but Kansas refused. The schools' women's soccer and softball teams met in NCAA postseason play, but as of 2017, the Border War had become the Cold War in terms of scheduling.

In Mizzou's final Big 12 season, the men's basketball teams played two epic games in 2012, both matchups of top 10 teams. After No. 4 Kansas held off No. 3 Mizzou in the final showdown in Lawrence, Jayhawks coach Bill Self squashed any hope of a Border War revival. "The next [Kansas] coach may play them. The next president, the next AD may force me to play. Who knows?" Self said. "We're their past."

On the football field, their past ended with some imagery from their origin. Before the Tigers and Jayhawks met at Arrowhead Stadium in the 2011 regular-season finale, Mizzou receiver T.J.

Moe hung in the locker room a version of Quantrill's flag, the one his Raiders had carried as they sacked Lawrence 148 years earlier. The series was dead. The rivalry...the hate...the history was alive. "If they don't want to play anymore, they don't want to play anymore. Take your toys and go home. Whatever," Moe told reporters that night in Kansas City. "I will miss them. It's like your brother. You fight with [him] every day, but at the end of the day, you need him to have your rivalry, and it's fun.... We're talking about we went over there and killed all their people and burnt their city down, OK? That's what makes [the rivalry]. They hate us. We hate them too." He added, "We were maybe on the wrong side [back then], but we're the good guys now."

12 Stipo

Norm Stewart was not fond of losing, and in 1979—come hell, high water, or Dean Smith—there was no way he was losing Steve Stipanovich. The seven-foot wunderkind from De Smet Jesuit High School in St. Louis—a young Bill Walton, some marveled—was among the most prized recruits in the country. Norm wanted Stipo. He needed Stipo.

He pulled out all the stops. Assistant coach George Scholz made De Smet's gymnasium a second home, hoping to fend off Stipo's other suitors. UCLA, Kentucky, North Carolina, and Notre Dame were Mizzou's top competition.

And Stewart wouldn't hesitate to call on his pals in St. Louis to see what they could do within the rules to help. Years later, he recalled telling one prominent businessman, "We're working our ass off on Stipanovich. Every day, every damn hour."

Stewart even tried hiring Stipo's high school coach, Rich Grawer. "Rich said, 'No, it'll look like you're hiring me to sign my players,'" Stewart recalled. "I said, 'I don't give a shit what it looks like. I want to hire you.'" (He would, a couple years later.)

At one point, North Carolina's Smith gave Stewart a call. "He said, 'Are you going to get Stipanovich?'" Stewart said. "I told Dean, 'To this point I've gotten every guy who's in that category in the state of Missouri.' He said, 'OK, that's what I figured. I'm going to help you…and next time I see him, I'm going to say his state university is a good choice.'"

As Stewart got settled into his seat in Salt Lake City for the 1979 Final Four—the year of the Larry Bird–Magic Johnson showdown in the championship game—his son Lindsey delivered some news that would change the Big 8. "He came running in and said, 'Dad, Stipo's on the phone. He's coming to Missouri," Stewart recalled.

Minutes later, back in Blue Springs, Missouri, Mizzou assistant coach Gary Garner relayed the Stipo news to Jon Sundvold, the high-scoring guard from the western side of the state. Sundvold had a recruiting visit to Arkansas scheduled, but Stipo's decision changed his plans. "I wanted to go where a big guy was going," said Sundvold, who committed to the Tigers on the spot, got word to Stewart in Utah, and officially formed the greatest scoring tandem in Mizzou history.

Stipanovich, the son of a funeral parlor owner, proved immediately he was worth all the fuss, averaging 14.4 points per game as a freshman in Stewart's triangle offense. His 445 points and 59.8 shooting percentage still stood as Mizzou freshman records in 2018. He scored 23 points in his first college game and later endeared himself to Mizzou fans with 29 points in a blowout of rival Kansas.

"Steve came in and gave us that presence inside," former MU center Tom Dore said. "He could score. He could rebound. And people don't talk about it, but he was a really good passer. You could see the talent from day one. He just made shots. He didn't do anything fancy. He'd take one dribble, catch, and turn and make a shot."

From the freshman's first practice, Stewart knew he had something special. Stipanovich puked before he could finish his first taste of post-practice conditioning runs but refused Stewart's offer to hit the showers early. Stipo insisted on finishing each and every run. That scene, Stipo bent over and losing his lunch in a pile of sawdust, solved two problems, Stewart told the freshman. Stewart told Stipo, "No one can accuse me of either babying you or showing any favoritism," the coach later wrote in his memoir. He added that he had also told him, "You are also willing to work harder than anyone else."

"He had a left hook, a right hook, a jump shot, a drop step," Sundvold said. "And his work ethic was unbelievable. And then there was his unselfishness. He didn't care that he was a great player. He didn't demand that he needed to score 20 points a game for his personal satisfaction. If he had six points a game but had 10 assists and 10 rebounds, he was fine. He never once had an ego to say he had to get the ball more."

In Stipanovich's freshman season, the Tigers would win their first of four straight Big 8 championships, and the average Hearnes Center crowd grew by 2,836, the biggest attendance increase in the country, *Sports Illustrated* wrote.

Stipo's sophomore year wasn't the same storybook season. In December Stipanovich made national headlines when he accidentally shot himself in the arm with a pistol. Initially, he made up a story that a masked intruder had broken into his apartment and shot him. Luckily, he avoided any serious injury but became an easy target on the road from rival fans. On the court, the Tigers won another Big 8 championship but flamed out in the first round of the NCAA tournament. Stipo's play had fallen off from his brilliant freshman season. The next year, his scoring took another dip to a career-low 11.6 points per game, but Mizzou reached No. 1 in the national polls, won the Big 8 again, and reached the second weekend of the NCAAs.

By his senior year, Stipanovich realized it was time to grow up. He embraced his Christian faith and gave up on past temptations. "I was kind of a wild guy and very immature," he told the *New York Times*'s Ira Berkow in 1983. "I didn't know what was real and what wasn't. Because you can play basketball, people tell you how great you are, and you start to believe them. You get bloated with ego and pride and self-satisfaction."

He added, "I partied a lot, ate junk foods and drank a lot of beer—I was drunk most of the time. And then the gun thing, and fans all over—outside of here—were on me terribly. It was very loud, very distracting. It was the lowest point of my life. I thought, what am I doing? Why should I continue? And I don't know why I did, but I did. And I'm glad. I fought back, and I'm here today. I knew things would get better, they had to…. That gun incident changed my life. Absolutely. It was in the past, and I had to look to the future. I mean, you can't unscramble eggs."

Fully dedicated to dominating on the court, Stipo closed his college career with his best season, averaging 18.4 points as the Big 8 Player of the Year and a first-team All-American. He scored double figures in 30 of 34 games as the Tigers recaptured a fourth-straight Big 8 title.

"He might have been the most overrated player in the country early in his career," Colorado coach Tom Apke said during the season. "Now he might be the most underrated."

The Tigers would bow out of the NCAA tournament again, but Stipo made his mark in a late regular-season game against Virginia superstar Ralph Sampson, the player to whom he'd drawn comparisons since high school. Virginia won the game, but Stipo took the matchup, scoring 27 points with 12 rebounds and five blocks.

Stipo finished his career ranked No. 1 in Mizzou history for points (1,836), field goals (709), rebounds (984), and blocks (149). Thirty-four years after his final game, he ranked among the program's top four in all four categories in 2018.

The Indiana Pacers took him at No. 2 in the 1983 draft—Sampson went No. 1 to Houston—and envisioned the skilled seven-footer becoming the team's franchise big man. The early returns were promising as Stipo scored in double figures and gave the Pacers consistent rebounding.

"He was a 6'11" guy who could trail the fast break for the Pacers," said Sundvold, the No. 16 pick to Seattle in the same draft. "They'd swing it to him, and he could shoot from the top of the key or put it on the floor. In the NBA he wasn't the best back-to-the-basket player even though he was in college, but he could do all those other things well."

"It was so close to home," Stipanovich later said of Indianapolis. "It was a great opportunity for me. But you have a lot of different emotions. You're nervous, you're excited. There was a lot of pressure. You wanted to be found worthy of that pick."

In 1988 the Pacers drafted Rik Smits, hoping to pair the 7'4" center with Stipanovich in the frontcourt. "That was going to free me up to play power forward," Stipanovich said. "I felt like I was just ready to make a jump in all of my statistical categories and play a more natural position for me."

It never came to be. Before the season tipped off, Stipanovich's left knee acted up and required two surgeries. Diagnosed with a degenerative knee disorder, he'd never play another NBA game. He retired at 29 with career averages of 13.2 points and 7.8 rebounds per game. "I think I was about ready to catapult myself to a whole other level," he said years later, "but the injuries cut that short."

13 A Shooter Ahead of His Time

Jon Sundvold spent more time playing basketball for Mizzou than any player in team history, but his timing was off. The NCAA adopted the three-point line for the 1986–87 season. By then, Sundvold was already hoisting them in the NBA. *His* game was ahead of *the* game.

In 1988–89 Sundvold averaged 10.4 points for the Miami Heat and set an NBA record for three-point accuracy. If only the arc had existed during his brilliant college career at Mizzou.

Sundvold left Missouri in 1983 as the program's second-leading scorer of all time, trailing only teammate Steve Stipanovich. Sundvold, a 6'2" guard from Blue Springs, Missouri, played more minutes (4,289) than any Tiger who came before him—a record that still stood in 2018—and scored 1,597 points with 628 field goals. Sundvold had the range to drill jumpers from 20 feet, but those baskets were worth no more than the two points rewarded for Stipo's hooks and dunks in the paint.

During Sundvold's junior season, the Atlantic Coast Conference experimented with a three-point line for league games. When the Big 8 coaches voted on adopting a three-point line, the final tally was 1–7, Sundvold recalled. "Norm was the only one who voted yes," Sundvold said. That would be Missouri coach Norm Stewart, who had won two straight Big 8 championships behind Stipo and Sundvold's lethal inside-outside dynamic.

"Most of my jump shots were past that line anyway," Sundvold said. "I could see why the other Big 8 coaches said, 'No, we'll wait a year or two.' It would have made our team better because we could have stretched defenses more."

For the top 10 three-point shooters in Mizzou history, three-point field goals accounted for an average of 51 percent of their baskets. Had 51 percent of Sundvold's field goals been worth three points, he would have finished his career with 1,917 points, moving him past Stipanovich as Mizzou's all-time points leader when they ended their college careers. With 1,917 points, Sundvold would have ranked as Mizzou's No. 4 career scorer instead of No. 11 (as of 2018).

"But I'll be honest," Sundvold said. "I'm so glad I never had [the three-point line] in high school because I never would have

Jon Sundvold (left) is one of six men's basketball players to have his number retired by the Tigers.

developed into a player. I would have just been a shooter. I could always shoot, but not having that line, I had to be an all-around player."

Sundvold, who played nine seasons in the NBA in Seattle, San Antonio, and Miami, described himself as "an introverted perfectionist" while playing under Stewart at Mizzou. As a freshman, he played alongside senior guard Larry Drew, a prolific scorer, playmaker, and treasured leader. Once Drew moved on to the NBA, the ball found its way into Sundvold's hands. He had to become more than a shooter.

"Running the show for Norm's teams, my job was [to figure out], 'How do we win games?'" Sundvold said. "I loved the challenge of going on the road. How can we go into a building, make them quiet, win, and go home?"

After Sundvold's junior year, his career reached a milestone when he made the U.S. national team for the FIBA world championships. Flying home from the tryout in Colorado Springs, Sundvold began to realize he'd emerged as one of the best players in the country. "It gave me a step," said Sundvold, who averaged 10 points for the U.S. team that lost to the Soviets in the championship game. "I was named to a few preseason All-America teams that year. It gives you confidence to say you're one of the best in the country. I just got better every year. I was never satisfied with my game."

As a senior, Sundvold put together his finest season, scoring in double figures in 31 of 34 games, including nine 20-point games. In December Sundvold blistered Oregon State for a career-high 32 points. "We did a good job on him for 15 minutes, and then it was Panicsville," Beavers coach Ralph Miller told reporters after Mizzou's 28-point win. "For a 6'2" guard he's a tough little guy. You have to defend him out to 22 feet. He's as good there as he is at 15."

Oregon State's William Brew was among the many defenders impressed that season. "He reminds me of Danny Ainge with the way he'll fight you on defense and the way he'll bust the jumper," Brew said. "He's an All-American, and you can tell him I said that."

Sundvold earned that honor and after the season watched as Mizzou retired his No. 20, along with Stipo's No. 40. Sundvold finished his career as the program's best free-throw shooter (84.8 percent), No. 2 scorer, and No. 2 in assists (382), trailing only Drew.

In the 1983 draft, Stipo went No. 2 to Indiana, and the Pacers hoped to reunite the Mizzou teammates by drafting Sundvold at No. 23. Instead, Seattle took the prized shooter at 16. "I was hopeful, like any kid, just to have a chance to go to a training camp," Sundvold said.

After two years with the SuperSonics, Sundvold was shipped to the Spurs two days before the start of the 1985–86 season. Alongside All-Star teammates Alvin Robertson and Artis Gilmore, Sundvold averaged a career-best 11.2 points per game in 1986–87. The next season, Sundvold played with a cracked shinbone, and the club left him unprotected in the 1988 expansion draft. He went to Miami with the ninth pick and became a trusted veteran sharpshooter. In 1988–89 Sundvold led the league in three-point accuracy, making a league-best 52.2 percent.

Sundvold required neck surgery prior to the 1991–92 season, and after three games, he decided he was done playing. He returned to Columbia to raise his family, opened an investment firm, and became one of the college game's top TV analysts.

And night after night, he watches players launch countless three-pointers.

14 Colorado Counts to Five

If and when Missouri ever builds a new football stadium—Memorial Stadium turned 92 years old in 2018—the deconstruction of the old haunt should start with an exorcism of the north end zone. It's seen its share of tragedy over the years, none worse than what unfolded on October 6, 1990. It would be just the Tigers' luck that one of the most infamous games in college football history—heck, maybe American sports history—came at their expense.

It was Bob Stull's second season as head coach. Mizzou was 2–2 and coming off an impressive win over nationally ranked Arizona State. Next up, defending Big 8 champion Colorado came to town. It was a critical test for Stull's Tigers. A good showing against the Buffs would earn the program some long-sought-after credibility. A win would be the first signature victory of Stull's time on the job. "They needed a big victory," Colorado coach Bill McCartney, a Mizzou grad, said years later. "They needed a big victory bad."

For a moment, the Tigers thought they had one. On fourth-and-1—or was it?—Colorado quarterback Charles Johnson lunged for the goal line to score the go-ahead touchdown in the game's closing seconds. Yes, in the north end zone on Faurot Field. Mizzou linebackers Tom Reiner and Mike Ringgenberg smashed into Johnson, the victory seemingly clinched. But Johnson spun loose, pushed forward, and landed on his back. It was enough to raise the arms of the officials. Touchdown, Colorado.

"He falls on his butt and reaches his hands out," Missouri safety Harry Colon later recalled. "We gave it our all and left everything we had on the field. But to this day, I'm still under the belief that he didn't score."

The officials saw otherwise, and instant replay was more than two decades away from entering the college game. Colorado won 33–31. Never mind that the Buffs used five downs to score the game-winning touchdown. Yes, indeed. Five downs. "I have that in my mind pretty well etched," J.C. Louderback, the referee that day in Columbia, said 20 years later. "Even up to today I wish it never would have happened so we would have had the true outcome of the ballgame.... I think about it all the time."

After a pass to tight end Jon Boman put the Buffs deep in Mizzou territory, here's how the notorious sequence unfolded:

First-and-goal, 3-yard line, 31 seconds left: Johnson spiked the ball intentionally to stop the clock.

Second-and-goal: Johnson handed the ball to tailback Eric Bieniemy, who crashed forward just short of the goal line. The Buffs called timeout to discuss their plan. Inexplicably, the chain gang never flipped the down marker from two to three, leaving the Buffs thinking they had three more downs to score.

Third-and-goal: Johnson called Geronimo in the huddle. It was a three-play sequence. Center Jay Leeuwenburg didn't understand. He told Johnson it was already third down. "The play clock started to run," Johnson later recalled. "I said, 'Jay, shut the hell up. Geronimo.' I had no idea what he was talking about." On third down, Bieniemy got the ball again, and the Tigers stopped him around the 1-yard line. Precious seconds melted away until Louderback stopped the clock at eight seconds.

Fourth-and-1: Johnson stuck with Geronimo, which called for another spike to stop the clock, setting up what the Buffs hoped was the game-winning play. But Missouri coaches knew better. By then, Colorado should have been out of chances. "Even though we were arguing whether that was actually the down or not, it didn't really make a difference because there was nobody who was indicating anything different," Stull later said. "Whether it was tenth down, we had to stop them."

Fifth-and-1: The down marker said four, and with two seconds left, Colorado got another chance to score. Johnson failed to find the crease behind his fullback on the right and instead dove left. He rolled on his back near the goal line and lifted the ball in the air. Forget that it was fifth down. Missouri players and coaches insist the defense stopped Johnson short of the goal line.

Fans seemed to agree as they poured onto the field and toppled the goal post. They apparently missed linesman Ron Demaree signaling a touchdown. Ahead 33–31, the Buffs headed to the locker room to celebrate. They had already sung their fight song when the officials came in and said they had to kick the extra point. They took a knee instead, officially crushing Mizzou's soul.

Missouri appealed the outcome to the Big 8 but to no avail. Colorado went on to win the national championship. The Tigers never recovered and finished 4–7. The officiating crew was suspended indefinitely. Years later, McCartney expressed remorse regarding the outcome. It came as no consolation to Mizzou. "The Big 8 sent me a football for being the Defensive Player of the Week for that game," Colon said later. "Every once in a while I take it outside and kick it around a little, just to take some aggression out. I want the last laugh."

15 Mel West and Norris Stevenson

Mel West and Norris Stevenson never asked to be pioneers. They just wanted to play football for their state school. In doing so, they earned a sacred place in Missouri history, becoming Mizzou's first African-American scholarship football players. Stevenson, a running back from St. Louis, came first, joining the Tigers in the spring of 1957. West, also a running back, arrived in the fall. Both players were recruited by Coach Frank Broyles, who left after the 1957 season to coach at Arkansas. Dan Devine, his successor at Mizzou, is often credited with integrating the football program, but it was Broyles who brought Stevenson and West to campus. Missouri was among the last schools in the Big 8 to integrate its roster, though Broyles later called West and Stevenson's recruitment "a routine decision."

"I guess I inadvertently never mentioned to him that he was going to be the first black player," Missouri assistant coach John Kadlec later said. "Norris, years later he brought that up to me. He said, 'You know, Coach, you never mentioned that to me.' And I go, 'Well, you know, Norris, I guess I recruited you as a football player—not as the first black player. I considered you a football player.'"

Both players became fixtures in the Missouri backfield. From 1958 to 1960, Stevenson ran for 1,184 yards in regular-season games and averaged a robust 7.2 yards per carry as a senior. West was the workhorse, becoming one of the most prolific backs in school history. He ran for 1,848 yards in regular-season games, plus another 108 yards in the 1961 Orange Bowl. He became the first MU player to lead the team in rushing for three straight seasons. (Only James Wilder and Brock Olivo have since done the same.) A first-team All–Big 8 selection in 1960, West finished his career as the school's No. 2 all-time rusher behind only Bob Steuber.

Unbeknownst to the college roommates at the time, West and Stevenson's impact on Mizzou history would transcend rushing yards. Their presence helped shape race relations within the athletics department and throughout the university. Soon after arriving at Missouri, Devine addressed two game-day traditions that he wanted changed, in part because of his two black players: the flying of the Confederate battle flag in the student section and the marching band's playing of "Dixie."

Multiple times in his first few years at MU, Devine's teams encountered restaurants and hotels that refused to serve Stevenson and West and the black players that joined them on the team, most notably in College Station, Texas, in 1958. The rest of the team walked out of the restaurant in support of their teammates.

Russ Sloan, an All-Conference end, described the scene in Texas as "demeaning" and "disgusting" years later in the *Missouri Alumnus* magazine. "They were first-class individuals and superb football players who carried the mantle of integration with tremendous dignity, composure and competitive spirit," Sloan wrote. "Mel and Norris always held their heads high and let their competitive deeds and accomplishments speak for themselves."

"I was shocked that this kind of prejudice was still taking place," Devine wrote in his memoir. "I broke down and cried, believing I had let my team down. I prided myself on preparation, every detail, and even though we had lost the game, having our players run into problems like this was far worse than losing the football game."

For many years after his college playing career, Stevenson was upset that Devine didn't do more to publicly support the black players in the face of the racism they faced. Their relationship was complicated, often described as cordial but not close. When Devine returned to Mizzou as athletics director in the early 1990s, he invited Stevenson to visit with him for a long talk. They cleared the air and became great friends. When Devine died in 2002, Stevenson gave the final eulogy at his funeral in Columbia. "He was a very good football coach," Stevenson said that day, "but when [my career] was over, he was much more than just a coach."

Stevenson told a story from the locker room following the 1961 Orange Bowl victory over Navy, the final college game for Stevenson and West. At the time, Stevenson was closer to Devine's assistant coaches, but their relationship began to mend when the coach asked the senior for a favor. "He asked me to pray for the team," Stevenson, the son of a Baptist minister, said during his emotional eulogy. "That's something I will always remember, particularly because it put me in a different venue.... He waged a battle on the gridiron—and on racism—and we all won."

Stevenson, who went on to coach college track-and-field in St. Louis, reconnected with his alma mater in the early 2000s after Gary Pinkel took over as head coach. Pinkel regularly invited Stevenson to talk to his players and leaned on the St. Louis native to help improve relationships with the city's coaches and players. In 2001, Pinkel's first season at Mizzou, the school dedicated the Norris Stevenson Plaza of Champions on the west side of Memorial Stadium, featuring a bronze plaque of the former player. Stevenson died in 2012 after suffering from colon cancer. "He'll be remembered around here," Pinkel said, "as a very important figure in our history."

West, though he came to campus just a few months later and was by most measures the more productive player, isn't held in the same reverence as his former teammate, perhaps unfairly. In 1993 Stevenson and West served as grand marshals of the Mizzou homecoming parade. West had returned to MU to earn his graduate degree but spent the rest of his life in Minnesota, where he became a teacher and school administrator. He died in 2003. His legacy might not carry the notoriety of his friend and teammate, but West's place in Mizzou's past is no less significant, and no less important.

16 Saint Brad

The most important Mizzou football player of the 21st century wore casts and braces on his legs as a young child. Born with an abnormality in his feet, Bradley Alexander Smith would struggle to walk, doctors feared. Surely, the boy would never run. Oh, were they wrong.

The world learned on August 31, 2002, that the kid from Youngstown, Ohio, could run...and run...and run...and run. Making his college debut that day as a redshirt freshman quarterback for the Tigers, Smith filleted an unsuspecting Illinois defense with 138 yards on the ground and another 152 through the air, leading the Tigers to a 33–20 season-opening victory in St. Louis, the first chapter in a legend that would take four years to complete.

"We have seen the future of Missouri football, and his name is Brad Smith," wrote *St. Louis Post-Dispatch* columnist Bernie Miklasz, putting a spin on the famous line by Jon Landau when he discovered Bruce Springsteen in 1974. By no coincidence, Springsteen had just played St. Louis the night before Smith's dazzling debut. Even a Bruce fanatic like Miklasz would agree Smith put on the weekend's better show.

"I don't think we'll put him on top of a monument yet," Pinkel marveled after the game. "But I suggest one day that may happen."

"The biggest memory from Brad Smith that I'll never forget until they put me under was his first start against Illinois," said A.J. Ricker, who started every game for Mizzou at center from 2000 to 2003. "He runs over to the sideline, but instead of running out of bounds, he gets waylaid. He runs back to the huddle with a big smile on his face. I said, 'Dude, get out of bounds or slide. What are you doing?' He just smiled and didn't say a word. I'm like, 'Wow.' That was amazing."

Pinkel's offense was a mess his first season at Mizzou, but he knew there was hope on the scout team. Pinkel's staff had discovered the mild-mannered, scrawny, 6'1", 170-pound QB before they came to Mizzou, back when they were bullying the Mid-American Conference at Toledo. The staff left for MU after the 2000 season but kept in touch with the prospect from Youngstown. Not knowing much about Missouri's program, the school, or the state, Smith put his faith in Pinkel and followed him to Mizzou.

By spring practices in 2002, Smith made a push for playing time. By preseason camp, he edged out senior Kirk Farmer for the starting job. Pinkel had some reservations thrusting the untested player into such a role—on national TV, no less, against Illinois in an NFL stadium. "It's too much to ask for a young guy," Pinkel recalled thinking. Think again, Gary.

Smith's debut was just a taste of his talents. By season's end Smith became the second player in Division I history to eclipse 2,000 passing yards and 1,000 rushing yards. As a sophomore Smith made the leap from prolific quarterback to winning quarterback, leading the Tigers to seven wins and an invitation to the Independence Bowl, MU's first postseason appearance in five years. Smith staged one of his most memorable games that year, a 41–24 win over Nebraska, the Tigers' first takedown of the Cornhuskers since 1978. He ran for three touchdowns and even caught one. Two weeks later Smith trampled Texas Tech with 291 rushing yards and a school-record five rushing touchdowns.

"I'm biased, but he's one of the best quarterbacks to ever play here," Ricker said. "He could do so many things. There were times I honestly thought we couldn't block anyone up front and they still weren't going to sack him."

With Smith established as one of college football's brightest stars, the luster wore off in 2004 when Mizzou coaches tried conforming the junior into a pocket passer. It didn't work. Smith ran for just 553 yards in 11 games as defenses helped comply with Mizzou's strategy and congested Smith's running lanes. He completed a career-worst 51.8 percent of his passes and threw a career-high 11 interceptions. Worse, the Tigers lost a Thursday night game at Troy and blew halftime leads in losses to Oklahoma State and Kansas State. The Pinkel-Smith honeymoon was over. The Tigers stumbled to 5–7.

In the off-season, Missouri's offensive coaches scrapped the playbook and installed a no-huddle spread system based on principles they learned from Urban Meyer's Bowling Green staff after

Brad Smith eyes his man.

he left the MAC school for Utah. Incoming freshman quarterback Chase Daniel piloted a similar offense in high school in Southlake, Texas, but Smith would get the controls first. It was a Hail Mary for Pinkel's staff. Another losing record could have sent them looking for new jobs.

But Smith thrived in the up-tempo attack. As a senior, he threw for a career-best 2,304 yards and ran for 1,301 more. He concluded a record-smashing run with his most heroic performance, rallying the Tigers from a 21-point deficit in the Independence Bowl to beat South Carolina 38–31. In his sendoff performance, he accounted for 150 rushing yards and 282 passing yards and had a hand in all four of MU's offensive touchdowns. "Quarterbacks will be remembered not so much for yards and touchdowns," Pinkel said after the game in Shreveport, Louisiana. "They'll be remembered for winning. And comeback wins. And big wins for your program's history. And that's [why] I'm very proud of him. For Brad, I don't think you could write a better story for a finish for his career." Smith left Mizzou holding 60 school, conference, and NCAA records and stood as the Tigers' career leader for rushing, passing, and total offense.

Without Smith, Daniel might never have arrived to take Mizzou's program to greater heights. Maybe Pinkel wouldn't have lasted long enough to leave as the program's career wins leader. Without Smith, maybe the SEC would never have come calling. "He was the catalyst," Pinkel later said.

In 2011 Smith was inducted into Mizzou's Intercollegiate Athletics Hall of Fame, joining the other MU luminaries with his typical grace and selflessness. "They really don't have to remember me," Smith said. "Honestly, they really don't. I was just a guy who gave everything he had on the football field. And that's all that really matters."

17 Leaving a Legacy

Missouri's 2008 basketball recruiting class came to Columbia as a party of six. Over time, the class lost some members and added a few more. On February 15, 2012, the core of Coach Mike Anderson's class, under the direction of a new head coach, made Mizzou history. An 83–65 victory over Oklahoma State was win No. 101 for the seniors, surpassing the senior class of 1983 that went 100–28 over four seasons.

From the 2008–09 season to 2011–12, a class headlined by guards Marcus Denmon and Kim English won 107 games with 34 losses. More important, they helped Mizzou fans rediscover winning basketball. "The fans really identified with us and knew us," said English, who scored 1,570 points over his four-year career, finishing No. 13 on the school's career scoring list. "We never had a doubt we were playing for them. Every win we wanted to share with them. Every loss we felt like we let them down."

The Tigers had gone five years without making the NCAA tournament when the class arrived in the fall of 2008. Denmon, a high-scoring combo guard from Kansas City, was suited for Anderson's maniacal full-court style. English, a shooter from Baltimore, Maryland, was a promising wing scorer. Laurence Bowers, a 6'9" power forward from Memphis, Tennessee, was raw but skilled. The Tigers also brought in Steve Moore, a big-bodied post player from Independence, Missouri; Miguel Paul, a point guard; Keith Ramsey, a lengthy junior college transfer happy to handle the dirty work; and Jarrett Sutton, a walk-on guard from Kansas City.

The young class joined a veteran core and helped the Tigers capture the 2009 Big 12 tournament championship, followed by a run to the Elite Eight in the NCAA tournament. Anderson's team fell just short of making the school's first Final Four appearance—Connecticut outlasted MU in the West Regional Finals—but the Tigers revived a fan base left in a stupor by the Quin Snyder regime.

The Tigers couldn't follow up with a strong encore the next season or the season after that, though both years ended in the NCAA tournament. In 2011, with the Denmon-English-Bowers core set to become seniors, Anderson left Mizzou for Arkansas. The night Anderson's departure became official, seniors-to-be Bowers, Denmon, and English gathered at Mizzou Arena for a news conference, unsure what the program's future held. "Deep down inside, you're mad, really disappointed," Bowers told reporters that night. "You know, 'Why us?'"

But there was only one thing the Tigers could do in the wake of Anderson's departure. "I think we'll reconcile it by winning," English said.

By then, Ramsey had graduated, Paul had transferred, and the Tigers had picked up junior college imports Matt Pressey, a versatile guard, and Ricardo Ratliffe, a 6'8" bruiser with a soft scoring touch in the paint. They combined with Anderson's leftover players to deliver one of the greatest regular seasons in team history under new coach Frank Haith. Even though Bowers missed the 2011–12 season with a knee injury, the senior-led Tigers won 30 games, beat five nationally ranked teams, and captured one more Big 12 tournament title in the school's final year in the conference. Denmon (17.7 points per game) earned second-team All-America honors, while English (14.5 PPG) enjoyed his best season and Ratliffe set a school record for shooting percentage (69.3). Moore, greeted by cheers of "Steeeeeeeeeve!" every time he took the floor at home, became a cult hero and valuable reserve.

"Frank made it work," English said. "He made it special. He inherited a bunch that was broken."

The four-year run ended sadly as Norfolk State, a No. 15 seed, upended the No. 2 seeded Tigers 86–84 in the first round of the

NCAA tournament in Omaha, Nebraska. But the class had made its mark along the way: the core of Denmon, English, Moore, and Sutton were 3–1 against Illinois and 7–2 in the Big 12 tournament with 15 wins over nationally ranked teams, including five victories over top 10 teams. They were nearly unbeatable at home, going 67–4 on Norm Stewart Court during the four-year run.

"I know we'll always be remembered as a bunch that gave Missouri fans a fun year, super-efficient, tough, unselfish brand of basketball," English said. "But I'm a realist, and I know we'll be remembered by the way we finished. It's a sore subject for me. I don't like to talk about the way the season ended. But we know. We know how amazing we were. But everything happened for a reason. You can't go back and change it. Not a day goes by that I haven't thought about it. It's tough. It's tough."

18 From Dixon to Stardom

A constellation of basketball stars played for Norm Stewart at Missouri over five decades, but few shined brighter than the first: John Brown. Brown, the rugged 6'7" forward from Dixon, Missouri, would leave Mizzou as the program's career scoring leader. How he got there came with a promise. Brown was a high-profile recruit who drew interest from all over the country— Cotton Fitzsimmons at Kansas State was MU's top competition for his services, Stewart recalled—but Stewart had an incentive no one else could offer. Mizzou was embarking on a new modern arena, and Brown would get to play his home games in the finest basketball facility in the country. That was part of Stewart's sales pitch.

Brown sought more than a sparkling new arena. He wanted to fill it with banners. "I came from a winning program in high school that won the state title, and coming into Missouri, I was fairly naive," Brown said years later. "I remember Coach Stewart telling me, 'Now, John, our goal is to win the Big 8 championship.' And I looked at him and genuinely said, 'Coach, I want to win the national championship.'"

That didn't happen, but for the first time under Stewart's watch, Missouri competed on a national stage with Brown as the centerpiece. He left Mizzou as the foundation to Stewart's rising program.

A foot injury delayed the start to Brown's career, but he made his debut on December 22, 1970, at UCLA against the top-ranked and eventual national champion Bruins. "Coach Stewart came up to me before the UCLA game," Brown said, "and he asked me, 'Do you think you can play? You'll probably never get another chance to play here.' At that point all I had done was shoot some free throws and run a little bit."

He did more than that against John Wooden's Bruins, scoring 14 points in a Mizzou loss. Brown made his Columbia debut three weeks later in a victory over Oklahoma with a team-high 23 points. As a junior, Brown emerged as Stewart's leading scorer, averaging 21.7 points per game. Forced to play center after Bob Allen suffered a knee injury, Brown powered an undersized front line to the program's first 20-win season and first postseason NIT appearance.

"He was the first great player under Coach Stewart, without a doubt," former teammate Gary Link said. "Honest to God, I can never remember a pass to John Brown that he didn't get. He got everything. Everything. He was so strong and worked so hard on getting to the right spot. He'd work and work and work. If he wasn't open, we'd move the ball around and he'd rework to get to the right spot."

Brown could punish opponents in the paint but also possessed unmatched skill as a shooter and passer. Reliable as the sunrise, Brown scored in double figures in all but six of his 72 games at Mizzou. "Coach Stewart would have us shoot 12 layups in a row in practice," Link said, "and watching John Brown was like watching a prizefighter hit a speed bag. *Dudda-duh, dudda-duh, dudda-duh.* He never missed. He was so smooth. His footwork and just everything about his game was just rock-solid. And he played both ends of the floor too. He was very, very special. He made us all a lot better." The 1971–72 team finished 21–6 and climbed into the national rankings for the first time under Stewart.

As a senior in 1972–73, Brown finally got his wish and was part of the first Mizzou team to play in the Hearnes Center. He christened the new arena with a short jumper, the first points scored in the building, in a victory over Ohio. The 1972–73 team, with Brown as captain, matched the 21 wins of the season before and went back to the NIT, again suffering a first-round defeat. Along the way, the Tigers peaked at No. 4 in the national polls and took down nationally ranked Ohio State, Kansas State, and Oklahoma. Brown again led the Tigers with 21 points and 11 rebounds per game, good for first-team honors on the All–Big 8 team.

Brown saved his best for a March showdown with Oklahoma State. Earlier in the conference season, Brown had an off night against the Cowboys with just 12 points, prompting OSU's Andy Hopson to get under Brown's skin with some postgame comments. "The next day in the paper, he said, 'If John Brown's the best player in the Big 8, then I'm better,'" Brown later recalled.

Uh-oh. The rematch fell on March 3. Brown needed 23 points to surpass Charles Henke as the team's career scoring leader. Brown set the record before halftime, scoring his 23rd and 24th points on a jumper. The game stopped as the Hearnes Center crowd saluted the newest Mizzou scoring leader. But Brown wasn't done. He finished with 41 points, third-most all-time at Mizzou and just five off Joe Scott's single-game scoring record. "[Hopson] just got me absolutely worked up," Brown said, "and I was just trying to show that I was the best."

Brown left Mizzou as the best to wear the school colors, finishing with 1,421 points and 720 rebounds. Brown, who made the 1972 Olympic team only to suffer a foot injury, was the 10th overall choice by Atlanta in the 1973 NBA Draft and played seven years in the league with Atlanta, Chicago, and Utah.

Big Stage, Big Disappointment

The Southeastern Conference invented the conference championship game in 1992. From 2007 to 2014, Missouri savored four chances to capture a conference title on the final weekend of the regular season. Only heartache ensued.

In 2007 the Tigers carried the No. 1 ranking into San Antonio, Texas, to face four-time Big 12 champion Oklahoma, the only team to beat Missouri during the regular season. The Sooners took the rematch too. Momentum shifted in OU's favor for good late in the third quarter when OU linebacker Curtis Lofton picked off a Chase Daniel pass deep in Mizzou territory, setting up the Sooners for a two-touchdown lead. "Mistakes are magnified in games like this," Daniel said after the 38–17 loss. A win would have clinched a spot in the BCS National Championship Game against Ohio State. Instead, the Tigers settled for the Cotton Bowl against Arkansas.

A year later, Mizzou was back in the Big 12 title game, this time on a friendly field at Kansas City's Arrowhead Stadium. But there was no home-field advantage against No. 1 Oklahoma and soon-to-be-crowned Heisman Trophy winner Sam Bradford, who led the Sooners to a 62–21 thrashing of Daniel's Tigers. "This one hurts the worst," said Daniel, who turned over the ball three times. "You can't beat a team like that when you're turning the ball over."

Few people, if anyone, at Arrowhead that day could have predicted that five years later Mizzou would be in Atlanta playing for another conference championship—in the SEC. But two years into their new league, the Tigers earned their way into a showdown with Auburn. The winner could slip into the BCS Championship Game depending on what happened later that night in the Big Ten title tilt. The teams engaged in what would become the most prolific scoring night in SEC Championship Game history. By the fourth quarter, Missouri couldn't keep pace as Auburn outlasted the Tigers 59–42. The teams set SEC Championship Game records for combined points (101) and combined yards (1,211).

A year later, Missouri was the last obstacle in No. 1 Alabama's path to the first College Football Playoff. The Tigers were no match for the Crimson Tide, especially after All-American defensive end Shane Ray was ejected for an illegal targeting hit on Bama quarterback Blake Sims. Ray objected to the call but had to watch the rest of the game from the locker room. The Tide washed away Mizzou's championship hopes 42–13.

Heading into 2018, the Tigers were still waiting to capture their first conference championship since 1969.

20 Michael Sam: Courage Under Fire

One of the most unlikely of Mizzou's All-American football campaigns unfolded in 2013 when Michael Sam, an unheralded recruit four years earlier, made the leap from part-time starter to SEC

Defensive Player of the Year. Sam exploded for a league-best 10 sacks and 18 tackles for loss. His production was sporadic—eight of his sacks came against hapless offensive lines from Arkansas State, Florida, and Vanderbilt—but by season's end his numbers were as good as any pass rusher in the country. Sam became Mizzou's first unanimous All-American since 1960.

All the accolades became footnotes on February 9, 2014, when Sam became a worldwide celebrity whose fame and courage soon transcended Mizzou football, all in five words: "I am a gay man." In two carefully crafted interviews arranged by his publicity team, Sam told the world via the *New York Times* and ESPN's *Outside the Lines* that he was gay.

Some of his Mizzou teammates had known for years. The entire 2013 Mizzou team had learned the previous August. At a team dinner at defensive line coach Craig Kuligowski's house during preseason camp, players went around the room sharing details about their lives. Sam didn't hold back. "He stood up," Kuligowski later recalled, "and said, 'My name is Michael Sam. I play defensive end. I'm gay.' It was that easy. And that was that."

"I know his teammates were excited," Mizzou strength coach Pat Ivey said. "When Mike finally came out to his teammates, they were relieved. They said, 'Good job, Mike. Now let's go play some football.' I think what that shows is when you are yourself, when you're comfortable being you around your teammates, it makes the whole environment conducive to that culture."

"I was kind of scared, even though [some] already knew," Sam told ESPN. "Just to see their reaction was awesome. They supported me from day one. I couldn't have better teammates.… I'm telling you what: I wouldn't have the strength to do this today if I didn't know how much support they'd given me this past semester."

Throughout the 2013 season, as the Tigers captured the SEC East on the way to tying the team record with 12 wins, teammates and coaches respected Sam's privacy and kept his sexual orientation within the sacred confines of the program. Some reporters following the team had heard whispers, but Sam declined interview requests throughout the regular season. The story remained his to be told, and not until rumors circulated at the Senior Bowl in January did Sam and his agents feel compelled to break the news worldwide. He became the first openly gay NFL prospect.

Missouri head coach Gary Pinkel, 61 at the time, was tackling a challenge he'd never encountered during his long career. His nuanced, progressive handling of such a sensitive topic became one of his finest moments at Mizzou. He knew there were mixed feelings within the locker room about a gay teammate, but he fostered an environment that allowed Sam to thrive without fear. "It's about being respectful to people," Pinkel said. "If you're part of our family, part of our football program, part of our team, we're going to be respectful of the differences amongst us and embrace and support each other. That's what we do here at Mizzou."

Sam became the first openly gay NFL draft pick when the St. Louis Rams chose him late in the seventh round. ESPN's cameras captured Sam getting the congratulatory call from Rams coach Jeff Fisher and the memorable image of Sam kissing his boyfriend, a former Mizzou swimmer, as they celebrated the news.

"Since February, since my big announcement, this has been a whole speculation of the first openly gay football player," he said on draft day. "But you know what? It's not about that. It's about playing football. Can Michael Sam play football? And yes I can. The St. Louis Rams know I can, and I'm gonna give everything I've got to the St. Louis Rams, to help the Rams win the championship."

Sam played well in the preseason but didn't survive the Rams' final cut. He resurfaced with Dallas's practice squad. The Cowboys later waived him. By 2017 Sam had never played in an NFL regular-season game. He did make it to prime-time TV as a contestant on ABC's *Dancing with the Stars* but was eliminated midway through the season. In May 2015 Sam signed with the Montreal

Alouettes of the Canadian Football League. At his introductory press conference, he was asked about his comparisons to Jackie Robinson, another barrier-breaker who played professionally in Montreal. "I'm just here to play football," Sam said. "I'm not trying to really do anything historic here."

He left the team and stepped away from football early in the 2015 season, briefly returning to Mizzou to pursue a graduate degree. Sam's legacy, though, was established long before his playing career stalled in Canada. Two months after Sam's groundbreaking announcement in 2014, Derrick Gordon, a shooting guard at the University of Massachusetts, became the first active Division I men's college basketball player to announce he was gay. Other young, gay athletes followed their lead, including Scott Frantz, an offensive lineman in Kansas State's football program.

At the 2014 ESPYs awards show, Sam won the Arthur Ashe Courage Award and gave a moving acceptance speech. "Recently a friend asked me to talk to his sister," he said, "a young woman who was considering killing herself rather than sharing with her loved ones the fact that she was gay. When we spoke, she told me she would never consider hurting herself again and that somehow my example had helped her. It's amazing to think just doing what we can, we can all touch, change, and even save lives." He added, "To anyone out there, especially young people feeling like they don't fit in and will never be accepted, please know this: great things can happen when you have the courage to be yourself."

21 Kellen Winslow: Late but Great Bloomer

Any discussion of the greatest football player to wear the Black and Gold of Mizzou has to include the player who forever changed the tight end position. Kellen Winslow was hardly a blue-chip recruit when he came to Missouri from East St. Louis, Illinois. He had played just one season of organized football at East St. Louis High. Mizzou assistant coach Tony Steponovich stumbled upon him while scouting two other prospects across the Mississippi River. But he couldn't take his eyes off the kid who didn't know how to put on his football pants when the season began. Winslow received his first scholarship offer that day in 1974. Four years later he was a consensus All-American.

But the future Pro Football Hall of Famer didn't find instant success as a receiver. As a freshman in 1975, he caught one pass for 12 yards against Kansas State. As a sophomore, he caught a pass in every game but never more than two. "But you could see the talent and the ability that he had," former quarterback Pete Woods said.

Tight ends weren't primary passing targets in Mizzou's offense. Winslow was mostly a blocker. "Didn't block worth a darn," said offensive tackle Howard Richards, whom Winslow often lined up alongside. "But he worked at it. He became pretty good at it."

As a junior in 1977, Winslow emerged as MU's second-leading receiver, catching 25 passes for 358 yards and three touchdowns. His world changed in 1978 when Warren Powers took over as head coach and installed a more pass-friendly system, a split-back veer offense piloted by sophomore quarterback Phil Bradley. Winslow became Bradley's No. 1 receiver and finished with career-high totals for catches (29), yards (479), and touchdowns (6). In an epic victory at Nebraska that year, Winslow hauled in six passes for a career-high 132 yards and a touchdown—his first and only 100-yard receiving game at Missouri. "The best thing I can say about him is I'm glad I didn't screw him up," Bradley said, "because what he turned out to be wasn't even close to what he was at Missouri."

The two-time All–Big 8 tight end was chosen for the East-West Shrine Game and the Senior Bowl and came out as the top tight end prospect for the 1979 draft. He became Missouri's second-highest-drafted offensive skill player since the NFL-AFL merger. Yes, skill player. Not a misprint.

Selected 13th overall by San Diego, Winslow became the final missing piece for a revolutionary offense designed by head coach Don Coryell, featuring strong-armed quarterback Dan Fouts and receivers Charlie Joiner and John Jefferson. The first of three major knee injuries to haunt his pro career limited Winslow to seven games as a rookie, but in 1980 he snagged 89 passes for 1,290 yards. In his first four full seasons in the NFL (1980–83), Winslow caught 319 passes. "To think whatever they saw [at Missouri], to become what it eventually became, somebody was really good in San Diego," Bradley said.

"Fouts and Coryell absolutely used him to the fullest," Richards said. "And Kellen changed the game at the tight end position."

Often put in motion or lined up wide, Winslow put together his most famous game in the 1981 playoffs, when he caught a playoff-record 13 passes for 166 yards and a touchdown against Miami. He also blocked a field goal to send the game to overtime. Winslow played that day with injuries to his neck and shoulder. He fought through cramps and spasms caused by dehydration and had lost 13 pounds by the time the game ended in overtime, he later told *Sports Illustrated*. "I'd never come that close to death before," he told the magazine.

Winslow's knee eventually betrayed his career and forced him to retire at age 30 after the 1987 season. For his career, he caught

541 passes for 6,741 yards and 45 touchdowns, plus another 28 catches in six playoff games.

Winslow was inducted into the Pro Football Hall of Fame in 1995—the first former Mizzou player to be enshrined in Canton—and had his No. 83 jersey retired the same year at Mizzou. In 2002 he made the College Football Hall of Fame. Winslow returned to Mizzou to complete his undergraduate degree and also served as Mizzou's radio analyst for four years. He later earned his law degree at the University of San Diego.

22 One Stinkin' Play

The euphoria set in as the Missouri football team flew home from Colorado on November 1, 1997. The Tigers had just beaten the Buffaloes 41–31 for their sixth win of the season, enough to qualify for a bowl game for the first time in 14 years. "It was one of those flights you don't even buckle up, doing everything you shouldn't do on a flight because you feel like you're on top of the world for an instant," said Brock Olivo, a senior tailback for the Tigers that year. "The guys in my senior class, we're like, 'Holy shit, what just happened? Are you kidding me? Just please let the plane land; let's get back to Columbia and enjoy this.'"

There wouldn't be much time to celebrate. Top-ranked Nebraska would visit Columbia in seven days for a nationally tele-vised showdown. The Tigers hadn't toppled the Cornhuskers since 1978. It was Missouri's chance to unshackle a program forever known as one of the country's sleeping giants. "We wanted more," Olivo said. "You get a taste of it, and it's like, 'This is what we've been missing out on? All those dynasties around the country—like

Nebraska—is this what they feel every week? Let's not let this slip away. Let's go get it.' Sure enough, those guys came to town and we didn't even see the No. 1 ranking. We didn't see Tom Osborne, the legendary coach.... We just saw an opponent."

And eventually everyone at Memorial Stadium on November 8 saw one of the most indelible plays in college football history—a kick, a catch, and more anguish for a fan base tormented by its near misses and north end zone mishaps.

With 4:39 left in the fourth quarter at a sold-out Memorial Stadium, MU's first home sellout since 1984, Corby Jones's touchdown pass to Eddie Brooks tilted the showdown back in Mizzou's favor, 38–31. Neither team could sustain momentum in the final minutes as both squandered possessions and had to punt. Taking over with 1:02 left and no timeouts, Huskers quarterback Scott Frost drove the length of the field and, on the final play of regulation, set the impossible in motion.

Third down from the Mizzou 12-yard line. Seven seconds left. Frost scanned to his left but threw right to Shevin Wiggins, who ran a slant pattern near the goal line. With Mizzou defensive back Julian Jones swarming him from behind, the ball popped loose from Wiggins. Mizzou safety Harold Piersey was in perfect position to grab the interception, his hands held out ready to squeeze the ball to clinch the victory. But Piersey would have been better off clasping those hands to pray.

As Wiggins fell back into the end zone—the same end zone, mind you, where Colorado had scored a game-winning touchdown on the infamous Fifth Down seven years earlier—the ball trickled down his leg and met his right foot before it could scuff the turf. Wiggins kicked the ball into the air, over his head, back into the end zone. Then along came Matt Davison to dive into history.

"The funny part was I knew he caught the ball," Jones remembered. "As soon as it went up in the air, I could see it and then saw Matty dive. I said, 'Dang it. That's going to be a problem.' It was in slow motion for me watching it. I saw it hit Shevin. I saw H.P. right there trying to grab it. I can still the see the whole thing in my head to this day." Just as Jones feared, Nebraska's freshman wide receiver made the diving catch, earning him free bar tabs in Nebraska for eternity. ABC's Brent Musburger had the call: "Third down...Frost to the middle...juggled...diving...*touchdown Nebraska!*"

The official signaled touchdown, which some Mizzou fans missed as they stormed the end zone to capsize the goal post. Reality set in soon enough as the Huskers' PAT sent the game into overtime. The Tigers never recovered. Frost's rushing TD put Nebraska back on top in OT; the Huskers swallowed Jones for a game-clinching fourth-down sack on the ensuing possession.

"Those were two warriors out there, banging away at each other, " Missouri coach Larry Smith said after the game. "I've never been prouder of a team, win or lose." But..."One stinking play," he added. "That's what it was."

Years later, the stink hasn't worn off. "It sends chills up your spine, man," Olivo said. "Even right now. I can remember the atmosphere that night. I don't think Faurot Field had been that electric for probably 20-some odd years."

"There's no reason they should have won," Missouri offensive lineman Craig Heimburger said. "It was really an illegal situation. What takes the wind out of your sails is the fact that we were right there, and to lose it on a technicality like that. It's so hard to live with."

The next week, Wiggins told reporters he kicked the ball unintentionally. Had the officiating crew thought he kicked the ball on purpose, they could have flagged Nebraska for a 15-yard penalty. The college rule book stated, "A player shall not kick a loose ball, a forward pass or a ball being held for a place kick by an opponent," and defined kicking as "intentionally striking the ball with the knee, lower leg or foot." But there was no flag—only heartache.

When he reached the NFL, Heimburger played with several of those Cornhuskers on the Buffalo Bills, including (briefly, for one training camp) Davison, whose place in both schools' histories—haunting for one team, heroic for the other—was captured with his catch, forever known as the Flea Kicker. Davison's touchdown salvaged the Huskers' perfect season. They'd ultimately win the national championship.

"When I met [Davison], I said, 'I've never met you, but I hate you,'" Heimburger said, laughing. "He smiled and chuckled. But deep down it's that dagger in your back that you live with forever."

King City's Finest

Just a few months before the start of the 1965 season, Missouri's football coaches found the final piece to their recruiting class—at a track meet.

Earlier that fall, following King City High School's season finale, Roger Wehrli peeled off his shoulder pads, assuming he'd never play organized football again. A standout basketball player, Wehrli thought he might play that sport in college, maybe even at Missouri. His father knew former Mizzou hoops coach Sparky Stalcup from their college days and had sent the current coaching staff some film of Roger's highlights. Months later, though, MU football assistant coach Clay Cooper attended the 1965 state track meet in Columbia, where he couldn't help but notice the high hurdles and long jump champion.

Cooper, MU's secondary coach under Dan Devine, offered Wehrli a scholarship to join the Tigers for the upcoming season.

"It was a chance I hadn't counted on," Wehrli said, "and an opportunity I couldn't pass up."

He would go down as one of Mizzou's great discoveries. As soon as he was eligible to play for Devine's varsity as a sophomore in 1966, Wehrli joined Cooper's secondary as a starting cornerback. By 1967 Wehrli was an All–Big 8 player. Later described by Mizzou historian Bob Broeg as Mizzou's "long-legged, lantern-jawed, pale-faced lad," Wehrli became a shutdown defender under Cooper's watch and an electric kick returner.

Wehrli's celebrated stay in the Mizzou secondary was a three-year thrill for the small-town star. "For me," he said, "coming out of the state of Missouri and coming out of high school in a small town, it was more than a dream come true."

Shortly before the 1968 season, the Tigers lost safety Dennis Poppe to an injury, prompting defensive coordinator Al Onofrio to shift Wehrli to safety. No sweat. Playing out of his natural position, Wehrli snatched a Mizzou-record seven interceptions, a school mark that stood for 39 years. He also led the country in punt-return yardage, setting Mizzou and Big 8 records with 40 returns for 478 yards, a whopping 12 yards per pop. With Wehrli patrolling the secondary, the Tigers ranked fifth in the country in pass defense, earned a Gator Bowl invitation, and smashed Alabama 35–10.

The All-American would go on to play in multiple postseason all-star games—Devine was his head coach in the Hula Bowl—and earned looks as a possible first-round NFL draft pick. The pale-faced lad from King City was the 19th overall pick in a draft full of star power. The St. Louis Cardinals snatched Wehrli in the first round and plugged him into a defensive backfield that already included future Hall of Famer Larry Wilson. By heading to St. Louis, Wehrli would continue his career in the state of Missouri.

"It was very special," he said. "You get all these letters from different teams your senior year in college, from Dallas and San Francisco, and you think, *Well, that'd be great to play there.* But being drafted by the Cardinals and coming to St. Louis...my parents were able to come to most of the home games. I had a background that people in Missouri knew who I was because I played at the University of Missouri. That was great for me."

Wehrli played 14 quarterback-terrorizing seasons for the Cardinals, intercepted 40 passes, recovered 22 fumbles, and appeared in seven Pro Bowls. "After a while," Cowboys Hall of Fame quarterback Roger Staubach once told the *Post-Dispatch*, "you just stopped challenging him. There was no point to it. He was the best cornerback I played against. The term 'shutdown corner' originated with Roger Wehrli."

In 1995 Mizzou retired the No. 23 jersey in honor of Wehrli and fellow All-American Johnny Roland, who wore the number before Wehrli arrived on campus. In 2003 Wehrli joined Roland and other Mizzou stars in the College Football Hall of Fame, but his crowing achievement came four years later in Canton, Ohio. Twenty-five years after he played his final pro game, with the Cardinals long gone from the Gateway City, Wehrli was inducted into the Pro Football Hall of Fame, becoming just the second Mizzou player to earn the honor, joining tight end Kellen Winslow.

Wehrli regretted that his parents weren't alive for his induction, but he savored the chance to join the game's most prestigious collection of players. He said during his induction speech:

> I've been asked many times since the selection if I regret that I had not been selected sooner, as though this were a given or something. The Hall of Fame is never a given. Being nominated over the years has put a sense of hope and "what-ifs" in my mind, but I never for once took it for granted that I should be or would be here. I consider this a great honor that has come because of the work of a lot of people that touched my life and helped me become the athlete that I did....

I was married my senior year of college. Started getting letters from pro teams about the draft. My wife, Gayle, who really wasn't much of a sports fan unless I was playing, she heard about the draft. She thought they were talking about the army draft in Vietnam. She was not ready for that. In fact, once we straightened her out on the draft, she said, "You mean like the NFL with Bart Starr?" That's the only player she knew in the NFL. Well, babe, I'm up here with Bart Starr, so maybe we made it.

Not bad for a small-town track star.

24 Out of the Coffin

Just 20 days separated the worst loss in Missouri basketball history from one of the most satisfying wins.

On December 2, 1993, Norm Stewart's Tigers headed to Fayetteville, Arkansas, to face the No. 2 Arkansas Razorbacks. It was Arkansas's "dedication game" for the sparkling, new Bud Walton Arena. Stewart had some history in the Razorbacks' former home: he had won his first game as Missouri's head coach in Barnhill Arena on December 2, 1967. Now, 26 years later to the day, his Tigers were the special guests for Arkansas's 19,200-seat palace. More like the appetizer, main course, and dessert.

An Arkansas team that went on to win the national championship propped the Tigers on a spit and roasted them on national TV, 120–68, the most lopsided loss in the history of Mizzou's program. "I'm scared to call home," MU guard Melvin Booker said after the game. "I'm trying to forget it already."

The Tigers did more than forget about the 52-point debacle. Three weeks later, following four nondescript wins over Jackson State, Arkansas State, SMU, and Coppin State, Mizzou needed three overtimes to outlast No. 19 Illinois 108–107 in the greatest installment of the Braggin' Rights game in St. Louis. It was the series's final showdown at the Arena before moving to the new downtown home of the St. Louis Blues.

The triple-overtime victory required Stewart to empty his bench and rely on several untested freshmen, but it became the launching pad for one of Mizzou's greatest teams. "We were just trying to find an identity," Julian Winfield, a sophomore guard, said years later. "We knew it was a big rival game. But nobody in their right mind knew it would be the game that it was."

Stewart had a senior-dominant team in 1993–94, led by Booker, Lamont Frazier, Mark Atkins, and big man Jevon Crudup, who dominated the first half in St. Louis, at one point scoring six straight points. "Jevon's tough to guard anytime," Stewart later said. "Some nights, in some situations, he would elevate his play."

That was one of those nights, as Crudup had 18 points at halftime. Marlo Finner's rare three-pointer off the glass beat the halftime buzzer and stretched Mizzou's lead to four.

The second half swung in Illinois's favor as Crudup headed to the bench with his fourth foul with eight minutes left. Illinois ripped off a 26–4 run to seize complete control. Down nine with 1:10 left, Frazier, the Tigers' senior captain, sparked a rally with an unlikely three-point barrage. "Lamont Frazier wasn't the person we'd go to for a three," Stewart said. "We had two or three other individuals who had a little better record shooting threes, but he hit a couple late, and that was the key."

Frazier and Atkins combined for four threes in the final two minutes to send the game into the first overtime. "There was no sense of panic," Winfield said. "There was more of a sense of, 'Here we come.'"

Mizzou's foul trouble became a foul emergency in OT. Atkins and Finner fouled out, prompting Stewart to empty his bench. Freshmen Derek Grimm and Jason Sutherland got their first Braggin' Rights tastes in the first OT. Sutherland quickly made an impact with a crucial three-point play. "It wasn't a leap of faith," Winfield said. "It was, 'Hey, guys, it's your turn.'"

Grimm's big moment came in the second OT, when he knocked down a game-tying free throw in the final minute. From there came the series's most memorable moment (or agonizing moment, for the Illini faithful).

Illinois freshman guard Kiwane Garris attacked the basket on the last possession of the second OT and drew a foul with no time left on the clock. Stewart went ballistic. Instead of swallowing their whistles, the officials handed Illinois the victory in the form of two free throws.

"I remember that play like it was yesterday," Winfield said 20 years later. "To this day I don't think it's a foul. You've got a Big Ten team playing a Big 8 team, two physical teams. And they call that one? But I was pretty gratified when I turned around and saw Coach Stewart go absolutely berserk. I said, 'OK, he's not mad at me. He's mad at the refs.'"

Had Frazier and Crudup not held Stewart back, the coach might have tackled referee Denny Freund. Mark it up as one of Stewart's many psychological ploys. His tirade delayed the game for a moment, giving Garris more time to think about his free throws. "Coach Stewart was his own Zou Crew section because he was raising a lot of hell while Kiwane was shooting his free throws," Booker said. "He was the one doing all the distractions."

"I didn't approve of the call because it was the last call of the ballgame," Stewart said. "There wasn't much contact. You just wait and see if he can make a free throw. Fortunately, for us..." Garris missed...both of them. On to overtime No. 3.

Sutherland splashed a three-pointer to open the third OT and the Tigers led the rest of the way. Garris finished with 31 points but missed 10 of 22 free throws. "They didn't put the nail in the coffin," Winfield said, "so we opened that coffin back up and stepped out of there."

"It was just destined for us to win," said Booker, who would go on to earn All-America honors as the Tigers went undefeated in Big 8 regular-season play. "That game turned our season around."

25 A.O.

The darkest day in Mizzou football history—maybe in all of Mizzou athletics—came on July 12, 2005. During an unseasonably cool summer day in Columbia, a group of football players gathered on Faurot Field for a typical off-season workout. Tragically, one player didn't survive. Aaron O'Neal, a redshirt freshman from St. Louis, struggled to complete the noncontact drills, staggered, collapsed, and later died when his body shut down. Viral meningitis was initially ruled as the cause of death, though medical experts later surmised that O'Neal's death was related to the sickle cell trait that he carried. The blood disorder can lead to organ failure and death during exertion. O'Neal's family filed a lawsuit against Missouri coach Gary Pinkel, athletic administrators, and members of the training staff. Four years later, the school agreed to pay the family a $2 million settlement.

Within the program, O'Neal's death forever changed the coaches and players who affectionately called the 19-year-old linebacker A.O. "That team grew closer," former linebackers coach Dave Steckel said. "They lost a brother."

Pinkel, who was vacationing in Las Vegas when O'Neal died, cut short his trip and returned to his team. "Being a head football coach, and you have players in your program, they're like your children," he said the next day, choking back tears several times. "I feel like I lost one of my children."

The 2005 Missouri football team honored O'Neal throughout the season with various tributes. In MU's comeback win over South Carolina in the Independence Bowl, players rushed to the 25-yard line to celebrate, to honor O'Neal's No. 25 jersey. In 2008, which would have been O'Neal's senior year, a different senior wore No. 25 for each game. At the end of the regular season, O'Neal was honored at the final home game with each of his classmates. His father, Lonnie O'Neal, attended the game, wearing his son's No. 25 jersey. Missouri gave Lonnie O'Neal a bowl ring for each of the four bowls Aaron would have played in during his Mizzou career. "Tonight was about him," quarterback Chase Daniel said after the emotional victory over Kansas State. "It wasn't about the seniors. It wasn't about this team. It was about him."

O'Neal's death brought out a side of Pinkel that players and colleagues had rarely seen during his first few years at Mizzou. He listened to players. He hugged them in public. He cried. He laughed. Players attributed the changes to O'Neal's death and the way it shook Pinkel and his program. "I know it's changed him," Steckel said. "Anytime something like that happens to you, it changes you."

To remember O'Neal's brief time at MU, the Tigers began a new tradition in 2009, giving his No. 25 to a young linebacker who would wear the number for the rest of his college career. Zaviar Gooden wore the 25 from 2009 to 2012, followed by Donavin Newsom from 2013 to 2016. The honor was especially meaningful for Newsom who, like O'Neal, attended Parkway North High School in St. Louis. "I said to him, 'You're going to be compared a lot to Aaron. Does that bother you?'" Parkway North coach Bob Bunton once asked Newsom. "Right away, without any [hesitation] at all, he just said, 'I'm proud of that. I'm proud of that.'" In 2017 freshman linebacker Jamal Brooks carried on the tradition as the team's new No. 25.

When Steckel moved to Missouri State in 2015 to take over as the Bears' head coach, his framed photo of O'Neal went with him, taking up a prominent place in his new office in Springfield. The darkest day in Mizzou history had passed. The memories were still fresh. "Death is an inevitable thing," Steckel said. "But when it's young, it's early, and it's tragic, people can't come to grips with it as much. It either separates people or brings them closer together. In our case, it brought them closer together."

At O'Neal's memorial service in Columbia, fellow linebacker Dedrick Harrington read a poem he wrote about his fallen teammate. The poem hangs alongside a framed photo of O'Neal in the team facility:

> I still hate waking up, getting the bad news that day.
> They say there's one life that we're living and time is slowly beating away.
> Who would've ever thought you would be gone so fast
> And just think yesterday us hanging out is now a thing of the past.
> Brotha, my Brotha, how I miss you so bad here today
> For you never really understand one's importance until they are gone away.
> Man, I'm sorry for if I could, I'd make this all just a bad dream and you'd soon awake.
> For my selfish self is so used to seeing you, your absence is so hard to take.
> I'm dying inside because now there's really no way to show how much I really care
> No way to let you know that in me there was a true friend and I was always there.

Though God always knows best no matter what the circumstances may be

I just wish he hadn't taken you from your family, as well as others and me.

I prayed for you and your family, asking God to take away the pain

But when the sunshine is gone, the only thing left is the rain.

So my Brotha, go enjoy sweet rest with the one who holds tomorrow

For soon the mourning will be over and we will smile instead of feel sorrow.

For your life is irreplaceable and I still see an awesome vision of your face

All the happiness and memories of you will forever fill this place.

I just pray that soon we can all somehow understand

That God needed an angel in Heaven, so he took you by the hand.

26 The Prince of Duke Who Would Be King

In hindsight, Missouri could have done better than Quin Snyder as the heir apparent to basketball legend Norm Stewart. Snyder, a 32-year-old coaching prodigy who learned at the hand of royalty—Duke's Mike Krzyzewski—was the choice in 1999 to take over the Mizzou program, picked ahead of fellow finalists Bill Self and John Calipari. Self, then the coach at Tulsa, would later thrive at Illinois and Kansas. Calipari, out of coaching at the time, would resurface at Memphis and Kentucky, where he'd reach four Final Fours in his first six seasons.

But in 1999 Snyder was the overwhelmingly popular pick, a former Duke player and assistant coach with a winning pedigree and the Coach K credentials to compensate for his head coaching inexperience. Besides, the pro-Snyder crowd reasoned at the time, how old was Stewart when he became head coach in 1967? Answer: 32.

"We believe without a doubt, unquestionably, that we have identified the finest head basketball coach for the University of Missouri, and it's an individual named Quin Snyder," Mizzou AD Mike Alden said on April 6, 1999. "I'm going to be very, very proud to be associated with and to work with him many, many years down the road through many successes. And it's going to be a lot of fun." Not always—but for the first few years…yes, indeed.

Snyder, from the Seattle suburb of Mercer Island, played point guard for Krzyzewski at Duke from 1986 to 1989 then earned graduate degrees from Duke in law and business administration before settling on a coaching career. He spent four seasons as a full-time assistant under Coach K and became the staff's top recruiter.

At Mizzou he made an immediate splash on the recruiting scene, landing Kansas City standout Kareem Rush then adding Detroit prep stars Arthur Johnson and Rickey Paulding, plus Travon Bryant, a McDonald's All-American from California. Under Snyder, the Tigers made the NCAA tournament in each of his first three seasons, reaching the Elite Eight as a No. 12 seed in 2002 with wins over Miami, Ohio State, and UCLA. It was as far as Stewart had taken the Tigers in 16 trips to the tournament.

A month later, Snyder planted the seed to his demise, signing a point guard from the College of Southern Idaho, Ricky Clemons, a gifted player and first-ballot nominee for the school's all-time Hall of Shame. The next year, Missouri failed to match preseason expectations and lost in the NCAA Round of 32. Clemons was arrested for striking his girlfriend, suspended, and ultimately dismissed. He then exposed the program to an NCAA investigation when he was recorded from his Columbia jail cell talking about receiving impermissible benefits. In 2004 the NCAA wrapped up its probe and placed MU on three years of probation and banned Snyder's staff from off-campus recruiting for a year.

By then, the program was on a steep decline. After the Elite Eight season, two of the next three years ended with first-round losses in the NIT, and the other ended with a second-round ouster. Snyder stepped down under pressure late in the 2005–06 season after a 26-point loss at Baylor, the team's sixth-straight Big 12 defeat. Synder's resignation launched not one but two campus-initiated investigations, one by the university chancellor and another by the university system president. Snyder finished with a record of 126–91. "I've had seven great years here with a lot of successes and a lot of challenges," Snyder said. "When someone tells you it's time to move on, you respect that, take it like a man, and you move forward."

Years later, the man remembered for delivering Snyder the news he'd been fired believes the former coach's early success at MU is too easily forgotten. "Quin and I were really close from the get-go," said former MU player Gary Link, the team's former radio analyst and special assistant to the athletics director. "He was like the little brother I never had. And you're damn right we were good [under Snyder]. In Mike Alden's defense, everyone says it could have been Bill Self, but Mike was hearing loud and clear that we need[ed] to go in a different direction. Bill Self was deemed to be Norm Stewart Jr. If you look at him, he pretty much was. He was the same kind of coach from the Midwest. Quin was the hottest associate head coach in America."

If Missouri erred with Snyder, it was in keeping him too long. The program was in deep decay once he was fired. "The toughest job an AD has to do is you have to pull the trigger one year too early instead of one year too late," Link said. "When you wait that extra year, that puts you in a hole for two years. Clearly, it was going bad for Quin at the end. Hindsight's 20/20, but it would have probably been better [to fire him] one or maybe even two years before."

Over time, Snyder found coaching success at the professional level. He led the Austin Toros of the NBA Developmental League to three winning seasons then worked as an NBA assistant with the 76ers, Lakers, and Hawks—interrupted by a stopover in Moscow, where he was an assistant in the Russian Professional Basketball League.

In June 2014, 15 years after landing his first and only college head coaching job, Snyder was named head coach of the NBA's Utah Jazz. In its first season under Snyder, Utah improved by 13 wins from the previous year. In his third year, he guided the Jazz to the 2017 Western Conference semifinals, their deepest playoff run in seven years.

Once Snyder relaunched his career, his Missouri days remained far behind in his rearview mirror. Rarely did he discuss the unraveling in Columbia. During a Yahoo! Sports podcast in 2017, Snyder said:

> You don't know what you don't know. Before I got to Missouri, I basically spent my adult life at Duke, from 18 to 32. I played there. I had gone to grad school there. Didn't think I was going to coach. Then started coaching and had an opportunity. There are some things that you can think you know, you can maybe know intellectually or rationally, but until you have lived through certain things, there is a level of knowledge and understanding, whether it's the profession or even on a personal level, that you just don't have. Life experience is the only way to acquire some of those things, whether we call them lessons or adversity or whatever the case may be.

27 Mizzou's Italian Stallion

Brock Olivo was born on June 24, 1976. Six months later, his idol was born on film. The two never met, but Olivo grew up wanting to be nothing less than the man he adored on the silver screen: Rocky Balboa. "As corny and cliché as it sounds, he was the underdog—and he was Italian," said Olivo, the pride of Washington, Missouri, who was among Coach Larry Smith's first recruits in 1994 and left Mizzou as the school's career rushing leader. "Rocky showed a generation of viewers who watched that movie how an underdog overcomes the odds," Olivo said.

From 1994 to 1997, Olivo became the Tigers' Italian Stallion, a workhorse running back who voluntarily played special teams… who set new standards in the weight room…who defined the rebirth of power running at Mizzou…who turned heads with a maniacal regimen, diet, and lifestyle. Bare-knuckled and bloody, Olivo changed the culture of Missouri football in the 1990s. "He's probably the most dedicated person I've ever seen in my life," former Mizzou offensive lineman Craig Heimburger said. "It was football 24/7 in his mind. He put so many distractions away that college kids don't. I've never seen a leader like that who sacrificed so much just to be a football player."

Before he became a prolific running back and return specialist at St. Francis Borgia Regional High School, Olivo found inspiration from his father, David, a former quarterback at the University of Miami. Brock remembered being distraught after losing a race in a middle school track meet. David brought home a poster that hung in his son's room until he left for college. "It said, 'When you're not training, someone somewhere else is. And when you meet them, they will win,'" Olivo recalled.

From there, the training began and never ended. When Heimburger reported to Mizzou in the summer of 1995, Olivo was the only player taking part in both the morning and afternoon running sessions during summer voluntary workouts. Olivo would lift weights in the afternoon, do more running in the evening, and finish the day with torturous abdominal workouts. Behind the Mizzou veterinarian school, Olivo discovered a steep grassy hill that became a staple for off-season training. Players would sprint up Brock's Hill in the searing heat, coating the grass with blood, sweat, tears, and breakfast. "All he could think about was football," Heimburger said. "And guys followed him."

As a senior in high school, Olivo jumped at the chance to play for Mizzou—literally out of his chair when Smith and assistant coach Curtis Jones visited him in January 1994. Olivo wasn't highly recruited by other schools but was dying to play for the state program, despite its 10-year losing streak. "When they visited

Former running back Brock Olivo waits on the sideline for his moment. His number 27 was officially retired by Mizzou on September 13, 2003.

my house, I was so excited, I was on the edge of my seat," Olivo said. "My dad had to put his hand on my chest as if to say, 'Take a deep breath, sit back in your chair; just calm down.'… For me it was a no-brainer. I would have run through a wall for both of those guys."

Instead, he ran through Mizzou's offensive line for the next four years. As Smith tried to develop an identity for Mizzou's offense, the ball usually found its way into Olivo's hands. He led the Tigers in rushing as a freshman, sophomore, and junior. As a sophomore in 1995, he lugged the ball 232 times, the second-most single-season carries in Mizzou history, trailing only Joe Moore's 260 carries in 1969.

"He wasn't the fastest guy on earth, but I've never seen a better power runner than Brock Olivo," said Heimburger, an All–Big 12 offensive guard with the Tigers. "I'd come around and pull and could always hear him going ahead of me slamming helmets with somebody, and always getting at least five yards on the play.… His feet hit the ground so hard. A lot of running backs are light-footed, but you always knew where Brock was because you could hear his feet and you could feel his feet coming."

With the emergence of quarterback Corby Jones, the Tigers became known for their dizzying option-based rushing attack, but it was the simple power-running play that became their calling card. "If you were going to define Missouri football in that era, it was the power play," Olivo said. "We called it 16 and 17. It doesn't get any more basic than that. It was Harry Heistand– and Andy Moeller–coached offensive linemen doubling down and kicking out with a 270-pound fullback and then our tailbacks slamming it up behind the double team. It was like, 'Here we come.'"

He added, "We knew we we're going to get five [yards]. It was like running through smoke. You don't know what's going to be on the other side, but you know you're going to come out clean if you hit the hole."

Olivo finished his college career as Mizzou's career rushing leader with 3,026 yards despite sharing the workload in his later years with Jones and tailback Devin West. His 31 touchdowns and 186 points were second all-time in scoring among non-kickers. He became the first Mizzou player with multiple 200-yard games, both in 1995.

As a sophomore Olivo begged Smith to let him play on every special teams unit. He got his wish with one exception: he wasn't part of the field goal block team. Otherwise, he spent his Saturdays chasing down returners on the punt and kickoff teams. He blocked on the return units. He relished the action, the explosions in the open field. "It's a different animal playing on special teams," he said. "You're doing things with your body that you can't do on offense and defense." As a senior, Olivo was named the inaugural winner of the Mosi Tatupu Award, given to the nation's best special teams player.

He did it all with his bare hands—literally. Olivo refused to wear gloves on the field. "For me, it was a statement," he said. "We were not fashionistas by any means, man. We had the bare bones. We didn't have names on our jerseys. We didn't have the fancy Nike uniforms. We were very simple. That reflected everything we did. You were going to get your knuckles dirty and bloody playing us. Because we had them too, and were proud to show them."

Missouri celebrated Olivo in 2003 by retiring his No. 27, a controversial decision for some who felt other former players were more deserving. For Olivo, the honor wasn't about his personal accomplishments. "My name on that wall is representative of everyone who came through there at that time," he said. "And for that I'm very proud."

After college Olivo went undrafted but spent four years with the Detroit Lions, mostly playing special teams. He abruptly retired after the 2001 season. After his pro career he worked in Washington, DC, for the National Italian American Foundation, a nonprofit organization that promotes Italian culture. After an unsuccessful Missouri congressional campaign in 2008, Olivo moved to Italy, where he became head coach of its national football team. He returned stateside and bounced around in some coaching jobs before joining the Kansas City Chiefs in 2014 as an assistant, coaching—no surprise—special teams. After a stint with the Denver Broncos, he joined the Chicago Bears in 2018 as a special teams assistant.

Olivo's rushing record has since been eclipsed at Mizzou, but statistics will never define his legacy. His former coach knew better. "His determination, his work ethic, his intensity, his love of the game of football, his love of the University of Missouri, his goals, his dreams…everything, from the day he walked in here, it's been there," Smith said in 1997, as Olivo prepared for his final home game. "But each year, each week, maybe each day, he's moved it to another level. He's been an…example." Perhaps the best.

28 Uncle Al

The first-floor meeting room at the Mizzou Athletic Training Complex is named after Al Onofrio, the Tigers' head coach from 1971 to 1977, the bespectacled coach who oversaw some of college football's great upsets of the 1970s. Since its construction in the early 2000s, the room has been where Mizzou coaches hold team meetings. That wasn't a specialty of the room's namesake.

"In some ways, he was the antithesis of a football coach," former offensive lineman Howard Richards recalled. "I rarely remember him talking to the team. It was not unlike Tom Landry, but Landry was more involved with the offense and defense. Al was almost reticent."

"He didn't put on airs," former quarterback Pete Woods said. "He was just a genuine guy."

"He was a father figure," former quarterback Phil Bradley said. "He was a quiet man who stood back and observed and watched his coaches coach. Then when it came time to bring the team in together at the end of practice, that's when the father figure in him really came out."

Uncle Al, as he's fondly remembered, was loved and widely respected as one of the game's great defensive masterminds, the brains behind the dominant Mizzou defenses of the 1960s under head coach Dan Devine. The son of Liberto Onofrio, who came to America from Naples at the turn of the 20th century, authored some of the greatest victories in MU history.

But first, he coached golf. In 1955 Devine had become head coach at Arizona State and needed to form his staff. Onofrio had been out of football coaching and found peace coaching the Sun Devils golfers. Devine talked him into joining the football staff. They spent the better part of two decades coaching together.

When Devine left Tempe for Mizzou in 1958, Onofrio could have stayed behind but opted to follow Devine. Under Onofrio, the Tigers made a pivotal defensive adjustment in 1959, shifting to a split-six system that unleashed the defensive ends to rush the passer. With Onofrio commanding the defense, the Tigers suffocated teams from week to week. From 1960 to 1965, Mizzou held opponents to single-digit scoring averages each season.

When Devine left Mizzou to coach the Green Bay Packers after the 1970 season, Onofrio became the natural successor in Columbia. "I was not an easy man to work for," Devine later wrote in his memoir, "so I know that those 16 years may not have been all pleasant. He hung in with me. I will always be indebted to him for his loyalty and skill."

After Onofrio's 1–10 debut season as head coach, Mizzou quickly recovered and became known as one of college football's great king slayers. From 1972 to 1977, his teams took down 14 top-15 teams, starting with No. 8 Notre Dame in 1972 in South Bend. Along the way, Onofrio's teams toppled No. 7 Colorado in 1972; No. 2 Nebraska in '73; No. 7 Arizona State in '74; and No. 8 USC, No. 2 Ohio State, and No. 3 Nebraska in '76.

But the big wins came with a price: the Tigers also lost 20 games to unranked opponents under Onofrio's watch. "Missouri is the kind of team that makes college football a wild trip for those who dabble in school loyalty and/or point spreads," *Sports Illustrated* wrote in 1976. "It is a squad with so many ups and downs that the players should take Dramamine before each game."

Missouri's nonconference schedules were brutal during those years, and the '76 team embodied the Onofrio regime. The Tigers went on the road three times that season and toppled teams ranked among the nation's top eight, at USC, Ohio State, and Nebraska— Onofrio called the 22–21 win over the Buckeyes "the greatest game Missouri has ever played"—but lost to unranked Illinois, Iowa State, and Kansas, and finished just 6–5. "We played so many big games at the beginning of the year that we got sort of worn out," said Woods, who quarterbacked the Tigers from 1975 to 1977. "Illinois was our only powder puff every year. That took a lot out of you. It was emotional because every week you had to be ready to play. If you try to keep that sustained emotion going every game, at some point you have a letdown. Unfortunately our letdowns were against teams that were good enough to beat us."

Losing to Kansas ultimately led to Onofrio's ouster after a 4–7 season in 1977. His teams were just 1–6 against the rival birds to the west, with three of those losses coming against unranked Jayhawks teams when the Tigers were in the top 20. Injuries limited Woods to parts of four games in 1977, forcing Bradley to pilot the offense as a freshman. The roster was loaded with future stars who went on to NFL careers, including Richards, tight end Kellen Winslow, and a stash of young defensive playmakers. But the latest loss to the Jayhawks was the final blow. Onofrio was fired after the 24–22 defeat by a Kansas team that had won just two Big 8 games that season.

"It was expected," Woods said. "There were a lot of A.O. Must Go signs in the stands and with the student body. A lot of people still remembered the Devine era, of course, and Al's first season when they went 1–10. It wasn't up to the level people hoped. We had won a lot of big games and showed we were able to compete against some of the great teams. But to not play as well against the lesser competition was disappointing, to say the least. Expectations were high."

Onofrio was 38–41 in seven seasons at Missouri, going 17–11 in regular-season nonconference games, 20–29 in Big 8 games, and 1–1 in bowls—a 49–35 loss to Arizona State in the 1972 Fiesta Bowl and a 34–17 win over Auburn in the 1973 Sun Bowl.

"I always told him he was so good as a coach that he could have tripped on his beard if he had just beaten Kansas," former *Post-Dispatch* sports editor and columnist Bob Broeg later said of Onofrio. "He was favored five of the seven times he played them and lost six of seven. It was diabolical."

Missouri replaced Onofrio with Warren Powers, a former Nebraska assistant who was coming off a winning season as head coach at Washington State. Powers had instant success at Mizzou, winning 31 games his first four seasons. In 1981 a school record–tying seven players were chosen in the NFL Draft—most of whom were recruited during the Onofrio years. That fact wasn't lost on the highest-drafted of the seven. "As much as we developed under Powers, the credit goes to Onofrio for getting us there," said Richards, the No. 26 overall pick to Dallas in 1981. "A lot of that credit hasn't been given to him for that."

"Who's to say how the next three years would have gone had the staff [not been fired]," Bradley wondered. "But the one thing you cannot dispute is they left a whole lot of talent at Missouri when they left."

Onofrio retired from coaching after he was fired and moved back to Arizona but often returned to Missouri for team reunions. Onofrio was elected to Mizzou's Intercollegiate Athletics Hall of Fame in 1993. In 2004 he died at 83 after suffering from non-Hodgkin's lymphoma. "He exemplified what universities want in a coach now," close friend and longtime Mizzou assistant John Kadlec told the *Post-Dispatch* when Onofrio died. "Integrity, honesty, loyalty, someone who will be concerned with football players other than as football players."

29 Mr. Smith Goes to the Basket

After missing the second half of 1988–89 while fighting cancer, Norm Stewart gathered his team before embarking on what became the greatest regular season in Mizzou history. Stewart returned a gifted core, led by junior forward Doug Smith and sophomore guard Anthony Peeler.

Stewart recalled the preseason meeting 25 years later. "I got them together," Stewart said, "and told them, 'Let me ask you guys a question. You're over in Rothwell Gymnasium and you're playing an important pickup game. Maybe you bet beer or you bet pizza. You need one bucket to win. Who are you going to throw it to if you need a bucket to get that pizza or beer? All of them said Doug."

No surprise. But Stewart wasn't satisfied. "'OK, but we've got a shot clock,'" he continued. "'Let's say we can't find Doug. Now who are we going to throw it to?' They said Anthony. I said, 'OK, good. So we've got our offense.' John McIntyre says, 'What about a third option?' Now, he's a hell of a shooter, but I said, 'John, three options screws up an offense.'"

So that was that. The 1989–90 Tigers would go as far as Smith and Peeler could take them. A strong supporting cast surrounded the tandem—Nathan Buntin, Lee Coward, Travis Ford, Jeff Warren and, yes, McIntyre too—but Smith and Peeler were Stewart's biggest stars. Smith especially.

The 6'10", 220-pound center from Detroit brought unique skills to the frontcourt. Smith dominated inside, but his game extended far beyond the paint. With a deadly turnaround jumper, Smith stretched defenses with his range. He rebounded, blocked shots, stole the ball, and set up teammates with passes out of the post. He did everything and did everything as well as anyone in the college game. "He doesn't worry about scoring," Stewart said of Smith in 1988. "He worries about playing defense, passing the ball, moving, learning the offense, [learning] what the other people are doing. Because he knows he has the confidence in himself that he will get points. If he can learn all those other things, he can get points."

With upperclassmen Derrick Chievous and Byron Irvin on the roster in 1987–88, Mizzou didn't need Smith to fill up the box score as a freshman. He averaged 11.3 points and gave Chievous a talented sidekick on the front line. As a sophomore, Smith emerged as Stewart's top-scoring big man, his average climbing to 13.9 points per game. As a junior, with Peeler entrenched in the backcourt, Smith reached a new level. He was the Big 8 Player of the Year while averaging 19.8 points and 9.2 rebounds while shooting 56.3 percent from the floor. The Tigers climbed to No. 1 in the national polls, led by the junior forward, whose game was more fierce than his personality.

"People say to me when they first meet me, 'Man, you look mean,'" he told the *Post-Dispatch* during his Mizzou career. "I don't know where people get the impression that I'm this mean person. I'm not a villain out there."

After MU's first-round exit in the 1990 NCAA tournament, Smith surprised everyone, Stewart included, by turning down the NBA to play one last college season, even though NCAA sanctions were looming over Stewart's program. "Basically I had made a commitment to the university for four years," Smith said years later. "I had a lot of fun with the guys I played with, and plus, I helped recruit several younger players. They came to Missouri thinking I would play for four years, so I didn't want to let them down."

Three weeks before Smith's senior year tipped off, the NCAA Committee on Infractions placed Mizzou on a one-year postseason ban, among other penalties. Smith's college career would end in the Big 8 tournament. "It was definitely a disappointment," said Smith, who averaged 23.6 points as a senior, earning a second Big 8 Player of the Year honor. "But we couldn't be concerned with those things. We had a season to play, so we just used the Big 8 tournament as our national tournament."

It was a disappointing season by most measures, as the Tigers finished fourth in the conference and quickly fell out of the national polls. But, as promised, Smith carried Mizzou to a championship. The Tigers swept Iowa State, Oklahoma State, and Nebraska to capture the Big 8 tournament in Kansas City. A week earlier, in his final home game, Mizzou had surprised Smith by hoisting his No. 34 jersey to the Hearnes Center rafters. No Mizzou player would wear the number again.

Smith left Missouri as one of the program's undisputed all-time greats. As of 2018, he still ranked as MU's career leader for field goals (897), No. 2 for points (2,184) and rebounds (1,053), No. 4 for blocks (129), and No. 5 for steals (178). His 14 30-point games are more than any player in team history. His 19 field goals against Nebraska in 1990 still stand as MU's single-game record.

The Dallas Mavericks took Smith at No. 6 in the 1991 draft, but he never became the sweet-shooting big man the franchise expected. He played five NBA seasons—four in Dallas, one in

Boston—and averaged eight points and 4.2 rebounds for his career. A lengthy contract holdout delayed his rookie year. He played for a different head coach every season. He gained too much bulk, which robbed him of agility. Smith would have been a prototype stretch forward in the modern NBA—a skilled shooter with the size to rebound and block shots—but coaches struggled to define his role. Smith would resurface in several minor leagues but lasted just 296 games in the NBA.

"If there's one regret I have about the time I spent in the NBA, it's missing training camp my rookie year," Smith said three years after his NBA career fizzled. "That put me behind, and in some ways, I don't think I ever recovered from it. But I played for five coaches in five years, which also made it tough."

He added, "There were some ups and down—when you're young, you make mistakes—but playing in the NBA was definitely a highlight for me. But it's not something I talk about much because I don't want to be one of those people who live in the past."

30 Perfection Spoiled in 1960

On top of the national polls for the first time in team history, Mizzou didn't wear No. 1 well in 1960. After thrashing Oklahoma 41–19 in Norman, the Tigers were feted all over town and thrown a parade through Columbia to celebrate the reward that was sure to follow, especially with No. 1 Minnesota's loss to Purdue.

Indeed, Mizzou climbed to No. 1 in the Associated Press and United Press International polls with one game left in the regular season. All that stood in Missouri's path was a home game against, naturally, rival Kansas. The Jayhawks were 6–2–1—with their only losses coming in nonconference play. The winner would be crowned Big 8 champion.

Nine games into the season, Oklahoma was the first team to score more than eight points on Al Onofrio's Mizzou defense. The Tigers had blanked three opponents and allowed just eight touchdowns through nine games. Until Oklahoma, no team had scored a rushing TD against MU. A national championship was looking realistic. "We were undefeated and looking like we were going the whole way," offensive lineman Ed Blaine remembered. "Then Kansas stepped up and whopped us."

Whopped them good. The Tigers could barely move the ball against the Jayhawks. The defense, stout all season, allowed halfback Bert Coan to rush for 67 yards and two touchdowns. Kansas won 23–7. Mizzou dropped to No. 4 and 5 in the national polls. The Tigers would get Navy in the Orange Bowl, but the national championship was shot.

Tigers coach Dan Devine blamed himself for the loss. "The shame of it was that it cost our kids the recognition they should have received from going undefeated and winning the conference championship as well as the national championship," he wrote in his memoir. "I learned a lot that week, lessons which I remembered and applied for years into the future. I realized it was the head coach's job to handle the distractions, and I didn't get it done."

There was an unexpected twist to the story: midway through the season the NCAA had placed Kansas on probation for illegally recruiting players, including Coan. As a freshman at TCU, Coan had accepted a plane ticket to an all-star game in Chicago, paid for by Kansas alumnus Bud Adams, who had a controlling interest in Houston's AFL team.

Kansas believed the issue would be tabled until after the season and kept Coan in the lineup, but Missouri athletics director Don Faurot reportedly filed a complaint with the Big 8, alleging that KU had illegally recruited Coan from TCU on Adams's behalf. "I did the wrong thing," Coan told the *St. Louis Post-Dispatch* years later. "I knew it was probably an illegal thing. I was unhappy at TCU, and I was open to recruiting. [Adams] did recruit me illegally off another campus, and I'm not going to try and smooth over that."

After the season, the Big 8 stripped Kansas of victories over Colorado and Missouri. Technically, Missouri was then 10–0 and Big 8 champions. Alas, the Tigers wouldn't be in the running for the national championship.

Missouri players took little consolation in the 10–0 record that came with an asterisk. "OK, but we lost," Blaine said. "[Coan] is a player just like every other player. The fact that he was ineligible to play doesn't change the game. The game was still lost and we had fallen off the pinnacle. We deserved the consequences.... It became Missouri's first undefeated, untied season in history. At least to me, that meant very little."

The Tigers beat Navy in the Orange Bowl and finished as high as No. 4 in the final polls. Devine never seemed to forgive himself for the loss that became a win but always felt like a loss. "That team was a national championship team and deserves to be recognized as such, and to this day my honest opinion is that I let it slip away from them," he wrote. "I can't go back and change it. That team bears a scar instead of a pat on the back, and it remains one of the biggest regrets of my life."

The NCAA, the Big 8, and Missouri gave the Tigers the credit for the win based on the league's ruling, but to underscore the rivalry between the two schools, Kansas still counted the game as a victory in its records.

31 Johnny Be Good

Johnny Roland could have been the greatest running back in Mizzou history. He could have been the greatest defensive back in Mizzou history. Instead, he split his time at both positions from 1962 to 1965—and just might have strengthened his legacy as the greatest *player* in Mizzou history.

At least one observer held that opinion 25 years after Roland played his last game at Missouri. When the university announced its All-Century Team in 1990 to commemorate the program's 100th birthday, the *St. Louis Post-Dispatch*'s Bob Broeg, the most prolific historian of Mizzou football, disagreed with voters who chose quarterback Paul Christman as the greatest player in MU's first century. "I'd give that recognition," Broeg wrote in 1990, "to Johnny Roland."

Was Roland truly the greatest to ever slip on a Missouri jersey? "Oh, I don't know," Roland said in 2015, well into retirement after a life dedicated to the sport. "I was a guy who was willing to do whatever it took to win."

Sacrifice defined Roland's legacy more than statistics. He came to Mizzou from Corpus Christi, Texas, after initially signing with Oklahoma, back when recruits weren't bound to national letters of intent like they are now. The Sooners' loss was the Tigers' gain. In his debut season with Dan Devine's team, Roland led the Tigers with 830 rushing yards as a sophomore, which ranked seventh in the nation, and earned All–Big 8 honors. In his first taste of college football, Roland scorched California for 171 yards and three touchdowns in what would go down as his career rushing performance. But his career was just getting started.

First, though, a detour through Kansas City. In 1963 the university accused Roland of stealing a set of tires when a mismatched pair was found on his car. At the time it was believed the tire switcheroo was a prank by one of Roland's teammates, but no one ever confessed. The school fined Roland $50 and expelled him before the 1963 season. He moved to Kansas City for the fall semester.

Devine strongly defended his star player. "I wouldn't blame him if he didn't come back," Devine said at the time, as reported by Broeg later. "What does he, a Texas boy, owe Missouri? He's too smart to have switched different-colored wheels from a car parked in the same block, but he's too proud to turn pigeon. He could go to Canada to play pro ball or transfer."

Instead, Roland was allowed to reenroll for the spring semester in 1964, but Devine approached him with a request before the season opener against Cal, a team featuring star quarterback Craig Morton, who'd eventually shatter every team passing record and some Pac-10 marks. Against the high-powered Cal attack, the Tigers needed Roland on defense. "You've got to remember who we were getting ready to play before I made the decision," Roland said. "Dan's strong suit was defense. He believed that you win with defense. We had a pretty young secondary and he thought if he moved me to the defensive side, it would at least give us some leadership on the back end. We had a couple pretty good running backs, so that if I moved, he thought we'd still be OK there."

Roland's move came with a caveat. "But [Devine] told me that when we got inside the 20 or on the goal line or in short yardage, I'd always be the running back," he said.

Roland made the move and transferred his talents across the line of scrimmage, becoming an All–Big 8 defensive back as a junior and senior. In 1965 he tied the school record with a Big 8–best six interceptions, earned All-America honors and, perhaps most notably, became the first African American player to serve as team captain in any sport at Mizzou.

That same season, the NCAA did away with the rule prohibiting substitutions, which allowed coaches to use a two-platoon system. Bruce Van Dyke remained the last of Devine's true "iron man" players, starting on both the offensive and defensive lines. But, as promised, Roland found his way on the field for offense too, as Devine's preferred back inside the 20-yard line. He finished the 1965 season with just 26 carries but visited the end zone five times. In between the 20s, Mizzou's Charlie Brown took over as Devine's top running threat and finished 10th in the country in rushing with 937 yards.

As the full-time back in Devine's power-sweep offense, Roland could have become one of the country's elite runners and perhaps challenge for the Heisman Trophy as an upperclassman. But Roland never questioned the move to defense. "I was always a team player," he said. "If that meant I had to move, then I'll move and we'll see at the end of the year what kind of decision it was."

Roland saved perhaps his most complete college game for his regular-season finale. In a 44–20 win at Kansas, Roland intercepted a pass, recovered a fumble, returned kicks, completed a pass, caught another, and crossed the goal line three times on short-yardage runs. He touched the ball 19 times for 178 all-purpose yards.

Roland was a first- and fourth-round draft pick in the 1965 AFL and NFL drafts, respectively, chosen by the New York Jets (AFL) and St. Louis Cardinals (NFL). His agent, former Mizzou player Jim Kekeris, helped convince Roland to accept the Cardinals' offer. Roland was the NFC Rookie of the Year in 1966 and rewarded the Cardinals with 3,608 rushing yards and 35 touchdowns and two Pro Bowl selections in seven seasons, becoming the franchise's career rushing leader. He finished his career with the New York Giants in 1973.

Roland became a favorite player of Devine, who later hired him as an assistant coach with the Green Bay Packers and at Notre Dame. In his memoir, Devine called Roland "a ferocious team player." "I always accused Johnny of taking notes," Devine wrote. "Whenever a player didn't know what to do or had a question, he went to Johnny. Everything on our schedule was timed out to the minute, and Johnny always knew exactly where everybody was supposed to be and when they were supposed to be there. He had to have a photographic memory; that was the only explanation for his knowing everything that he did."

Roland went on to a long coaching career in the NFL, working for the Eagles, Bears, Jets, Rams, Cardinals, and Saints. He was Walter Payton's position coach during the Hall of Fame running back's peak years with the Bears. In fact, Roland was Payton's choice to be the head coach of the expansion team he tried to bring to St. Louis in the 1990s.

In 1995 Missouri retired No. 23, first worn by Roland and later by NFL Hall of Fame defensive back Roger Wehrli. In 1998 Roland was inducted into the College Football Hall of Fame, where he's listed as…a cornerback.

In one of the feel-good moments of Mizzou's 2017 football season, Roland's grandson, senior walk-on lineman Adam Roland, surprised his family when he jogged onto Faurot Field for the season's final game wearing the retired No. 23 in tribute to his grandfather and the family legacy.

32 The Fixer

The 1997 Tigers were about to do something no Missouri football team had done since 1983: take the field for a bowl game. As Mizzou players lined up inside the tunnel at San Diego's Qualcomm Stadium before the start of the Holiday Bowl, their leader was in his usual spot in front of the pack. Larry Smith was about to coach his fourth college team in a bowl game, something only three other coaches had done in Division I history.

"Someone said, 'Coach, you're on, we're going,'" former offensive guard Craig Heimburger recalled. "Coach had to turn around and put his back to the entrance because he could not control the tears coming down his face. All because he'd taken us to a bowl game." Heimburger added, "We couldn't get him a *W* that day, but it was still a win for Missouri, considering how many years it had been."

Gary Pinkel is lauded as the coach who built Missouri into a consistent winner in the 2000s, but sometimes lost in the praise is the man who truly led a lost program out of the wilderness of irrelevancy. That man was Smith.

Smith, Missouri's coach from 1994 to 2000, guided the Tigers to consecutive winning seasons in 1997 and 1998, snapping a 13-year string of losing. Smith couldn't sustain the success, but he proved it was possible to revive the program often hailed as one of college football's "sleeping giants."

Smith earned a reputation as one of the game's great turnaround artists after reconstruction jobs at Tulane, Arizona, and Southern California. A native of Van Wert, Ohio, Smith was out of coaching in 1993 when Mizzou fired Bob Stull and, for the fourth time in 16 years, needed a new head coach. While also undergoing a change at athletics director—in-house candidate Joe Castiglione would replace Dan Devine—the school considered West Virginia's Don Nehlen and offensive coordinators Skip Holtz (Notre Dame) and Tommy Bowden (Clemson) but narrowed its focus to two prime candidates: Chicago Bears assistant Vince Tobin—a former Mizzou player and assistant coach—and Smith. Smith, 55 at the time, was the choice, and brought his proven pedigree to Mizzou. He became an instant hit with his new players when he promised to rip up the dreaded artificial turf on Faurot Field and replace it with natural grass.

"I told the team today, 'I didn't come in here to lose. I came in here to win. Waiting around two or three years, that's a bunch of baloney,'" Smith said his first day on the job. "I don't think the cupboard's bare. I don't think we're ready for a national championship yet, but I just got a chance to meet with those young people and eyeball a few. I tell you what: there are some fine-looking athletes."

Brock Olivo, an in-state star running back from Washington, Missouri, was among Smith's first recruits. He was starstruck when Mizzou made the hire. "When we found out—and by 'we,' I mean the state of Missouri, the few loyal Tiger fans that were left in that era—but when we found out Larry Smith was going to be the new head coach, that was huge news for us," Olivo said. "He was a rock star name for us. You knew that you were going to be a part of something special if you jumped on board with him."

The Tigers went through typical growing pains in Smith's first years, but the foundation took shape. Losing had become an autumn tradition in Columbia. That was about to change. "I've never known a man who hated losing more than Coach Smith," Heimburger said. "It changed every cell in his body. You could see it in his face, in the way he walked. It wasn't put on. I know a lot of coaches who could put on that face to let you know they're mad after a loss. But losses ate him alive. That resonated to all of us, from the top down."

Smith's staff built its smash-mouth offense around massive, Missouri-bred offensive linemen. They blocked for a platoon of power runners in an option-oriented attack. Halfbacks Olivo and Devin West and fullbacks Ernest Blackwell and Ron "Rhino" Janes teamed with quarterback Corby Jones to give the Tigers one of the Big 12's most prolific rushing attacks. As the Tigers controlled the line of scrimmage, the losing culture became part of Mizzou's past.

Smith was never one to hide his emotions, especially once the Tigers became winners. "After victories he'd get emotional," Olivo said. "Then we'd get emotional and you'd have these locker rooms full of testosterone, but at the same time half of the guys are crying, weeping, and hugging each other. It was cool, though, because you saw the sensitive side of the guy. He humanized that role for us. He wasn't just this guy who stood up on a scaffolding with a megaphone and barked orders at you. He rolled up his sleeves and got his hands dirty just as much as we did."

The real breakthrough came on November 1, 1997, in Boulder, Colorado. That day, the Tigers took down Colorado 41–31 for their sixth win of the season. Mizzou was bowl eligible for the first time in 14 years. "That's when players and coaches and fans thought maybe it [was] possible," Olivo said. "Maybe Mizzou football [was] a real thing."

A week later, Mizzou nearly shocked college football with a home upset of No. 1 Nebraska—only to watch Matt Davison snag a game-tying touchdown pass off the foot of teammate Shevin Wiggins in the infamous Flea Kicker Game. The Tigers lost in overtime but earned nationwide attention for the program Smith was building.

After losing the 1997 Holiday Bowl to finish 7–5, the Tigers proved the breakthrough season was no fluke. Smith's 1998 team went 8–4 and edged West Virginia in the Insight.com Bowl for the school's first bowl win in 17 years. "They're probably the most mentally tough football team I've ever been around," Smith said after the win. "We've had a lot of adversity...but you know what? Nobody complained. They just kept playing."

That was the last great highlight for the Smith years. The Tigers couldn't replace the lost production of offensive playmakers Jones and West and finished 4–7 in 1999 and 3–8 in 2000. Mizzou gave Smith the options to retire, resign, or be fired after the 2000 season finale. Tough as always, Smith didn't flinch at the offer. He was fired. He left Mizzou with a 33–46–1 record in seven seasons and an overall coaching record of 143–126–7.

Smith and his wife, Cheryl, retired to Tucson, Arizona, but he stayed involved with college football with some radio and TV work. He later revealed that he'd been diagnosed with chronic lymphatic leukemia during his final season at Missouri. Smith died on January 28, 2008, at 68 years of age.

Three months earlier, he made it back to Mizzou for a reunion of the 1997 team. He visited with his former players, caught up on their lives, and shared stories. Smith politely declined interview requests that weekend. His story had already been told.

33 Band-Aid

The irony was impossible to ignore. Norm Stewart spent his career sparring with student reporters from Mizzou's famed School of Journalism and also reignited Mizzou's basketball program in 1984 thanks to...Mizzou's famed School of Journalism.

Derrick Chievous, one of the nation's prized recruits, a flamboyant and highly skilled swingman from Jamaica, New York, wanted to study journalism. Mizzou happened to have one of the nation's best schools to do just that—none finer if you ask any partisan product of the world's first journalism program. Mizzou's J-school, the object of Stewart's annoyance for so many years, became the ultimate trump card in landing one of the country's top recruits.

The irony thickens. Once he got to Mizzou, Chievous, the most prolific scorer ever to wear a Tigers jersey, didn't particularly like talking to the media, especially after games in which he routinely scored more points than any player on the floor.

Chievous, famous for wearing his trademark Band-Aid on his forehead, was Stewart's first high-profile recruit from beyond the state border. A McDonald's All-American, Chievous averaged 29 points a game at Holy Cross High School in Queens. "We had the John Browns and the Kim Andersons, but Chievous was New York," Stewart said years later. "He was the first player that you just wanted to make sure that he got so many touches. A guy told me a long time ago, 'You take your best player, put him in the center of the floor, throw him the ball, and tell the others to get the hell out of the way. They can figure out where to go.'"

Chievous arrived on campus a year after All-Americans Steve Stipanovich and Jon Sundvold had graduated and not only gave Stewart a much-needed jolt of offense—he averaged 13.1 points as a freshman and 18.8 as a sophomore—but delivered a new, exciting style of play to the Hearnes Center, straight from the New York City playgrounds. "No one wanted to forget Stipanovich and Sundvold," Stewart wrote in his memoir, "but in college basketball if you want to maintain your program, you have to change with the times. We scored more points with Derrick and we attracted more fans to the arena with him."

Just 16 when he came to Mizzou, the 6'6" Chievous was a scoring machine. He could shoot from outside with a soft jumper. He could corkscrew his body around defenders inside and pile up points from the paint. Unlike any player in Big 8 history, Chievous could draw contact and get to the foul line. He finished his career with conference records for free-throw attempts (963) and makes (764).

That part of his game wasn't universally admired in the conference. "I think he charges every time he gets the ball," Iowa State coach Johnny Orr said in 1988. "He's been in this league four years and they haven't called it yet. I don't expect them to start now."

In the 1987 Big 8 tournament, Chievous became Mizzou's career scoring leader—as a junior. He led the conference in scoring that year at 24.1 points a game. "It's not what I came here for," Chievous said before setting the record against Kansas State. "I came here to get a degree and a Big 8 championship ring. I didn't come here to break any records.... As I told Coach, one day I was going to get one of those rings that he had on his finger." Chievous followed up on the pledge that season, leading Mizzou to the Big 8 regular-season and tournament championships.

That season, *Sports Illustrated* got an exclusive inside look at the Mizzou star as Alexander Wolff wrote an extensive piece for the magazine. Chievous put his colorful personality and unique lexicon on full display in the 2,700-word profile, telling Wolff:

> When I get my degree I'm gonna have on nothing but punk panties under my gown and a big rope with a medallion around my neck and a Word-Up hairdo. Have a city graduation, instead of a Missour-uh one. Then, get a job— nine to five, behind the scenes. Think about the future.
>
> For so long I lived life day to day. Living in this different atmosphere gets me thinking, "Hmmmm, maybe I will be around tomorrow. Maybe I won't walk outside my apartment building and get shot at." "Paper" is my new word. Represents money. Once I make that, I'll pay back my dues to my mother.

(The New Yorker had faced some culture shock getting acclimated to campus life in the middle of Missouri. On an episode of his player interview segment, "Band-Aid Court", that ran during Stewart's TV show, Chievous once asked teammate and avid hunter Greg Church about that time he "caught a 12-point deer," setting Church and the camera crew into fits of laughter.)

Chievous's senior year wasn't a storybook finish to his Mizzou career. Stewart benched him for the start of several games and criticized his star for taking too many shots after a loss to Illinois. Still by season's end, he led the Big 8 in scoring again at 23.4 points per game and padded his lead as MU's top scorer, finishing 744 points ahead of Stipanovich.

Chievous's college career ended with 35 points and 8 rebounds in a first-round loss to Rhode Island in the NCAA tournament. "Derrick Chievous came to Missouri at a time when we were really changing over in our program," Stewart told reporters after the game. "We needed a great player like he is, and we needed somebody who really had the things that he had. He gave them to us. He gave us a lot of wins.... Fantastic ballplayer."

The Houston Rockets drafted Chievous 16th overall but traded him to Cleveland for three draft picks after a promising rookie year. He lasted just 32 games with the Cavaliers before he was out of the league at 23 years old.

Chievous remains Mizzou's all-time scoring leader—only Doug Smith has joined the 2,000-point club since Chievous's career—and returned to school to earn his degree in 2000. Oddly, though, his No. 3 is not among the retired jerseys hanging in the Mizzou Arena rafters.

34 Elite but Nevermore

The path was paved for the Tigers in 1982. If Missouri couldn't finally reach the Final Four with this loaded roster and the most favorable bracket imaginable, then maybe the Tigers never would.

Gary Link, eight years since he'd played his last game at Mizzou, bought a ticket to the 1982 Midwest regional and climbed the stairs to the highest seats at the St. Louis Arena, where he'd watch his Tigers cruise past Houston and either Boston College or Kansas State to finally punch a Final Four ticket. Or so he thought.

The Tigers never got past Houston, one of many Mizzou dream seasons shattered on the second weekend of the NCAA tournament. At the start of the 2018 NCAA tournament, only Brigham Young had made more tournament appearances without reaching the Final Four, with 27. The Tigers have reached the Elite Eight four times under three different coaches but have never taken that final and most rewarded step.

As he watched Norm Stewart's 1982 team fail to escape the Sweet 16 in what amounted to a home game against Houston's Clyde Drexler and Hakeem Olajuwon—the Tigers were loaded too, with Ricky Frazier, Jon Sundvold, and Steve Stipanovich—Link wondered if his team and his coach would ever break through. He cried. "I thought, *Man if this team can't get there...*" he told me. It was more than 30 years later as Link stabbed at his plate of spaghetti over lunch in Columbia. He couldn't finish the sentence.

The pain of being sooooooo close first came in 1976. Led by prolific scorer Willie Smith, the Tigers won the Big 8, then edged Washington and Texas Tech to reach the NCAA Midwest regional final against Michigan. In Louisville, Smith exploded for 43 points against the Wolverines. He helped the Tigers erase an 18-point deficit and take a late lead. But foul trouble depleted Stewart's lineup. Michigan won 95–88 and later fell to Indiana in the National Championship Game.

Eighteen years would pass before the Tigers again rung the Final Four doorbell. After a magical 1993–94 regular season that saw Stewart win his eighth Big 8 championship with an unprecedented 14–0 run through conference play, the Tigers earned a No. 1 seed in the NCAA tournament for the first time in program history. In the West Region, Mizzou took down Navy and Wisconsin then held off Syracuse in overtime to reach the Elite Eight in Los Angeles. This time, Lute Olson's Arizona Wildcats were the final roadblock to the Final Four. Like Stewart, Olson had never won a national championship. "They were on his ass like they were mine about not going to the Final Four," Stewart said in 2015. "I told him [before the game], 'One of us is going to break through.' It was Lute." Arizona handed Mizzou a 92–72 defeat. Stewart would never get closer to another Final Four.

For Quin Snyder's 2001–02 Tigers to shatter their Final Four glass ceiling, they'd have to do it the hard way. Ranked as high as No. 2 in December, the Tigers could never sustain success during the regular season. With a sixth-place finish in the Big 12, Mizzou squeezed into the NCAAs as a 12 seed in the West. The Tigers promptly made tournament history, becoming the lowest seed to crash the regional finals. In Albuquerque, Snyder's Tigers upset Miami and Ohio State then held off 8 seed UCLA in San Jose. But they met an old nemesis in the Elite Eight and lost to Oklahoma for the ninth consecutive time. Senior guard Clarence Gilbert— Mizzou's heart, soul, and three-point gunner—couldn't find the basket in San Jose, shooting just 1-for-16 in his college finale. "There's no shame in what we did today," Snyder lamented.

Seven years later it was Mike Anderson's turn to guide the Tigers to the brink of glory. As the 3 seed in the West, Mizzou survived Cornell and Marquette then eliminated 2 seed Memphis in

Glendale, Arizona, securing a showdown with Connecticut for that elusive Final Four berth. Denied again. The Huskies, the region's No. 1 seed, held off the Tigers 82–75.

"I thought I could get them to that magical place," Anderson said. Close—again—but not there yet.

35 A True Dual Threat

From the time he moved to Columbia from Macomb, Illinois, then left for Bellingham, Washington, Phil Bradley underwent a metamorphosis. "I came here as a baseball guy who played football," he said. "I left being a football guy who played baseball."

He also left as the most decorated two-sport athlete in Mizzou history. Bradley was a three-time first-team All–Big 8 quarterback from 1978 to 1980 and broke the league record for career total offense, a record that stuck until Oklahoma State quarterback Mike Gundy broke it in 1989. Bradley guided the Tigers to three bowl games and became one of the core players of Mizzou's loaded 1977 recruiting class, the final group assembled by Al Onofrio, who was fired after the '77 season.

Bradley never expected to play as a freshman. The Tigers had an entrenched senior quarterback in Pete Woods. Bradley could serve as Woods's apprentice in '77 and, if he was fortunate, win the quarterback competition in '78. "To be honest, I didn't even know I could play at this level," Bradley said. "I chose Missouri over Iowa simply because they had an established quarterback and I could come in and try to figure things out and see if I could get into position to play. As it turned out, that lasted about a quarter and a half."

In the 1977 opener, John Robinson's USC Trojans visited Columbia, and linebacker Clay Matthews Jr. got up close and personal with Woods's knee. Woods's day was done early and Bradley got his first taste of college football in a 27–10 loss to the visitors from Los Angeles. Onofrio went back and forth between Bradley and Woods the rest of the season—sophomore quarterback Jay Jeffrey played some too, then transferred to Baylor, where he led the Bears to the 1980 Southwest Conference title—but the Tigers struggled offensively most of the year. "Phil was a great athlete," Woods said, "but obviously when I was there, he didn't particularly distinguish himself. Playing as a freshman is a tough thing to do."

Playing as a sophomore produced better results, especially under new coach Warren Powers and his split-back veer offense, a dramatic change from Onofrio's favored I-back attack. Surrounded by dangerous receivers Kellen Winslow and Leo Lewis and a seemingly endless supply of running backs in James Wilder, Earl Gant, and Gerry Ellis, Bradley thrived as the captain of Powers's ship.

By the time his career ended with the 1980 Liberty Bowl, Bradley had accumulated 6,459 yards of total offense, breaking Paul Christman's school record that stood for 40 years. Bradley also broke the Big 8 career record, set by Kansas State's Lynn Dickey in 1970. "He just had this attitude, and in the huddle, I trusted the guy," offensive tackle Howard Richards said. "We always felt like he was going to put us in position to win and score at will."

Bradley's senior class established itself as one of the best in team history. Six players were selected in the 1981 NFL Draft, including Richards, a first-round pick by Dallas, and Wilder and defensive back Eric Wright, both second-rounders. Bradley was easily among the best pure players of the bunch—but his name was never called during the draft. The 6-foot, 180-pound quarterback was born a generation too soon for the NFL's tastes at the time. He lacked the prototypical size the NFL craved at the position, and his dual-threat nature was made for another era.

You can't tell Richards otherwise. "People said his size was the factor [that explained why] he didn't go the NFL," Richards said. "But if you look at what Russell Wilson has done [with the Seattle Seahawks], Phil was that type of quarterback. I'm absolutely sure he could have played and been successful in the league. I've seen a lot of quarterbacks who couldn't do what he could do in terms of running ability. Even some of the backup quarterbacks I played with in Dallas, he would have been head and shoulders above them."

But that chance never came, despite Bradley's production as Mizzou's full-time signal caller for three seasons. "It was disappointing," Bradley said of not playing in the NFL. "You feel like your credentials should have allowed you, especially back then with 10 rounds in the draft. It turned out it didn't happen."

Luckily for Bradley, he had a pretty lucrative hobby. Powers allowed Bradley to moonlight with Gene McArtor's Mizzou baseball team after his sophomore and junior seasons. Following his senior football season, Bradley had offers to play professionally in Canada, but teams wanted a commitment before the professional baseball draft in the summer of 1981. By then, Bradley was immersed in an All–Big 8 season in the MU outfield. As a senior Bradley set MU single-season records for hits (84), runs (77), and walks (56) while hitting .457, which still ranks as the third-highest single-season batting average in school history. For his career, Bradley hit .362, one of five career accomplishments that still ranked among MU's 10 best as of the 2018 season.

The Mariners chose Bradley with the first pick in the third round of the draft—five spots before the Padres took another standout college outfielder, future Hall of Famer Tony Gwynn. Bradley made minor league pit stops in Bellingham; Bakersfield, California; and Salt Lake City before making his Major League Baseball debut with the Mariners in 1983. An American League All-Star in 1985, Bradley played eight years in the big leagues and amassed 1,058 hits. He might have left Mizzou as a football player who dabbled in baseball, but in the pros, Bradley made his mark as an outfielder. In 2003 Mizzou made him the first baseball player—and the only one as of 2018—to have his number retired. His No. 15, the same number he wore on the football field, hangs on the outfield wall looking over Simmons Field.

36 Mister Magic

Norm Stewart knew he couldn't afford blips. That's what he called recruiting lulls, empty years between the great classes that lifted the program to new heights. In 1973 the Tigers said good-bye to John Brown, the program's biggest star and greatest scorer. The next year, Stewart bid farewell to Al Eberhard, another productive player. The 1974–75 season would see the debuts of promising sophomores Kim Anderson and Jim Kennedy, but Stewart needed a stopgap talent to avoid another down year before the wave of newcomers would blossom. Enter William Smith, better known as Willie. Soon to be known as Mister Magic.

Stewart first met the 6'2" guard from Las Vegas at the National Junior College Tournament in Kansas, where they exchanged what Stewart later described as "an unorthodox handshake." "The soul shake was in vogue then," Stewart wrote in his 1991 memoir.

Out of that handshake was born one of the great Mizzou basketball careers. Smith gave Stewart two instant qualities. "He was a playmaker and a leader," Stewart recalled years later.

One problem: the left-handed shooter couldn't shoot. "When he came here, he shot like this," Stewart said, holding his left elbow out and high like he was about to freshen up with a stick of deodorant.

The incomparable Norm Stewart was as talented a recruiter as he was a gameday coach.

When Smith left campus for a visit home to Las Vegas, he asked Stewart what he could work on while he was away from the team. "I said, 'One thing is, take your elbow and move it under [the ball],'" Stewart said. "I told him, 'For Christ's sake, nobody shoots with a flying elbow.'" Stewart added, "He came back and was dynamite."

In his Mizzou debut, Smith led the Tigers with 24 points against Wisconsin-Oshkosh. A week later he scored 27 against Portland. In December he paced the Tigers with 37 points in a double-overtime win over Oklahoma. Mizzou finished third in the Big 8 and Smith emerged as the program's biggest star since Brown, averaging 22.4 points while leading the Tigers in scoring 20 times in the 27-game season. His scoring average was second-best in team history.

Smith got to Mizzou three years before a certain point guard arrived at Michigan State in 1977, and legend has it, Smith earned his nickname when he asked the Mizzou pep band to play his favorite jazz groove, "Mister Magic" by Grover Washington. The name stuck.

As a senior, Smith was even better, averaging a school-record 25.3 points per game, a figure that still stood in 2017 as MU's prolific single-season average. Guiding the Tigers to a Big 8 championship and into the NCAA tournament regional final, Smith led MU in scoring in 26 of 31 games, including a career-best 43 points in his finale, a loss to Michigan that would have sent the Tigers into the Final Four.

But he was more than a scorer. He dished a school-record 138 assists as a senior, helping develop teammates Anderson and Kennedy. He also pulled down nearly six rebounds a game. Smith was an extension of Stewart on the court. "He was a coach on the floor and off the floor," Stewart said. "He and I could communicate."

Smith bounced around the NBA with four teams in four years, never able to duplicate his scoring prowess from college. Despite playing just two years in the Black and Gold, his No. 30 jersey hangs from the rafters at Mizzou Arena. Smith's 1,387 points in just 58 games were more than all but one player who came before him at Mizzou.

37 A Star Shines in the Split T

When All-American quarterback Paul Christman exhausted his eligibility, Tigers coach Don Faurot had to discover a new centerpiece to the offense. Christman left as the school's career passing leader, but the offense didn't leave with him.

The 1941 season marked the debut of Faurot's split T formation, the offensive system that changed college football and established Faurot—for those paying careful attention to history—as one of the game's offensive pioneers. Faurot's creation borrowed some elements of Stanford's version of the T-formation, but Faurot added bigger splits between his offensive linemen. The quarterback became more of a running threat as Faurot scrapped the quarterback pivot with the snap and had the QB slide into his next move, either a handoff or keeper.

There was another crucial change: Faurot moved 6'2", 210-pound Bob Steuber from end to halfback. It proved to be one of Faurot's most prescient coaching moves at Mizzou. The powerback from St. Louis became one of the country's elite ball carriers and the most prolific rusher in team history—and for decades to come.

The results were overwhelming. The Tigers led the country in rushing in 1941, averaging 307.7 yards per game, while Steuber, the converted receiver, ranked third in rushing yards (885) and first in yards per carry (7.6). In 1942 he became the first 1,000-yard rusher in team history, totaling 1,098, which ranked second nationally. He again led the nation in yards per pop (7.4) and scored more touchdowns (18) and accounted for more points (121) than any player on any team. Steuber earned All-America honors as Missouri won the Big Six but somehow he didn't contend for the Heisman Trophy—even though he outran and outscored the six running backs who finished among the top 10 vote-getters.

He might not have earned nationwide acclaim, but teammates and coaches knew what he meant to the Mizzou attack. "To this day, I still think that guy was the best athlete ever to go through the University of Missouri," former All-American center Darold Jenkins once said of Steuber. "I don't think he ever understood the necessity for training rules. He'd have a beer or two or get a hold of some of that 'Boone County homemade,' but it never did slow him down at all."

Steuber was a three-sport letterman in Columbia and inspired legends like this one from Mizzou historian Bob Broeg: "Steuber could do incredible things. One Friday he played a baseball doubleheader in St. Louis for Mizzou, caught a bus back to Columbia, drank beer until 4 a.m., it was said, suited up with his black and gold thinclads for a track meet, and then went out and won the 100-yard dash, the 220, and the broad jump, and took third in the high jump."

Steuber finished his Mizzou football career with a team-record 2,030 rushing yards—remember, he didn't move to halfback until his junior year and the Tigers played only 10 regular-season games per year back then—and held the rushing record for nearly 30 years. His 222 career points stood as the Mizzou record until 1992, and entering 2018, his 1942 scoring total (121 points on 18 touchdowns and 13 PATs) still stood as the most by a Missouri player who wasn't exclusively a kicker.

After Mizzou, Steuber was a first-round draft pick by the Chicago Bears but played only one game before joining the navy to serve in World War II. While assigned to preflight training school, Steuber attended DePauw University and later Marquette and Iowa and played multiple sports at each spot. After the war, Steuber bounced around several professional football organizations but suffered a career-ending back injury in 1948. His pro career never got off the ground, but Steuber's college exploits weren't forgotten. He was inducted into the College Football Hall of Fame in 1971 while Mizzou retired his No. 37 jersey. In retirement, Steuber returned to St. Louis and launched a business career and also served as an analyst on football Cardinals broadcasts. The first great running back in Mizzou history died in 1996 at age 75.

The Physics Professor Who Changed Everything

Missouri fans can have a healthy debate to decide the most important football coach in the program's history, with Don Faurot, Dan Devine, and Gary Pinkel the obvious leading candidates. But Austin Lee McRae deserves a prominent place in the conversation. You won't find McRae in the school's Intercollegiate Athletics Hall of Fame, which is hard to believe considering he's the person solely responsible for bringing the sport of football to the university.

In 1889 McRae was a newly arrived physics professor on campus. A Georgia native and alumnus of the University of Georgia with a graduate degree from Harvard, McRae had played some football at Harvard but noticed the sport had not caught on at Missouri. Sparked by McRae, professors got together and organized some games, forming teams from the school's four core divisions: academic, law, engineering, and medicine. McRae coached the academic team. They wore black-and-gold caps. They defeated the law school team to claim the campus championship in the spring. The sport was still an infant on campus, but college football was crawling at Missouri.

Later that fall, McRae and a group of students formed a team as part of a school-wide athletic association. They held tryouts, hoping to find a team suitable to play Washington University a month later in St. Louis. On October 17, 1890, a Friday, the team was formed. Three days later, McRae organized a dress rehearsal against an outfit of students forever known as Picked Team in the Mizzou history books. McRae's squad won 22–6. A football team was born, led by a 29-year-old physics professor.

"He found here plenty of brain and brawn, enthusiasm and ambition, but all chaotic, undirected, and undisciplined," fullback

Burton Thompson said during a speech on campus 32 years later, as chronicled by the *Missouri Alumnus*. "To that man, more than to any other individual is due the credit, honor and glory for all that you may claim for your track and football teams today.... For it was [McRae] who inspired and encouraged us to our first efforts at football, which, if somewhat unseasonable were none the less fruitful of good results."

Here is the roster for McRae's team of pioneers:

Starters
Benjamin Goslin, right end
George Whitsett, right tackle
Aytchmonde Shull, right guard
William Littell, center
William Records, left guard
William Gordon, left tackle
Charles Keith, left end
Dennis Kane, quarterback
Mordecia Bogie, left halfback
Daniel Shawhan, right halfback
Burton Thompson, fullback

Reserves
Benjamin Graham
John LaMotte
James Denny
Henry Terrill
Harris Moore
Oliver Axtell

A month later, McRae's team headed east to face Wash U. It did not go well for the visitors. "We went at our training with all the zeal of gladiators about to enter an arena where the struggle meant life or death," Thompson recalled during his speech in 1922. "We had no training table; no regulations except those each man chose to observe; no gymnasium; no baths or showers except at our several homes; but I believe each man faithfully played the game with all fairness and took the grilling without a murmur or a break."

Washington University won the game 28–0. Four days later, McRae's team accepted a challenge from the de-facto junior varsity team, a group of students back in Columbia called the Engineering Eleven. The score, a 90–0 dismembering of the understudies, still stands as the highest scoring output in MU history and the most lopsided victory.

After the season, McRae and the football players formed the school's first athletics association, the precursor to the modern-day athletics department. McRae served as president over a board of committees for football, baseball, hare and hounds, and tennis. The association also organized the school's first track meet.

McRae was one-and-done at Missouri. In 1891 he left Columbia to become the chair of the physics department at the state campus in Rolla, known then as the Missouri School of Mines and Metallurgy, where he also coached that school's first football team. He'd later teach briefly at the University of Texas. McRae eventually returned to Rolla, where he made his mark as a professor and department chair. He died in 1922 at 61 after suffering from pneumonia. The university in Rolla and all the town's public schools closed all of their classes on the day of his funeral.

McRae's lone season coaching Missouri's first football team was but a footnote in his biography. A sketch of his career published by the Phelps County Historical Society only briefly mentions football and devotes far more to his contributions to science.

39 Devine in '69

In January 2015 the 1969 Missouri football team was inducted into the Missouri Sports Hall of Fame in Springfield, where 57 living members of the Big 8 championship team gathered to celebrate a season that's widely considered one of the greatest in team history. The reunion came with a surprise.

The players from that Dan Devine–coached team had never collectively watched the Orange Bowl that concluded their 9–2 season. "After we lost, Devine never showed it to us," linebacker John "Nip" Weisenfels said of the 10–3 loss to Penn State. But Weisenfels had obtained a DVD copy of the original broadcast. He brought it to the Hall of Fame weekend.

The players poured some cocktails, got comfortable, and watched their younger selves battle Joe Paterno's Nittany Lions. Of course, they knew what happened that night in Miami. The Tigers turned over the ball nine times, including seven interceptions, but hung with the nation's No. 2 team down to each team's last gasp.

"The thing that made you understand why this team was special was those guys were watching it for the first time and every one of them, to a man, made a comment like, 'If I had only done this, we would have scored or if I had only done this, we would have made a big play,'" Weisenfels said. "Nobody was talking about themselves or any individual achievement. Everyone was talking about what they could have done to make the team great. That's what set that team apart."

Extraordinary talent made the 1969 Tigers great too. Terry McMillan quarterbacked Devine's penultimate team—he left after the 1970 season to coach the Green Bay Packers—and the Miami native by way of a Joplin junior college set a Big 8 single-season record with 18 touchdown passes, including a Mizzou single-game record four TD passes, in a 48-point annihilation of Kansas. He shared the backfield with Joe Moore, the mighty 200-pound running back who'd finish his career as the team's career rushing leader even though he came to college wanting to play along the offensive line. The brilliant Mel Gray was McMillan's favorite target, averaging 27 yards per catch and a touchdown for every three receptions. Up front, All-American guard Mike Carroll cracked open holes for Moore, while Larron Jackson was among the Big 8's best tackles. The 1968 Gator Bowl champion Tigers relied on a punishing defense—they held five opponents to 10 points or fewer—but the '69 team won with offense, scoring at least 37 points in six games. Flanker Jon Staggers doubled as an electric return specialist while fullback Ron McBride added another backfield threat. The defense featured All–Big 8 tackle Mark Kuhlmann, Weisenfels at linebacker, and Dennis Poppe at safety.

The season began with three straight nonconference wins: a 19–17 squeaker over Air Force, a 37–6 bludgeoning of Illinois in St. Louis, and a 40–17 statement victory at Michigan, clinched by Moore's 62-yard touchdown run in the fourth quarter. On that day in Ann Arbor, the Tigers dealt new Wolverines coach Bo Schembechler his first defeat. Michigan would go on to share the Big Ten title and didn't lose another home game until 1975.

The Tigers were undefeated and ranked No. 5 when they visited Colorado on October 25, the site of a crushing 31–24 loss, MU's only regular-season defeat. "Frankly, we beat ourselves in Colorado," Weisenfels said. "If that game had gone on another five minutes, we would have won. But it didn't, and we lost."

A snowstorm had blanketed Folsom Field that weekend, and Colorado used bulldozers to remove the snow for the game, leaving divots throughout the field that were filled with sand, a nightmare for McMillan, Moore, and MU's fleet of playmakers. "But

[Colorado] was playing on the same field," Weisenfels said, "so it doesn't excuse the fact that we lost."

The Tigers recovered the next week and outlasted Kansas State 41–38, a game that saw KSU quarterback Lynn Dickey throw for 394 yards and stage a wild comeback. Missouri led 21–6 at halftime, but the Wildcats scored four touchdowns in an eight-minute span to go ahead 31–28. The Tigers answered with a pair of one-yard touchdown runs by McBride and McMillan to clinch the win, the first of four straight to finish the regular season as co–Big 8 champs with Nebraska. The Tigers won the head-to-head showdown with the Cornhuskers 17–7 to secure the Orange Bowl invitation.

If Notre Dame could beat Texas in the Cotton Bowl, the Orange Bowl would decide the national championship. By kickoff in Miami, it was a moot point: Texas held off the Irish to capture the national title. The breaks didn't fall Mizzou's way in Miami. Devine worried about McMillan playing in front of friends and family in his hometown, and the quarterback played a role in MU's struggles, throwing five interceptions. Devine later regretted he didn't use a more conservative game plan. "I blamed myself for the loss because I only did an average job of coaching and I didn't design enough help for our quarterback," Devine wrote in his memoirs.

The Orange Bowl loss left a bruise on the legacy of the '69 Tigers, who set a team scoring record with 365 points. But years later, Devine's selfless bunch still resonated as one of the program's greatest teams. "I was disappointed by the loss," Devine wrote, "but I couldn't let it dampen our spirits too much for what had really been an exciting season.... Looking back on it, that team might just have been the best team Missouri ever had."

40 Hearnes Center

In 1972 Norm Stewart's Missouri basketball team made its long-awaited move out of cozy Brewer Fieldhouse and into the Hearnes Center, a multipurpose building decked in drab. Built just east of Memorial Stadium, the Hearnes Center—named after Missouri governor Warren E. Hearnes—was unlike anything Stewart's players had ever seen. Coming from 6,000-seat Brewer, the Tigers stepped into the towering structure that seated 12,600 and were amazed by two features: its size and silence. "It was so big; it [was] like we [were] playing outside," said Gary Link, a junior on the first Mizzou team to inhabit Hearnes. "It was like the Grand Canyon. It was so huge, it blew us all away."

Rather than install a traditional wood floor, Missouri covered the court with a gray rubber surface called Tartan. It made for unusual acoustics. "On that rubber floor," Link said, "you don't hear the ball bounce."

Hearnes, Missouri's Democratic governor from 1965 to 1973, was inspired to propose a new campus arena after visiting Assembly Hall at the University of Illinois in 1966. The state appropriated $7.65 million for a more modern basketball arena for the 1967–68 budget, and student fees would cover the remaining costs. The building was designed by St. Louis architectural firm Sverdrup & Parcel, which also built Busch Stadium II in St. Louis and the Superdome in New Orleans.

Construction took three years to complete—were it not for the promise of a new arena, Stewart never would have convinced Dixon, Missouri, star John Brown to play for the Tigers—and the structure was unveiled on July 24, 1972 (and officially dedicated on August 4). The $11 million building sat on 4.4 acres and filled

324,000 square feet. Construction required 20,000 cubic yards of poured concrete, 3,000 tons of structural steel, and 1,600 tons of reinforcing steel. The final product favored practicality over aesthetics.

As the last stages of the arena came together, the athletics department asked Stewart to settle on a surface for the court. Stewart suspected he might not get his wish. He wanted wood. He requested wood. He got Tartan. Tartan floors had become popular in the Big 8, mostly because they were cheap to install and maintain. "It was awful," Stewart said.

"The odd part of Tartan was if you were sliding defensively, your shoes stuck and you just fell over," former MU guard Jon Sundvold said. "It didn't even feel like basketball. Ankles would turn, knees would get hurt. The floor didn't have any give."

The first event held in the new building was the Missouri Farmers Association convention in August 1972. In the fall, Stewart's team hosted its Black and Gold Scrimmage, followed by an exhibition victory over the Chilean Olympic Development team.

Finally, on November 25, the Warren E. Hearnes Multipurpose Building had its first official college basketball game, when Stewart's Tigers played host to the Ohio Bobcats. Brown scored the first basket in the new building with a midrange jumper as Mizzou opened the arena with an 87–75 victory. The Tigers went 12–1 in their new home that season, suffering their only loss to Colorado. Crowds rarely filled the cavernous arena to capacity that first season, but over the next 32 years, the Tigers would go undefeated five times at Hearnes and never lose more than five home games in any given season.

"The structure of the building is so unique because it goes up so high," Brown later said. "It's almost like a pit, and I think that could really be intimidating for the opposing team. So there was a real advantage for us from day one."

Hearnes produced its share of memorable moments. Among them:

- The first sellout came on Kansas's first visit, January 20, 1973. The Tigers took down their rival 75–72 in overtime as Brown pulled down 21 rebounds, which stood as the Hearnes record when the Tigers moved out 31 years later.
- On February 28, 1981, Mizzou clinched a second-straight Big 8 regular-season title on Ricky Frazier's game-winning shot over Kansas State in a 46–43 victory, a game in which the Tigers held the ball for nearly eight minutes late in the second half.
- On February 11, 1987, MU's Derrick Chievous outdueled Kansas's Danny Manning in a 63–60 win as Lee Coward hit the game-winning jumper in the final seconds.
- Corey Tate knocked down what might have been the most famous shot in Hearnes history on February 4, 1997—a jumper to beat No. 1 Kansas 96–94 in double overtime.
- The longest Hearnes game came on January 13, 2001, when Mizzou outlasted Iowa State 112–109 in four overtimes, led by Clarence Gilbert's 43 points.
- In 2004, with the Tigers set to move into what is now called Mizzou Arena, the final basket at Hearnes came on March 7, a buzzkill for the Tigers as Kansas's David Padgett closed the building with a late jumper to secure an 84–82 win for the Jayhawks.

Over time, Hearnes underwent many facelifts. The Tartan floor was replaced with a portable hardwood surface in 1980–81. That same year, a black border surrounded the court. In 1989 gold paint replaced the black, and an outline of the state of Missouri was painted at center court. The black apron returned in 1999, plus the new modern Tiger head logo on both ends of the floor. In 2001 the floor was named Norm Stewart Court in honor of the first and greatest coach to roam its sideline. Also that year, bleachers for a student section went up behind the west basket and the teams' benches switched sides along the north sideline.

Some more Hearnes history:

- Mizzou was 476–72 all-time in the building. Kansas won more games (13) than any other visitor, followed by Oklahoma (8) and Kansas State (7).
- The Tigers went undefeated in the building five times: 1974–75, 1980–81, 1988–89, 1989–90, and 1993–94.
- The highest official attendance for a game came on January 22, 2000, when 14,098 were on hand to watch the Tigers beat No. 7 Kansas 81–59.
- Only 18 nonconference teams won games in the building, led by Arkansas, which beat the Tigers four times at Hearnes. Marquette and Memphis, with two wins apiece, were the only other nonconference teams to win multiple times in the building.
- Missouri's longest winning streak at Hearnes lasted 34 games, starting with a win over Oklahoma on March 3, 1988, and lasting until Arkansas beat the Tigers on December 8, 1990.

41 The Catalyst

Larry Smith's quarterback timeshare plan fell apart midway through the 1996 season. Smith had been splitting snaps between sophomore starter Corby Jones, a bruising runner, and sophomore backup Kent Skornia, the more polished passer. A hip pointer sent Jones to the bench for Mizzou's sixth game, against Kansas State, but after Skornia threw three interceptions in what became a 25-point loss, Smith benched Skornia in favor of Jones, still nursing his sore hip.

That didn't sit well with Jones, whose father, Curtis Sr., was part of Smith's coaching staff. But Curtis wasn't the parent who marched into Smith's office after the loss to Kansas State. Nope, it was Gwen Jones, Corby's mother. Jones Jr. recalled:

> She knew Coach Smith pretty well. Our families were close. And unbeknownst to my father, she went in and said, "Here's my problem. If he's not healthy enough to start, he's not healthy enough to play. If he's not good enough to play for you, put him on the bench and I have no problem with you. But you're not going to jerk my son around."
>
> Coach Smith said, "Gwen, I respect that." And that was the end of the conversation. From that point on, Coach Smith called me in and said, "This is your team. We're going to win or lose by you." And that's when things started to take off.

The Tigers won the next week, beating Oklahoma State, and won three of their final five games. Jones would start every game the next two seasons, become the centerpiece to a prolific offense that ended the program's long postseason drought, and finish his career as one of the great offensive playmakers in school history. Thanks, Mom.

Actually, Smith had put his faith in the young quarterback long before that conversation in his office. After a 30–0 loss at Kansas State dropped the Tigers to 2–3 in 1995, Smith climbed on the team bus in Manhattan, Kansas, and made an announcement that changed the course of the program. "He said, 'Monday morning, you guys all better come in and be ready to strap your helmets on because we're changing everything we're doing,'" recalled Craig Heimburger, a freshman offensive lineman on that team. "The word he used was *revamp*: 'We're going to revamp the offense and challenge the defense.' We were all scared for our lives."

Smith closed practices to reporters the following week and kept his quarterbacks from doing interviews. But the players knew of Smith's plans. He planned to unwrap his rookie quarterback. Yes, Jones. The true freshman. The guy who hadn't played a game in almost a year, not since November 4, 1994, his final game at Columbia's Hickman High School, a loss to rival Jefferson City. Even more daunting, Jones would make his college debut against undefeated No. 2 Nebraska. In Lincoln. Gulp.

The Tigers hadn't scored a touchdown in six quarters when they pulled into Nebraska. Jones walked off the bus confident he could spark the sputtering offense. "The only reason I was playing," Jones said, "was because we couldn't do anything else." He added, "I thought I could do something. Clearly, I couldn't. But I was too young and stupid to know better."

Skornia started but Jones would see the field, running eight times for just seven yards. He threw two passes. Only one was completed—to a Cornhusker. By day's end, Nebraska made corn mash of the Tigers in a 57–0 rout. It didn't faze the rookie. "I got pummeled this week, but I just thought, *There's always next week*," he said. "[Nebraska] does that to a lot of people."

As the season continued, Smith gave Jones more chances. By the halfway point of 1996, the offense belonged to No. 7. Smith and offensive coordinator Jerry Berndt constructed a lethal option-based running attack around Jones. Behind a massive offensive line, Jones and his parade of running backs spent the next three years applying tread marks on Big 12 defenses.

In 1997, no longer sharing the quarterback duties, Jones set a single-season Mizzou record for total offense with 2,545 yards. More important, he carried the Tigers to consecutive road victories over Oklahoma State and Colorado—he accounted for eight touchdowns in the two wins—with the latter securing the Tigers bowl eligibility for the first time since 1983.

Along the way, Jones became the program's biggest star and unquestioned leader. "Corby was a winner, man," former running back Brock Olivo said. "His freshman year he was wide-eyed and running for his life. As he matured, you knew when he stepped in the huddle that it was going to get serious. One way or the other we were going to find the end zone. You always knew. Once he got to the point where he was confident and was seeing the field, he became a very dynamic quarterback. He wasn't just a one-trick pony. He was that guy [about whom] defensive coordinators would say, 'How are we going to stop this guy?'" Olivo continued, "He was the catalyst. He was the guy that put Mizzou football back on the map. It was so much fun to watch him grow as a quarterback in those years."

After a loss to Colorado State in the 1997 Holiday Bowl, Jones was poised for an epic senior season and appeared on most preseason Heisman Trophy lists. Instead, the worst came true. Curtis Sr. was hospitalized during the summer after having a heart attack on Father's Day. A month later, Curtis Sr. suffered another heart attack, this one fatal. Corby buried his father on August 1, five weeks before the start of his senior season as the Tigers began the year in a state of mourning. "The support I had from everyone else is what got me through losing my dad, from my family to the team," Jones said. "It was interesting because it would have been completely different if my dad hadn't been like a dad to [the other players] too. Everyone was experiencing the same loss. That made it easier for me. I wasn't out there on an island. I was with a bunch of people mourning just like I was."

On the field, Jones played through a series of injuries, including a nasty case of turf toe that stripped the quarterback of his greatest skill: his ability to freelance and demoralize defenses with his legs. "I couldn't be me," he said. "I couldn't create."

He was fortunate to have help, starting with All-American tailback and close friend Devin West, a group of maulers along the offensive line, and an underrated defense that featured freshman defensive end Justin Smith, a future All-American and NFL All-Pro.

Jones couldn't duplicate his 1997 numbers, but he delivered one crucial missing piece from his catalog of achievements: he ran for three touchdowns and accounted for 181 yards in a victory over West Virginia in the Insight.com Bowl. "That was the peak," said Jones, who returned to Mizzou and earned his law degree. (He now practices law in Kansas City.) "Accomplishing that was such an overwhelming feeling."

Jones left Mizzou holding a batch of records and ranked among the top five for career rushing yards, passing yards, and total offense. "I'd like to be…remembered as a guy who motivated people around him and got the best out of the people around him," he said. "That's what I want. Not everybody liked me on Saturdays, but they respected me on Saturdays. I wasn't always sunshine and butterflies, but I was a competitor. They knew that. My O-line knew when I showed up and stepped on the field they'd have to carry me off it."

42 Captain Jenks

Before Darold Jenkins played his final college football game, Missouri's All-American center had no illusions of playing professionally. "The army is my future," he told the Associated Press as the Tigers prepared for the Orange Bowl on January 1, 1942. "I'm going to stick with it as long as possible."

Jenkins, nicknamed Captain Jenks at Mizzou, was the first great All-American offensive lineman to play for the Tigers and the only one to have his number retired. But his post-Mizzou career was every bit as remarkable.

Jenkins, who centered Don Faurot's offensive line in 1940–41 and also played linebacker, became a B-17 fighter pilot in World War II and fought 27 combat missions. On his 27th mission,

Darold Jenkins in 1941, shortly before entering military service in World War II.

Jenkins was shot down over Germany on March 16, 1944, and captured by Nazi forces. The All-American spent 17 months at Stalag Luft III, a German prison camp. "Interrogation by the Nazis was child's play," Jenkins later said. "I'd already run the gauntlet of tough questions and answers from [Faurot] when I'd seek to borrow five dollars of my own money for a heavy date."

Coincidentally, a fellow war prisoner in the camp was a former Fordham player—from the 1941 team that beat Jenkins's Tigers 2–0 in the Sugar Bowl. "We used to walk the perimeter of that prison camp for exercise," Jenkins told Mizzou historian Bob Broeg. "We'd play that game over and over and over—and it always came out 2–0."

Jenkins was liberated in 1945, and upon returning to his home state, the Higginsville, Missouri, native earned his law degree. He became a prosecutor and later worked for the Missouri highway commission. "Football competition helped in the courtroom, and so did recognition, a football residue that's pleasant and an icebreaker," he later said. "But I'm a pretty good trial lawyer for a country boy, and I think that helps also. Now and then, some of those metropolitan lawyers do what I learned in football you never do—they underrate me."

As a player, Jenkins played a pivotal role in Faurot's split T offense. Back then, centers were described as skill players, having to make the crucial snap back to the quarterback. Jenkins was no exception. His No. 42 was retired shortly after his playing career, an honor that had only been bestowed on former quarterback Paul Christman at the time. Jenkins was inducted into the Missouri Sports Hall of Fame in 1971, the College Football Hall of Fame in 1976, and was part of the inaugural 1990 class of Mizzou's Intercollegiate Athletics Hall of Fame.

"He was well-known to many ball carriers suddenly brought to a violent halt by his crushing tackles as he backed up the Tiger line," the *Savitar* wrote of Jenkins in 1941. "Few indeed were those who eluded him as he patrolled the area behind the Missouri forward wall. His defense signals were always dependable, his ability to diagnose plays uncanny, and a bad pass from center was unheard of with the Higginsville lad to snap the ball back."

43 "Let's Go Kick Their Ass!"

If you were at Memorial Stadium on October 23, 2010, you'll never forget what unfolded. Chances are your night ended down on Faurot Field, surrounded by thousands of other delirious Mizzou fans. Oklahoma, ranked No. 1 in the Bowl Championship Series standings, was in town for homecoming. It was the biggest Mizzou home game of the Gary Pinkel era.

For this chapter, we turned the writing duties over to T.J. Moe, a sophomore wide receiver that season, to refresh our memories of that epic victory.

* * *

The lead-up to the Oklahoma game was unlike anything I'd ever experienced. Coming off a season in 2009 that we finished 8–5, the college football world didn't have very high expectations for the 2010 Tigers. Nonetheless, we were sitting at 6–0 and looking to become the first Mizzou team since 1960 to start the season with seven straight wins.

The No. 1–ranked Oklahoma Sooners were coming to town. As players, we were constantly reminded to ignore the media and focus on what we could control. But don't think that we weren't aware of everything that was being talked about throughout that week. Did I know that Gary Pinkel had never beaten Oklahoma?

Yep. Did I know that Mizzou had never beaten a No. 1–ranked team in program history? Yep. Did I know that ESPN's *College GameDay* was coming to Mizzou's campus for the first time in history and deeming our game the biggest of the college football weekend? Yep.

Every Thursday before practice, there's a team meeting that usually lasts around 25 minutes. This is the most difficult meeting for players to stay awake in. It's after a long week of class, a few hours past lunch, and feels like nap time. Coach Pinkel would walk in the room, and everyone would sit up in their chairs and listen to him go through his speech. Coach would keep notes on every Thursday speech he'd ever given. Oftentimes he'd bring the notes from previous speeches that he gave before big wins and share those. This Thursday was different, and he knew it. Instead of a 25-minute meeting, it lasted about three. I don't recall how he opened the speech, but it ended with these words: "Men, they don't respect me. They don't respect you. Let's go kick their ass!"

The team stays in a hotel Friday night before games, even home games. We have a team meal together, go through all of our final meetings, and make last-second adjustments. Saturday night games are miserable for the players. Most guys wake up at 8:00 AM wired and ready to play but have to sit in the hotel with sporadic meetings for seven hours. So what did we do? Watched *College GameDay*, of course. Mizzou fans, by the way, set the attendance record for *GameDay* that day with more than 18,000 fans scattered across the quad. We all watched as Kirk Herbstreit, Lee Corso, Desmond Howard, and Chris Fowler discussed our game. When it came time to make their picks, Corso brought out the Mizzou helmet from underneath the desk but said, "Not so fast, my friend." He pulled on Boomer's headgear instead, declaring Oklahoma his pick for the night.

The drive from the hotel to the stadium always gives the players a good indication of how wild the crowd is going to be that night.

You look to see how far down Stadium Boulevard the cars are parked. People tailgate for every game, but Mizzou never had a day like this. Cars were parked miles from the stadium. They lined the streets on both sides of the road. Many fans just wanted to be in Columbia for a possibly historic day and didn't have a ticket to the game. Oklahoma fans left their tailgate to line the streets as we drove by, cheering, screaming, and making their presence felt. We parked across from the stadium at the training complex. It was time for a Mizzou tradition, the Tiger Walk. There's routinely great fan support for the Tiger Walk, but this day was different. There was a line on both sides of our walkway, five to six fans deep the entire walk. It was that way from the second we stepped off the bus until we entered the locker room. The fans were letting us know they'd be there that night like never before.

Mizzou generally had great fan support during my four years in school, but five minutes before kickoff, there were usually a lot of empty seats soon to be occupied by people still funneling inside from their tailgate. But on this night, I walked out of the locker room for warmups and you would have thought it was already the second quarter. The place was packed to the brim. Extra seats were brought in on the field. The stage was set. *GameDay* was on campus, undefeated No. 1 Oklahoma was in town, and fans were present like never before. It was time to play.

We were set to receive the opening kickoff. Marcus Murphy, a future All-American return man, was back to receive. Oklahoma kicker Patrick O'Hara kicked it short. The ball bounced at the 20-yard line, right to the off returner, Gahn McGaffie. Gahn hesitated, found a seam, and hit the jets. He found the left sideline with only one man to beat. You'd have thought an earthquake erupted. It was incredible. Gahn cut back straight into the end zone, and the other 10 guys on the field piled on top of him. That was the loudest I've ever heard Faurot Field. Others who were there that night tell me the same.

We played one of the best games we could have imagined. As we led 36–27, the final seconds ticked off the clock, fans began to rush the field. We did it. After all the build-up, we delivered what everyone had hoped for. We made Mizzou history.

44 Sir Anthony

"He's the left-handed Michael Jordan." That's how ESPN's Dick Vitale described Missouri sophomore guard Anthony Peeler moments before tip-off at Kansas's Allen Fieldhouse on February 13, 1990. It was No. 1 Kansas against No. 2 Missouri. Four of Norm Stewart's starting five were from the Detroit area. The exception was Peeler, the Kansas City kid who grew up in the middle of the Mizzou-Kansas Border War.

When the prized recruit from Paseo High School settled on his college choice, it came down to the archrivals. Just like that night in Lawrence, Mizzou won. "They've got too many guards, and you never know when Larry Brown's going to leave," Peeler said when he signed with Stewart's Tigers. "[Kansas] probably thought I didn't want to be bothered. Plus, I'm a resident of Missouri."

There was never a dull moment during Peeler's prolific four-year Mizzou tenure, especially for the writers assigned to cover his volatile career. The Tigers rose to national prominence with Peeler in the backcourt—he shared the headliner duties with forward Doug Smith, a year older—and he left Mizzou as arguably the best guard the program ever produced. A shooter, a slasher, a playmaker, Peeler had unique size (6'4") in the backcourt and gave Norm Stewart an explosive outside threat to pair with Smith, Nathan Buntin, and Jevon Crudup over the course of four years.

But the dynamic guard wasn't low-maintenance. After his freshman season, Peeler spent time in a Kansas City in-patient substance-abuse rehab facility. Stewart benched him a few times for missing classes. He was declared academically ineligible for the first semester of his junior year and missed the season's first seven games. Peeler could have followed Smith to the NBA in 1991, but it was Smith's decision to stay in school his senior year that inspired Peeler to do the same. "I feel that I should stay and help the team effort," Peeler said, "because guys came up here to play with me, just like I came up here to play with Doug."

Peeler vowed he had matured for his senior season, giving credit to MU's Total Person Program for sharpening his focus off the court. On the court, Peeler was a brilliant scorer with 21 career games with 25 points or more, but he was hardly a one-act show. A ferocious dunker. An unselfish playmaker. A rugged defender (most of the time). His scoring increased each season, from 10.1 points per game to 16.8 to 19.4 to 23.4. Peeler improved his three-point shooting percentage each season, topping out at 41.7 as a senior. He was a willing rebounder, pulling down 6.2 as a junior. He scored in double figures every game his senior year.

Peeler was at his best against Mizzou's greatest rival. In eight career games against Kansas, Peeler averaged 21.5 points…25.3 in his last three…and 36.5 in his final two. In his final regular-season game in 1992, he torched the Jayhawks for a career-high 43 points in Lawrence. "He had a glare in his eye," Kansas's Alonzo Jamison told reporters after the game. "He was unconscious. He wasn't even hitting any of the rim—he was hitting the bottom of the net."

Twenty-five years after his final college game, Peeler still ranked among Mizzou's top five in several career categories: points (No. 3), field goals (No. 5), free throws (No. 2), assists (No. 2), and steals (No. 1, tied). By any measure, he had the best statistical career of any guard to come through the program.

That was Good Anthony. Not-So-Good Anthony showed up shortly after his final college game when Peeler was arrested on suspicion of assault among other charges when a woman said he bit her and pointed a gun at her head—with the NBA Draft right around the corner. Peeler pleaded guilty to reduced charges and was placed on probation. Six years later the victim was awarded more than $2 million in damages in a civil suit.

The incident might have hurt Peeler's draft stock some—he went No. 15 to the Los Angeles Lakers—but he outlasted the initial baggage with a 13-year NBA career in L.A., Vancouver, Minnesota, Sacramento, and Washington, averaging 9.7 points per game. Peeler's top scoring season (14.5 PPG) came in 1996–97 with the Grizzlies, but he was an especially valuable guard for six Timberwolves playoff teams from 1998 to 2003. A 35 percent three-point shooter as a freshman at Mizzou, Peeler was the NBA's most accurate shooter behind the arc in 2003–04, his penultimate season, at 48.2 percent with the Kings.

45 Tigers Go Bowling

Glenn "Pop" Warner's first Stanford team won the Pacific Coast Conference in 1924 and earned an invitation to play Notre Dame in the Rose Bowl, just one of two bowl games on the college football calendar that year. But Los Angeles wasn't content with hosting Stanford while the hometown USC Trojans were left out of the postseason. So the city created something called the Los Angeles Christmas Festival, a new bowl game set for Christmas Day, hosted by USC at Memorial Coliseum. They just needed an opponent. Hello, Missouri. Gwinn Henry's Tigers, winners of the

Missouri Valley Conference, became the team of choice. Proceeds from the game would go toward MU's new stadium project back in Columbia.

Mizzou's travel contingent left Columbia on December 19 and arrived in Los Angeles four days later, the start of a jam-packed week that included a tour of the Metro-Goldwyn-Mayer movie studios, where the Tigers met several movie stars, including silent film star Rudolph Valentino, Bob Broeg later chronicled.

When the game arrived, Missouri couldn't keep up with the home team. "For two quarters the Missouri 11 played as brilliant football as was ever seen on the Pacific Coast, sweeping the heavier and faster Californians aside and driving through them," reported the 1925 edition of the *Savitar*. "Again and again the Tigers were in scoring position and just missed…. When the Tigers came back upon the field after the intermission between the halves, it was quite a different 11. The long trip had done its work, and battled desperately as they might, the Missourians could not compete with the inexhaustible reserves which the Trojans were able to send against them."

Missouri's 20–7 loss marked the first and last Los Angeles Christmas Festival but not the last postseason bowl game for the Tigers. Missouri returned to bowl season when the 1939 Tigers accepted an invitation to the Orange Bowl to face Georgia Tech. That too was a defeat. The Tigers didn't win their first bowl game until their eighth try, the 1961 Orange Bowl victory over Navy.

Through the 2017 season, the Tigers had played in 32 bowls, making the most appearances in the Orange (four), Cotton (three), Gator (three), and Independence (three).

Along the way, Missouri produced many memorable bowl performances. Among them, these superlatives:

- Tony Temple shredded Arkansas in the 2008 Cotton Bowl for an MU bowl-record 281 rushing yards and four touchdowns.

Tony Temple scores a 22-yard touchdown in the first quarter of the 2008 Cotton Bowl.

- Blaine Gabbert picked apart Iowa in the 2010 Insight Bowl for a slew of MU bowl records: 41 completions on 57 attempts and 434 passing yards.
- T.J. Moe, Gabbert's top target that night, caught an MU bowl-record 15 passes for 152 yards.
- In the 1981 Tangerine Bowl against Southern Miss, Bob Lucchesi kicked an MU bowl-record four field goals.
- Bill Tobin's 77-yard run in the 1962 Bluebonnet Bowl still stands as MU's longest play from scrimmage in a bowl game.

46 The Gainesville Gunner

Who owns Mizzou's single-game basketball scoring record? Gotta be Derrick Chievous? Nope. Doug Smith? Try again. Steve Stipanovich? Good idea...but no. Joe Scott, the pride of Gainesville, Missouri, scorched Nebraska for a school-record 46 points on March 6, 1961. The record performance came long before college basketball added both the three-point line and the shot clock. It was a rare highlight during an otherwise difficult 11–13 season for the Tigers.

The 6'4" Scott, gangly with a buzz cut fit for his generation, was known as the Gainesville Gunner. One of the state's most prolific high school scorers before he came to Mizzou, Scott wasn't shy about uncorking shots from all over the court, often clashing with Coach Sparky Stalcup's preferred ball-control style.

That day against the Cornhuskers, MU's penultimate game of the season, Scott shot 18 of 30 from the field and made 10 free throws. His 18 field goals also set a Mizzou record in the 97–76 win, the most points the Tigers had ever scored in a conference game. "It was the wizardry of Scott that disturbed Nebraska and the pigeons trying to roost in the Brewer field house rafters, while the crowd chanted, 'Let 'er go, Louis Joe,' during the final few minutes," wrote the *Kansas City Times* the next day.

With the victory long secured and a minute to play, Scott had tied the Mizzou single-game scoring record of 44 points, set by Lionel Smith against Marquette in 1957. With 45 seconds left, Scott broke the record with a one-handed 20-footer. "When you have a game like that, you don't remember a lot of it very clearly," Scott told the *Post-Dispatch* years later. "You remember spots of it, but you're kind of in your own world when you shoot the ball that well."

"I knew I was on and scoring a lot of points," he later told *Rural Missouri* magazine. "That's about all I knew. When the game was over they carried me off the floor, so I knew something special had happened."

Over the next 50 years, many would come close to Scott's record. Doug Smith scored 44 in 1990, also against Nebraska. Clarence Gilbert, a fearless three-point sniper, went for 43 in a quadruple-overtime win over Iowa State in 2001. Anthony Peeler dropped 43 on Kansas in 1992. Willie Smith also scored 43, an NCAA tournament record for Mizzou in the 1976 regional final against Michigan. But at the end of the 2017–18 season, Scott's record still stood.

47 Mizzou Arena

Billed as the "finest on-campus arena in the country" when its doors opened in 2004, Mizzou Arena will forever be remembered for its awkward origins. Designed in the likeness of modern NBA arenas, the sparkling $75 million basketball facility was set to replace the antiquated Hearnes Center but first had to overcome a naming snafu. The building was originally called Paige Sports Arena in honor of Elizabeth Paige Laurie, the daughter of Walmart heir Nancy Walton Laurie and her late husband, Bill. The couple's $25 million donation helped make the project possible. At the time, the Lauries owned the St. Louis Blues NHL franchise, while daughter Paige, 22, was a recent graduate of the University of Southern California. The name was unpopular with some alums who objected to naming an on-campus facility after someone who never attended the school.

Their dissent wouldn't last long. It didn't have to. A month after the arena opened, ABC's *20/20* interviewed Laurie's former USC roommate who alleged being paid $20,000 to write papers and finish other assignments for the Walmart heiress. Within a week of the story's broadcast, Missouri dropped Paige from the building's name when the family relinquished the naming rights. The university curators voted unanimously to rename the building, simply, Mizzou Arena.

The state-of-the-art arena borrowed concepts from nearly 20 facilities that Mizzou officials visited before settling on a design, including the NBA's Conseco Fieldhouse in Indianapolis and American Airlines Center in Dallas.

Taking 20 months to complete, the arena stood 117 feet, 9 inches tall—about seven feet taller than its predecessor and neighbor, the Hearnes Center—could seat a capacity crowd of 15,091, and featured 26 private suites. Norm Stewart Court, the hardwood floor named after the Hall of Famer who spent most of his coaching career roaming the Hearnes Center sideline, made the move from Hearnes to the new building.

Construction required 21,600 cubic yards of concrete, 2,006 tons of reinforcing steel, 1,500 tons of structural steel, 104,074 bricks, 67,934 concrete blocks, 460 doors and frames, 237 lockers, 77,400 square feet of carpet, and more than 37 miles of communications cable.

The new home for Mizzou men's and women's basketball included locker rooms, weight rooms, equipment rooms, a full-court practice gym, and an academic study center, plus offices for coaches and athletics administrators. Just behind the west basket, MU arranged a student bleacher section with approximately 3,000 seats. Sportswriters would have to crane their necks to get a full view of the court; press row became press corner, tucked away in the arena's northwest pocket and surrounded by fan seating.

The new arena didn't give the Tigers much of a home-court advantage initially. Under Coach Quin Snyder, Mizzou lost its third regular-season game in the building to Davidson and finished 14–5 overall at home during the debut season. The Tigers managed to beat two nationally ranked teams in the new building that first year: No. 16 Oklahoma and No. 7 Kansas. The inaugural season at Mizzou Arena ended with a disappointing first-round defeat to DePaul in the NIT.

Heading into the 2017–18 season, the men's basketball team had two undefeated seasons at Mizzou Arena: 2008–09 and 2012–13. In the team's first 11 years in the building, the Tigers were 161–33 in regular-season and postseason games for a winning percentage of 83 percent.

"The atmosphere was great when we were good and in league play," said former guard Kim English, whose senior class lost just four games in four seasons at Mizzou Arena. "And it was quiet early in the year. You learn[ed] to accept it and know that if you won, the fans would finally come out. And if you didn't [win], they wouldn't come out.... The place really can get rocking, and it was especially an advantage before the benches were flipped."

When Mizzou joined the SEC in 2012–13, league rules mandated that Mizzou's bench move to the west end of the floor by the student section, which meant the visiting team played in front of the students in the first half, not the second. English recalled several high-profile opponents in the Big 12 who missed crucial free throws while shooting into a backdrop of screaming students, including Kansas guards Sherron Collins and Tyshawn Taylor and Oklahoma All-American Blake Griffin. "A big reason we won those games," he said, "was the missed free throws in the second half."

48 Too Much Time

Julian Winfield's layup gave the Tigers a 74–73 lead with 4.8 seconds left. Four point eight. That's all that separated Mizzou from toppling No. 1 seed UCLA at the 1995 NCAA tournament in Boise. Ninety-four feet and 4.8 seconds. "UCLA [called] a timeout, and as we [went] to break, I [said], 'Oh, baby, I love this tournament,'" Missouri radio broadcaster Mike Kelly recalled.

During the commercial, Kelly scribbled a note to radio analyst Jim Kennedy, who did likewise. Both notes said the same: "Too much time." The rest is NCAA tournament history—and Mizzou torture.

Mizzou's tragic history of last-second misery has its own collection of names that will haunt fans for generations. By 1995 Colorado's Charles Johnson had already scored the Fifth Down touchdown. In two years, Nebraska's Matt Davison would catch the Flea Kicker. That day of the 1995 NCAA tournament in Boise, the Hall of Heartbreak would expand to include Tyus Edney, UCLA point guard—a 5'9" flash who could freeze time and destroy hope faster than you can tie your shoe. Tyus Effin' Edney.

"Cameron Dollar inbounds the ball, Edney takes it and comes up the sideline," Kelly recalled. "He goes behind the back at half-court, and before 'Buck' Grimm knew what could hit him, Edney goes up, and I said, 'Flips it up and in. UCLA, the No. 1 team in the nation, survives and advances. Jim, what a gallant effort by Ol' Mizzou.'" Kennedy sat stone-faced as the shock and horror set in. "Then it's pause, pause, pause, pause," Kelly said. "Finally, 'Mike, I don't know what to say.' I'm thinking, *Jesus, say something!*"

As Edney caught the inbound pass a few steps behind the free-throw line and raced upcourt, Mizzou's Jason Sutherland ran with him step for step but didn't get close enough to foul. Edney dribbled six times, once behind his back from his left hand to his right, reached the right side of the lane, and lofted a one-handed prayer over the outstretched arms of 6'9" Derek Grimm. Backboard... net...prayer answered. UCLA 75, Missouri 74.

For Mizzou, there was no time left for anything but commiseration and second-guessing. Should the Tigers have denied Edney the ball on the inbounds? Should they have sent a stronger double-team at halfcourt? Should Grimm have done more to block the shot? "I would say that if Derek Grimm wouldn't have cut his fingernails, he would have blocked it," former UCLA assistant coach Lorenzo Romar later told the *Post-Dispatch*.

Twenty years later, the pain hadn't faded for Stewart, who'd returned to the NCAA tournament just one more time in his final four seasons at Missouri. But when Stewart thinks back to Mizzou's crushing loss—the Bruins would go on to win their 11th national championship—he chooses to remember the build-up to Boise. The team had gathered at his house that Sunday to watch the tournament selection show. The Tigers drew the No. 8 seed in the West Regional, which meant they'd face top-seeded UCLA in the second round—if they survived the first round, no guarantee for a Stewart-coached team. The psychological game began immediately that day.

"We drew Indiana," Stewart recalled. "The next game is the winner of UCLA and Florida International. I didn't look at the rest of the bracket. I said to the players, 'You guys, let me tell you something: the toughest game you're going to have is Indiana. It's the opening game. You're all looking at the next game, UCLA. That will be an easier game for us to win. Because they're looking at the bracket and thinking Indiana will beat Missouri. So they're not even thinking about playing you.'"

Stewart continued, telling the team, "The first thing that happens to [UCLA] is they're going to wake up and say, 'Shit, we're playing Missouri.' They're not going to be ready to play Missouri. 'But we have to beat Indiana first.'" They did. The Tigers took down Bob Knight's Hoosiers 65–60 behind Paul O'Liney's 22 points.

Two days later, it was Mizzou-UCLA for a spot in the Sweet 16. The Tigers gained control early with hot shooting from outside and led the Bruins by eight at halftime. Would MU finally lift Stewart's March curse? Instead, the Tigers would play a role in one of the game's most indelible moments, forever replayed every March.

Years later, Mizzou's voice behind the stunning finish could appreciate its place in history. "At the end of the day, despite all the glitz, the glory, the national TV, the essence of college athletics is about kids making plays," Kelly said. "On that day, on that stage, that kid made the biggest play he could have made."

Kim Anderson Comes Home

The timing couldn't have been better. On March 29, 2014, Kim Anderson experienced the peak achievement of his coaching career, leading Central Missouri to the Division II national championship. Nineteen days later, Missouri coach Frank Haith boarded a plane in Columbia bound for Tulsa, Oklahoma, to interview for the Tulsa head coaching job, a position he'd accept the next day. That left Anderson's dream job open for the fourth time since his days as Norm Stewart's assistant coach at Mizzou. This time, though, Anderson's credentials included a national championship, albeit at the Division II level.

Anderson, the Big 8 Player of the Year for the Tigers in 1977, spent 11 seasons on Stewart's bench but wasn't Mizzou's choice to succeed his mentor in 1999. Instead, the chance came 15 years later. Anderson, the No. 6 scorer in MU history when he finished his playing career, was introduced as the Tigers' head coach on April 29, two weeks shy of his 59th birthday.

Former Mizzou teammates and players Anderson coached at MU widely praised the hire, hoping the new coach would reconnect the program to its glory years under Stewart. Missouri's last three coaches—Quin Snyder, Mike Anderson, and Haith—had guided the Tigers to nine NCAA tournaments over 15 seasons, but they came and left as outsiders to the state and to the program. Kim Anderson, a native of nearby Sedalia, dreamed about becoming the head coach at his alma mater. Though MU initially targeted Wichita State's Gregg Marshall as its choice to replace Haith, campus administration backed Anderson as the No. 2 choice. "There just aren't many people better than Kim Anderson, and there aren't many better representatives for the University of Missouri than Kim," former Missouri center Tom Dore said. "The guy can coach. He's everything you'd want in coaching. I know he's got the ties to Norm, but Kim's his own man. To me, that stands above everything else."

When Marshall turned down Mizzou's offer, the job belonged to Anderson. Questions immediately surfaced about his age—he was the oldest head coach in the SEC when the 2014–15 season tipped off—and his lack of Division I head coaching experience. His peers at the D-II level scoffed at the skepticism. "He can coach the socks off most Division I guys," said Bob Chipman, the head coach at Washburn University. "That Division II thing doesn't mean anything. He was around Norm, so he knows the blueprint. He saw how the best practices in the history of basketball operate. And he's a great game coach."

Anderson's debut season was historic—for all the wrong reasons. Anderson inherited a roster with only six scholarship players and added six newcomers to the mix. Freshmen and sophomores formed the nucleus of a team that became wildly inconsistent on the court and troublesome off of it as Anderson suspended seven different players during the course of the season. The Tigers lost their season opener—a dreadful defeat to Missouri–Kansas City—and finished with a 9–23 record, the worst Mizzou season since 1966–67. MU suffered a 13-game losing streak, the longest in team history, and finished last in the SEC at 3–15.

Anderson reshaped the roster for his second season with a promising freshman class, hoping to revive a program that had seen better days, but the Tigers made only subtle progress, going 10–21. Even worse, the school slapped itself with self-imposed sanctions for NCAA violations that mostly occurred on Haith's watch. Anderson returned for his third season in 2016–17 working for his third athletics director and needing to win to secure his job for a fourth season. It didn't happen. The roster was gutted again and composed exclusively of players Anderson recruited, but the Tigers finished last in the SEC for the third-straight season and won just eight games overall, dropping his three-year record to 27–68. With a couple weeks left in the season, AD Jim Sterk told Anderson he wouldn't be back for a fourth season. Being a good guy wasn't enough to save his job. The native son with deep ties to the area couldn't overcome three years of historic losing and swaths of empty seats in Mizzou Arena.

"I certainly hope that whoever the [next] coach is that we have provided a little bit of a building block for them," Anderson said. "I maintain that when I was hired I was pretty much asked to stabilize this program. It took a while. It obviously took too long. But I'm proud of what we've done. I know there's a lot of people out there that aren't. But no one out there sat in my shoes for the last three years. No one out there knows the challenges we had."

Anderson's players gave their coach one last highlight, a buzzer-beating overtime victory over Auburn in the SEC tournament. The Tigers bowed out of the bracket with the next night's loss to Ole Miss.

Six days later, Sterk hired Anderson's replacement, Cal coach Cuonzo Martin, an established Division I coach with a reputation as a recruiter. He quickly reeled in a big catch, perhaps the biggest in Mizzou's history: Michael Porter Jr., the top-ranked high school player in the country. Porter asked out of his national letter of intent to the University of Washington and agreed to play at Mizzou, where Martin had just hired his father as an assistant coach. Martin would open his debut season that fall with a remade roster, supplementing the core of Anderson's roster with one of the nation's top recruiting classes.

Anderson, meanwhile, returned to the level where he had once thrived, across the state border at Division II Pittsburg State in Kansas.

50 Ol' Mizzou's Treasured Scribe

Bob Broeg was to Mizzou football what William Faulkner was to the American South. Yeah, they weren't the only ones who wrote about their chosen subjects, but damned if they weren't the very best.

Broeg, a St. Louis native, attended Missouri's School of Journalism in 1941, then joined the *St. Louis Post-Dispatch* in 1945, where he first covered the St. Louis Browns (then the Cardinals). Missouri Tigers football became his second passion. His words appeared in the newspaper until 2004, many of them devoted to the Tigers.

Best known for his trademark bowtie, verbose writing style, and close association with Missouri coach Dan Devine, Broeg sometimes second-guessed his loyalty to the man he called Dan'l.

"Dan Devine, with Stan Musial the special journalistic joy of my mature years as a sportswriter, became the new Mizzou coach and soon a good friend," Broeg wrote in his 1995 memoirs. "Maybe too good, considering the need for balance between newsprint personal and professional views. As my wife, Dorith, suggested, Devine looked like a corner druggist, but his soft-spoken words had the power to inspire." Broeg wasn't the only reporter who chronicled the Tigers' glory years, but he was the writer Devine trusted most.

After the Tigers lost the 1960 Orange Bowl to Georgia, Broeg and Devine shared one of their many private moments, later retold in Broeg's prose. "Breathing the sweet orange scent of fashionable Miami country club afterward," he wrote, "Devine told me softly and prophetically, 'We lost a football game, but I think this young team is matured and ready.'"

More than a decade later, when Devine was offered the head coaching job with the Green Bay Packers, it was Broeg's advice he sought. "Naturally," Broeg wrote, "I hoped Dan would stay at Mizzou, but if he expected me to make a strong appeal, I disappointed him. As Shakespeare said, to thine ownself be true.... Devine hung up after telling me he would recite his rosary in a prayer for guidance. I felt he was gone. And he was. Missouri football has never been the same."

Broeg went on to author *Ol' Mizzou: A Story of Missouri Football*, the unrivaled history of Tigers football, published in 1974 and later updated in 1990. The bible of Mizzou football lore opens with typical Broegian prose: "Late in life when Mark Twain was a Connecticut Yankee, someone asked the famous humorist, 'Mr. Clemens, what kind of days do you like best?' 'October days in Missouri,' said the man from Hannibal, without the benefit of ever having watched a football game back home in that delightful Indian-summer time of the year when leaves are as bright as a coed's cheeks and as colorful as Ol' Mizzou's fight song."

The university awards multiple scholarships in Broeg's name. In 1969 he was given the university's Faculty Alumni Award. In 1971 he earned the Missouri Honor Medal for Distinguished Service in Journalism, the first sportswriter to receive the award.

When Broeg died in 2005, a treasured part of local sports history and Mizzou sports history left with him. He covered the games and the people who played them with an unbridled enthusiasm, painted words with a poet's appreciation for style and color—but free of cynicism and meanness. "So many writers in our profession sour and turn bitter as they age and move aside to make room for younger colleagues and modern athletes. Not Broeg," former *Post-Dispatch* columnist Bernie Miklasz wrote after Broeg's death. "He stayed in the moment, able to apply his old-school wisdom to new-world issues and make it fit. Broeg evolved and kept up."

Over time, Broeg pulled off the ultimate trick performed by only the greatest writers of history and sport: he became every bit as iconic as the icons about whom he wrote. "In past times writers, including me, hero-worshipped," Broeg wrote. "Now they denigrate. Isn't the latter simply a compensation for the former? Why not find a middle ground....? Above all, damnit, I believe it's essential to be able to write according to what your heart and head tell you."

No Mizzou scribe mastered that skill better.

51 The King of Shake and Bake

Ricky Frazier came and went like a powerful gust of wind. He was the patriarch of the greatest high school basketball dynasty in Missouri—Charleston High—located on the tip-top of the Missouri Bootheel in Charleston, Missouri. The Blue Jays won

11 state championships from 1975 to 2012, the first captured by Frazier, the 6'6" forward who was impossible to guard anywhere on the court. His nephews Corey and Lamont came later, excellent college players in their own right. But nobody could touch Uncle Ricky. "When the Lord waved the talent wand over Ricky Frazier, he lingered more than he did over everybody else," former Mizzou coach Norm Stewart famously said about the All-American.

Frazier grew up across the street from the most popular playground in Charleston, and from there one of the great Mizzou basketball careers was honed at an early age. First, though, a pit stop at Saint Louis University. Playing for the Billikens in 1977–78, Frazier was named Freshman of the Year in the Metro Conference after averaging 13.7 points per game. His time there was short: after one season at SLU, Frazier transferred to Missouri to play for Stewart. He was an instant hit in Boone County, adding scoring punch to a nucleus that included point guard Larry Drew, forwards Curtis Berry and Mark Dressler, and freshman stars Steve Stipanovich and Jon Sundvold. "He was tough," Sundvold said. "His basketball IQ was way up there, A+-type student on the court. Like most of Coach Stewart's players, he was a great team player."

As a sophomore, Frazier averaged 13.8 points, 5.6 rebounds, shot well from the field and the foul line, and led MU with 20 blocks. The Tigers won the Big 8 by three games before losing in the second weekend of the NCAA tournament.

Frazier's game soared to another level as a junior, when he led the Tigers in scoring (16.3 PPG) and helped capture another Big 8 title. In the regular-season finale, Stewart decided the best answer for Kansas State's zone defense was to play keep-away. The Tigers held the ball for nearly eight minutes late in the second half of a tie game with a plan for Frazier to play hero. Frazier freelanced on the final possession and drilled a jumper with seven seconds left. The Wildcats fouled him on the play, and for good measure, he hit the free throw for a 46–43 win and another Big 8 crown.

Former Mizzou center Tom Dore said:

> One-on-one, Ricky was just about unstoppable. If we
> were late in the game and it was tight, Norm was going to
> Ricky. We were going to isolate him on the left side. He'd
> make a move to the baseline and come to the middle and
> finish at the basket, because he just didn't miss.
>
> He wasn't a great standstill jump shooter, but on the
> move, for some reason, he could do so much more by going
> to the basket. He was so slippery. I don't know another
> word that really fits him. He wasn't unbelievably quick. He
> was a great jumper. And he would read you; he'd make a
> little move going the other way, and the ball would go in.

The player Al McGuire called the King of Shake and Bake
didn't let up his senior year—he averaged a team-best 16.1 points,
playing on one Stewart's most talented teams. Frazier. Sundvold.
Stipo. All in their prime. Frazier was the Big 8 Player of the Year
and earned third-team All-America honors as the Tigers won
another conference championship.

Two weeks before the Big 8 tournament, Mizzou faced
Georgetown in a nonconference showdown, a matchup of elite
big men Stipanovich and freshman Patrick Ewing. The Hoyas
dealt MU its second loss, but Frazier commanded the spotlight
with 24 points. "I was afraid of Frazier," Georgetown coach John
Thompson told reporters after the game. "He's everything they said
he [is]. Stipanovich knows more about positioning himself than
Ewing does, but it didn't make any difference to Frazier. He was
going over us all day.... I must have said Frazier's name 100 times
in the huddles during the timeouts. We had three guys run to him
every time he got the ball."

That Missouri team reached No. 1 in the national rankings,
but like always, the Tigers fell short in the NCAA tournament,

losing to Houston in St. Louis at the Midwest Regional. Frazier went out strong, scoring a career-high 29 points in his final college game. That gave him 1,448 points for his career, the most in team history, though Sundvold and Stipo, four-year players, would surpass him the next year. Frazier's scoring mark for three-year players stood until Kareem Rush passed him in 2002.

Numbers, though, didn't define Frazier's career. It was about the creativity, the finesse, the will. "He was a really unique guy with the ball in his hands," Dore recalled. "He needed the ball. That wasn't a negative, but that's how he was creative. He was special. He never had the huge numbers, but he didn't have to. Ricky just wanted to win. If he got 25, great. If he got 9 and we won, great. He never complained. Never."

Frazier could have been an NBA star with his scoring touch and explosiveness. The Chicago Bulls thought enough to draft him in the second round, but a groin injury and an emergency dental procedure cut short his rookie year. The Bulls released him before the regular season tipped off. Frazier was the ultimate NBA tweener: too small to play in the frontcourt, not sharp enough a shooter to play in the backcourt. He resurfaced in lesser leagues and overseas but never made a mark professionally. Sadly, Frazier became a cautionary tale of the great depths into which athletes can plunge when sports no longer matter. He was arrested for felony shoplifting in Sikeston, Missouri, in 1986. In the 1990s he was diagnosed with glaucoma. His vision betrayed him.

"I've been a really depressed person," Frazier told the *Columbia Tribune* in 2000. "I kind of isolate myself from a lot of people. I'm half-afraid most of the time. You're used to knowing and seeing everything and then you lose so much of it."

For Missouri fans in the early 1980s, visions of No. 32 will forever outlive the fiercest gust of wind.

52 40 Minutes of Hell 2.0

The Mike Anderson coaching era of Mizzou basketball had an unusual beginning and an unfortunate ending, but in between, he gave the Tigers five solid seasons on the court.

The basketball program had unraveled under Quin Snyder's watch, to the point that university leaders questioned athletics director Mike Alden's handling of the coach's departure. But after a disastrous 2005–06 season, Alden was tasked with finding Snyder's replacement. A few names surfaced as possible candidates: Rick Majerus, Bob Huggins, Dana Altman, John Beilein, Steve Alford…and Anderson. The former Arkansas assistant coach had installed Nolan Richardson's 40 Minutes of Hell system at Alabama-Birmingham and taken the Conference USA program to the NCAA tournament three times in four years, including a march to the Sweet 16 in 2004.

Just as Alden settled on Anderson as his top choice, the university system board of curators called an emergency meeting to vote on Alden's job status after the botched handling of Snyder's resignation. Alden survived, and Anderson took over a fledgling program without much established talent on the roster. "When Quin left, of course, it's kind of like Daddy's gone," Anderson said. "They don't know what's going to take place. But now there's light at the end of the tunnel. Now it's my job to make sure I can reach out to them and let them know, 'Hey, we're going to be OK.' As a matter of fact, it's a new day, it's a new era, and there's no question I want them to be a part of it."

Anderson coached the Tigers to 18- and 16-win seasons in his first two years, respectively, both times missing the postseason. Some off-court incidents marred the mild progress the Tigers made on the court, notably a bar fight that led to an arrest and five suspensions. But it all came together for Anderson in his third season, led by DeMarre Carroll, a skilled power forward transfer from Vanderbilt who happened to be Anderson's nephew. Carroll, fellow seniors Leo Lyons and Matt Lawrence, junior guards J.T. Tiller and Zaire Taylor, and a promising collection of freshmen led the Tigers to 31 wins; regular-season victories over nationally ranked USC, Kansas, Texas, and Oklahoma; and a third-place finish in the Big 12—MU's best showing in conference play since 1999, Norm Stewart's final season on the bench. Then, for the first time since 1993, Mizzou captured the conference tournament, beating Baylor to clinch the Big 12 title in Oklahoma City. "We have seen this program when it was at its worst and best—and [the latter is] right now," Lyons said.

In the NCAA tournament for the first time since Snyder's 2002 Elite Eight team, the Tigers did the same, riding their relentless defense to victories over Cornell, Marquette, and Memphis. The season ended with a loss to Connecticut in the West Regional final, the fourth time MU had come one game short of the Final Four. Anderson was rewarded with a raise and seven-year extension. The program was back on solid ground and the Tigers had the man responsible locked up for years to come.

Or not. Anderson's next two teams were solid but hardly spectacular, both going 23–11 with fifth-place finishes in the Big 12. Young guards Marcus Denmon, Kim English, Mike Dixon, and Phil Pressey showed signs of promise, but under Anderson, their talents couldn't get the Tigers past the first weekend of the NCAA tournament.

Anderson had flirted with job openings at Georgia and Oregon, but in March 2011, his dream job became a reality: Arkansas, where Anderson had coached alongside Richardson from 1985 to 2002. Twenty days after saying he planned to retire at Mizzou, Anderson was introduced as the Razorbacks' head coach on March

24, turning down a lucrative raise at Missouri that would have paid him $2 million a year. Anderson left behind a program in far better shape than the one he had inherited from the Snyder fiasco. He also left behind a team of veteran players resolved to carry on without him. They would the next season, winning the Big 12 tournament under Anderson's replacement, Frank Haith.

Anderson didn't have instant success at Arkansas. The Hogs failed to make the NCAA tournament until 2015, his fourth year. Missouri joined Arkansas in the SEC in 2012–13, setting up a pair of rivalry clashes each year between the Tigers and their former coach. Anderson and Haith had a heated exchange during the 2013 game at Mizzou Arena—neither coach explained what caused the brief shouting match—but Haith had the last say, a 30-point victory in Anderson's Mizzou Arena debut as the visiting coach. But Anderson left with some pride in the program he helped revive. "When I got here, [Mizzou Arena] was empty, " Anderson said. "It was like, 'Man, they've got a program over there?' All of a sudden now it's changed. I think that's good."

53 Missouri's Man in Charge

Only one person ran Mizzou's athletics department longer than Mike Alden. There's no shame in finishing second to Don Faurot.

Faurot, the legendary MU football coach, also served two stints as AD, from 1935 to 1942 and 1946 to 1966. A generation later, Alden ushered Mizzou athletics out of the 20th century and into the Southeastern Conference. Alden's regime as Mizzou's athletics boss spanned from 1998 to his stunning retirement in 2015. During those 17 years, Alden expanded Mizzou's athletics budget from

$13 million to nearly $100 million and completely overhauled its facilities. When Alden stepped away from college sports to join MU's faculty in the College of Education, his epitaph was already written, headlined by two major achievements: he hired football coach Gary Pinkel, who became the school's all-time wins leader, and navigated Mizzou's safe landing in the SEC after conference realignment redrew the college sports map.

The latter may not have happened without the former. Pinkel, Alden's handpicked successor to Larry Smith after the 2000 season, made Mizzou football relevant on a national scale for the first time in nearly 40 years—relevant enough to earn an invitation to the SEC, the country's foremost football conference. Together, the Alden-Pinkel tandem worked together for 14 years. "I'm so fortunate," Pinkel said when Alden stepped down in January 2015. "We can agree to disagree, so not everything was fun and roses all the time. But it's very unusual for an athletic director to stay in one place for that many years, let alone a football coach. He's so well respected nationally and so well respected in the SEC for what a great man he is, his honesty and great integrity."

The sun didn't always shine on Alden's watch. After some early success, the men's basketball program collapsed under Quin Snyder, Alden's chosen successor to longtime coach Norm Stewart, who retired in 1999, less than a year after Alden took office. The basketball program never enjoyed sustained success under Alden. Evidence: he had to hire four head coaches in 15 years. Also, Mizzou absorbed national scrutiny for mishandling several sexual-assault allegations involving athletes. Almost a year after Alden announced his resignation, MU self-imposed sanctions for major NCAA violations that took place under former basketball coach Frank Haith, whom Alden had hired in 2011.

"Have we made some mistakes along the way?" Alden asked in 2015, presciently. "Absolutely we have. Have we stumbled along the way? Absolutely. Have we had challenges? There's no doubt about that. But I believe, and we believe, that each and every one of those stumbles...those challenges...those mistakes...that we learned from that. We grew from that."

During the Alden years, MU basketball moved out of the Hearnes Center and into Mizzou Arena, football's Memorial Stadium underwent several major renovations, and the school approved a new softball stadium that opened in 2017. Under Alden, Missouri teams for golf, tennis, gymnastics, swimming, and wrestling all moved into new facilities. A handful of missteps complicated Alden's legacy—that's inevitable considering he served the equivalent of four presidential terms—but most would agree he left Mizzou in better condition than it was in when he first arrived. Mack Rhoades, his successor, conceded that much his first day on the job in 2015. "This," Rhoades said, "is not a fixer-upper."

In 2016 Mizzou colleagues and supporters found a new sense of appreciation for Alden's tenure when Rhoades suddenly left for Baylor after just 14 months on the job.

54 Mr. Mizzou

Seemingly out of tears to cry, John Kadlec Jr. stood behind the lectern at Our Lady of Lourdes Catholic Church in Columbia. It was November 1. All Saints' Day on the Catholic calendar. Of course it was. John said good-bye to his father that morning in 2014. He hoped thousands more would join him later that day at Memorial Stadium, where the Tigers would host Kentucky. "For those of you going to the game," he said, "bring home a win for Mr. Mizzou."

Dozens of men have coached football at Missouri since the school formed its first team in 1890. Only one became known as

Mr. Mizzou. But John Kadlec Sr. was so much more than an assistant coach during his 86 years. He was a Mizzou player. A Mizzou administrator. A Mizzou fund-raiser. A Mizzou broadcaster. A Mizzou icon.

The St. Louis native began his college career at Saint Louis University—his mother insisted he attend a Catholic school—but he dropped out after a semester and got a job driving an ice truck. Soon enough, Tigers coach Don Faurot dispatched an assistant coach to recruit Kadlec to Missouri. Kadlec became an All–Big 7 offensive lineman for the Tigers, lettering from 1948 to 1950. He joined Faurot's coaching staff after graduating and served two long stints on the staff under Faurot, Frank Broyles, Dan Devine, and Al Onofrio.

Remembered former offensive lineman Ed Blaine:

> He was friendly but could be stern. He was like a father figure to most of us coming up. He could put his arm around you and tell you everything was all right…or he could kick you in the butt. I'm not sure John would be the right choice to be the head coach because he was too nice a guy, but he was critical to how the players responded to things. He was the buffer zone. If Devine gets carried away and slams you on the head or something to emphasize his way, John would come over, put his arm around you, and say, "It's OK. He doesn't really mean it."

Kadlec belongs in a small class of assistant coaches who spent two decades on multiple Mizzou staffs. Clay Cooper spent more years than anyone on Mizzou's staffs, 29 years from 1947 to 1975. Chauncey Simpson coached for 21 seasons, from 1934 to 1954. John "Hi" Simmons, more famous as Mizzou's head baseball coach, was a football assistant for 20 seasons, from 1937 to 1956. Andy

Hill, a wide receiver for the Tigers in the 1980s, is the modern-day Mizzou lifer. He entered his 22nd season on the staff in 2017.

Kadlec was done coaching when Onofrio's staff was fired after the 1977 season, then spent a few years in Kansas State's development office. He returned to his alma mater in the 1980s and later reunited with Devine, brought back as Mizzou AD, and ran the department's fund-raising office.

In 1995, AD Joe Castiglione talked Kadlec into filling in as the team's radio analyst after Kellen Winslow abruptly quit shortly before the season. Kadlec agreed, reluctantly. He wasn't the most

Missouri players wore an emblem on their helmets honoring the late John Kadlec in 2014.

polished broadcaster, but he was a perfect match with play-by-play voice Mike Kelly. After the season opener, Castiglione persuaded Kadlec to finish out the year. "That was in his wheelhouse," Castiglione said. "He had such a unique style that related to everybody." The temporary gig lasted 16 years: Kadlec became a fixture in the booth and worked alongside Kelly through the 2010 season.

"I can't think of anybody who's had or will ever have the longtime devotion to Mizzou both as a servant and certainly as a coach," Kelly said after Kadlec died in 2014. "Fifty-plus years of his life dedicated to Mizzou. You think about the countless thousands of people he came across during that time."

Twice in the radio booth Kelly saw emotions overcome his longtime partner. First, on November 1, 1997. (All Saints' Day. Coincidence?) The Tigers beat Colorado in Boulder for their sixth win and became bowl eligible for the first time since 1983. The long, cold 14-year winter was over. "As that last drive [was] unfolding and Missouri [was] grinding out the clock and exhausting any life Colorado [had] left, I looked over, and there [was] a tear coming out of John's eye," Kelly remembered, "because his program that he loved so much was finally putting to bed the years of losing."

Ten years later, the Tigers throttled Arkansas in the Cotton Bowl for their school-record 12th victory. "At the end of that game," Kelly said, "I could see he [was] getting emotional and there [were] tears in his eyes because the football program he cared about and loved, and his university, was finally back on the platform and the stage that he thought it should be."

In 2005 Missouri named its practice fields in Kadlec's honor. A lifetime dedicated to Mizzou began on those fields but extended far beyond for decades to come. "John was a great example of how one can live life to its fullest," Castiglione said. "He was just an authentic man and ever the gentleman." And the one and only Mr. Mizzou.

55 Tough, Raw-Boned Iowa Farmer

There are statistics that encapsulate the college basketball career of Al Eberhard, starting with this remarkable fact: he's one of only four Mizzou players to average a career double-double, at 16.8 points per game and 10.1 rebounds. Here's another: Eberhard was 6'5" in his sneakers and managed to finish his career averaging double-digit rebounds. Only three other Mizzou players in team history could say the same. None were named Steve Stipanovich or Doug Smith.

But the way a former teammate tells it, neither numerical measure defines Eberhard's career as much as the ooze that poured out of his knee one day in the training room. Gary Link, take it from here.

"Al was the toughest guy I ever saw," Link said. "He played through stuff. I remember I had a little ankle injury and I was in the training room whining about putting my foot in the ice. He's in there getting his knee drained. They bring in a needle this big..." Link spread his hands about the length of two iPhones. "And then this red, yellow, orange concoction comes out of his knee," Link continued. "I'm almost sick looking at it. They take it out, and I go, 'Al, doesn't that hurt?' He says, 'Yeah, it hurt pretty bad.' Then he taped it up, went out, and played. Tough, raw-boned Iowa farmer. He'd go through a wall for you."

Eberhard, a signature Norm Stewart player during the formative years of the Stewart regime, often had to do just that. Part of an undersized front line headed by 6'7" superstar John Brown, Eberhard was the ideal sidekick in 1971–72 and 1972–73. The pride of Springville, Iowa, and the son of a hog farmer, Eberhard finished right behind Brown in scoring and rebounding in both seasons.

In his memoir, *Stormin' Back*, Stewart recalls one of his fondest memories of coaching, when he tried urging Eberhard to sit out a Big 8 Holiday Tournament game because of a severely sprained ankle. Eberhard convinced Stewart to let him go through pregame warmups in Kansas City. "I swear," Stewart wrote, "he couldn't even hobble." Eberhard won the argument, played in the game, and produced as always, scoring a game-high 24 points in the win over Kansas State. "It was the most courageous thing I have ever seen," Stewart wrote.

Stewart recalled seeing Eberhard's father, Marvin, embracing his son in the shower back at the team hotel after the game, overcome with pride over his son's grit. Stewart considered it one of the most emotional scenes he'd ever witnessed.

After Brown graduated, Eberhard and Link captained Mizzou's 1973–74 team. The year unraveled into a rare losing season under Stewart, but Eberhard admirably stepped into Brown's role as MU's leading man. He averaged 19.7 points and 12.0 rebounds and finished his career ranked No. 2 on MU's career scoring list, trailing only Brown. Drafted 15th overall by the Detroit Pistons, Eberhard played four years in the NBA. In 1989 Eberhard joined Mizzou's staff on an interim basis while Stewart recovered from cancer surgery. Eberhard worked closely with Smith, MU's burgeoning star forward, and earned credit for boosting his performance in the second half of the season.

56 Faith in Haith

The collective reaction around the state of Missouri on April 3, 2011, came in one word: "Who?" Hiring a third head basketball coach in 12 years, Mizzou AD Mike Alden went with Frank Haith, who in seven years as the head coach at the University of Miami led the Hurricanes to one NCAA tournament appearance and sported a conference record of 43–69. Alden had reportedly offered the job to Purdue coach Matt Painter, but the deal fell through before contracts were finalized, leading Alden to Haith, whose job security at Miami began to erode—until Mizzou threw him a $1.6 million life preserver and the keys to a program coming off three straight NCAA appearances. It wasn't exactly love at first sight when Haith arrived. "When I hear…'Who is this guy, Frank Haith, and what has he done?' I get it," he said at his introductory press conference.

It turns out, Haith did more in his first season than anyone expected. He also did more at Miami than Missouri had known. Before he ever coached a game at Mizzou, Haith became one of several figures to come under investigation for possible recruiting violations at Miami. A former Miami booster, imprisoned for running a $930 million Ponzi scheme, told Yahoo! Sports that he lavishly spent thousands of dollars on Hurricanes athletes from 2002 to 2010, leading to an exhaustive NCAA investigation into Miami's program, including Haith's time at the school. Missouri stood behind its newly hired coach, but a cloud of uncertainty hung over MU for the next two years as the NCAA plodded along in its investigation.

It didn't distract the Tigers on the court. In Haith's debut season, with an undersized lineup loaded with talented guards—Marcus Denmon, Kim English, Phil Pressey, Michael Dixon—Mizzou finished 30–5, took second in the Big 12, and captured the 2012 conference tournament in Kansas City, Mizzou's final appearance in the tourney before leaving for the SEC the following year. English later said:

> If Frank [didn't] come in, I would have transferred to Maryland. Mike Dixon was on the verge of transferring. I'm not sure Phil Pressey was planning on coming back. It was an ugly team. It was selfish basketball. We didn't guard. We did a lot of things the wrong way. Coach Haith came in and grabbed the reins. We had a lot of natural ability.... He identified roles right away. He gave us a system to play out of right away. He gave us defensive principles in the halfcourt. He took a team that was 1–7 on the Big 12 road the year before and we [won] the most regular-season games in Missouri basketball history with seven scholarship players.
>
> I think it's underappreciated what he did. He did an amazing job with a team that was on the verge of falling apart.

After winning the Big 12 tournament, the Tigers earned a No. 2 seed in the NCAA tournament. It was the peak of the Haith era. It was mostly downhill from there. A week later, Norfolk State earned an eternal place in the consciousness of Mizzou fans with a punch-to-the-gut first-round stunner, an 86–84 upset, a game that will never escape Haith's legacy at Mizzou. The Tigers' run to the school's first Final Four was over before the first lap was complete. Mizzou was favored by 21 points, making it the biggest loss as measured by Las Vegas point spreads in tournament history. "The coaches did a great job getting us ready, but they can't go out and get loose balls on the floor, can't make free throws or get rebounds," Denmon said. "That's for the players to do, and we came up short."

Haith guided the Tigers back to the NCAA tournament in his second season, but it was another one-and-done cameo. Mizzou lost by 12 to Colorado State, wrapping up a lackluster 23–11 season.

Other than first-round NCAA losses, Haith's short time at Mizzou was defined by the swarm of Division I transfers to join the roster—eight in all. Former coach Mike Anderson left behind a nucleus of English, Denmon, Pressey, and forward Laurence Bowers, but Haith opted for quick fixes to restock the roster, a philosophy that temporarily kept the program afloat with the first wave of additions: Keion Bell (Pepperdine), Earnest Ross (Auburn) and Alex Oriakhi (Connecticut). Transfers Jordan Clarkson (Tulsa) and Jabari Brown (Oregon) became the SEC's highest-scoring guard tandem in 2013–14, but Haith didn't supply much of a supporting cast as the Tigers settled for the NIT, snapping the program's five-year run in the NCAA tournament. Clarkson and Brown left early for the NBA, while the next wave of transfers—Deuce Bello (Baylor), Zach Price (Louisville) and Cam Biedscheid (Notre Dame)—gave Mizzou next to nothing. Price and Biedscheid were discarded before ever playing a game for the Tigers. Bello transferred in 2015.

As for the Miami scandal, the NCAA botched the investigation and Haith got away with a five-game suspension to start the 2013–14 season, seemingly fraying his relationship with his bosses at Mizzou. His long-term job security in doubt, Haith settled for a fresh start in April 2014, leaving Mizzou for the head coaching job at Tulsa. He left Columbia with a 76–28 record in three seasons and the best winning percentage (.731) in team history among head coaches who spent at least three seasons on the bench. Under Haith, the Tigers had wining records against nationally ranked opponents (10–7) and top-10 opponents (6–5).

57 Lost in the Wilderness

At his introductory press conference as Mizzou's new football head coach in 1934, Don Faurot famously quipped, "I don't know one thing, not a single thing, more overconfident than for a Missouri football coach to buy a house." At that point, Missouri had chewed up and spit out 21 coaches in 44 years, only one lasting more than four years on the job.

A generation later, from 1978 to 1993, Mizzou upheld that reputation as three men were handed the keys to the head coach's office then had them snatched away. Warren Powers, Woody Widenhofer, and Bob Stull all had varying results at MU and faced different challenges, but none could discover and sustain a formula for winning like Dan Devine had done in the 1960s and Gary Pinkel achieved later in the 2000s and beyond.

Powers, a Kansas City native who played at Nebraska and with the Oakland Raiders, turned Washington State into a winner in his only previous head coaching job. He made a smashing debut in 1978 with a 3–0 win at No. 5 Notre Dame, the defending national champion. With brilliant offensive talent collected during the Onofrio years—quarterback Phil Bradley, running back James Wilder, tight end Kellen Winslow—Powers won at least seven games in each of his first four years on the job. Malaise eventually set in. Once Onofrio's recruits filtered out of the program, the Tigers went just 15–16–3 from 1982 to 1984. Attendance steadily declined. A year after giving Powers a three-year extension, AD Dave Hart fired him following his first and only losing season in 1984. Powers's winning percentage (.580) stands fifth among Mizzou head coaches who lasted at least three years.

Next was Widenhofer, the first Mizzou alum to come home as head coach since Faurot. A former defensive assistant with the Pittsburgh Steelers and head coach in the USFL, Widenhofer promised to build the Tigers around a punishing defense. "You entertain with offense and win with defense," he said when he arrived. The Tigers, all aboard Woody's Wagon, barely entertained and definitely did not win, going just 12–31–1 in four seasons under the first-time college head coach. There were comically bad losses to Oklahoma—51–6 in 1985 and 77–0 in 1986—and a 0–10 record against nationally ranked teams. Widenhofer's departure was termed as a resignation—he was in the final year of his four-year contract—but he suffered the same fate as his two Mizzou predecessors.

Widenhofer returned to the NFL as an assistant and resurfaced as the head coach at Vanderbilt in 1997. He was no more successful there, going 15–40 in five seasons. Retired from coaching, Widenhofer later took a job working in a tollbooth near Destin, Florida.

Thern there was Stull, who unlike Widenhofer came to Mizzou with college head coaching experience. A disciple of Hall of Fame coach Don James, Stull had pulled off winning seasons at Massachusetts and Texas–El Paso. "UTEP had been the armpit of college football," said Dirk Koetter, Stull's offensive coordinator at UTEP and Missouri and later a head coach in college and the NFL. "Our expectations were we were going to go in there and light [Missouri] up, return it to the Dan Devine days when Missouri was winning eight, nine, ten games every year."

Not quite. Despite a loaded staff that included coaches who would thrive in college and the pros—Koetter, Andy Reid, Marty Mornhinweg, Ken Flajole, and Dave Toub—Stull couldn't deliver a winner at Mizzou, going 15–38–2 in five seasons. The Tigers never won more than four games on his watch and suffered 10 losses by 40 or more points.

Stull, who later returned to UTEP as the school's athletics director, long held that three hurdles stood in the Tigers' way during his tenure: brutal nonconference schedules, shoddy facilities, and lofty admission standards that prohibited Stull from recruiting some players who thrived at rival schools.

Stull's final season, a 3–7–1 campaign in 1993, included a 73–0 loss at Texas A&M and ended with a 28–0 loss at Kansas. It marked 10 straight losing seasons for the program. Stull stepped down after the season and accepted a post in MU's administration. "He had a record for turning programs around," MU chancellor Charles Kiesler said, "but five years is a reasonable time to do it." Like they had been every four years for the past 16, the Tigers would become someone else's problem to solve.

58 Battle Royal at Brewer

Charles Henke didn't go down without a fight. One of the great Mizzou players of the pre–Norm Stewart era—Stewart's playing career predated Henke but not his coaching years—Henke still ranks as one of the program's greatest scorers and rebounders.

A 6'7" forward from Malta Bend, Missouri, a tiny town northwest of Columbia, Henke became Mizzou's all-time scoring leader and averaged a robust 18.1 points per game for his career. Only four MU players have eclipsed Henke's average: Willie Smith, Derrick Chievous, John Brown, and Kareem Rush. Henke closed his career averaging 24.6 points as a senior in 1960–61. Only Smith has posted a better scoring season (25.3 in 1975–76) in all of Mizzou history. Henke's rebounding average (9.8) ranks fifth all-time. Henke played for three losing teams, but his contributions were noted: he earned All–Big 8 honors as a junior and senior and All-America recognition as a senior.

Henke's Tigers never reached the postseason, but his final day in a Mizzou uniform embodied the Border War and introduced the Missouri-Kansas feud to a national audience. The date was March 11, 1961. The place was MU's Brewer Fieldhouse. It was the regular-season finale. The Jayhawks were in town, led by star forward Wayne Hightower. ABC broadcast the game with Jack Buck at the microphone. Early in the second half, with the rivals locked into a tight game, Hightower intercepted a pass from Henke and swooped in for a layup. He missed but corralled the rebound. He missed his next shot too, as Henke fouled him from behind. Uh-oh. Hightower spun around and swung a right hook at Henke's head. The blow missed and Henke returned fire, setting off a melee as players, coaches, and fans turned the Border War into WrestleMania.

"We've got a wild one!" Buck said during the telecast. "Kansas and Missouri! Brother, they are really slugging in there!"

Mizzou football assistant coach Harry Smith sprang to his feet and urged the student pep band to play a song, anything to settle down the crowd. On cue, the band played the Tigers fight song—not exactly a plea for peace. "There's going to be more than one shiner coming out of that crowd," Buck said as the fists kept flying.

Tension between the schools had been broiling since the fall, when Kansas got caught using an ineligible football player against the Tigers. KU suspected Mizzou athletics director Don Faurot blew the whistle. The lingering bad blood spilled onto the court at Brewer. "As America watched on television, what began as a rumble between rival gangs turned into chaos when hundreds of fans cascaded out of the bleachers," wrote Michael Atchison in *True Sons: A Century of Missouri Tigers Basketball.* "Some acted like marauding thugs, others like warriors for peace. Some looked for Jayhawk blood, others fought off the vigilantes."

Eventually, the officials and coaches restored order and the game resumed—without the rivalry's two best players. Henke and Hightower were ejected, ending the career of the Missouri great. Mizzou hung on for the victory, snapping a 10-game losing streak to the Jayhawks.

The two schools discussed ending the series, but cooler heads prevailed and the Border War survived—until conference realignment extinguished the fire a half-century later.

Wilder Runs Wild

By any measure, James Wilder is among the great running backs to carry the ball for Mizzou, but one game stands above the rest from his three-year stint in the backfield. Few players are defined by a singular performance, and it's unfair to Wilder's legacy to limit his career to one game. But few players have played as he did on November 18, 1978, in Lincoln, Nebraska.

The Big 8 cochampion Cornhuskers were bound for the Orange Bowl, but not until serving as prey for the Tigers in the regular-season finale. "Whenever you say 'James Wilder,' some people think that's the only game he ever played," said former Mizzou quarterback Phil Bradley, who handed the ball to Wilder 28 times that night and watched him blister the Huskers for 181 yards. "That's his staple game. That's the game [when] he left his mark on Missouri football."

Wilder, a Sikeston, Missouri, native who came to Mizzou in 1978 by way of Northeastern Oklahoma A&M College, could have broken Mizzou's single-game rushing record that night in Lincoln—at the time, 240 yards, set by Harry Ice in 1941—but four of Wilder's carries ended in the end zone, none more famous than a seven-yard score with 3:42 left, the game-winning TD in Mizzou's 35–31 victory.

Running through the left side of the offensive line, Wilder paused and blasted linebacker Bruce Dunning with his forearm. TV announcers Steve Bassett and Bob Rowe erupted on the call:

> Rowe: "Did you see that? Did you see him? Did you see him take that man and throw him down?"
>
> Bassett: "You will not believe what Wilder did!"
>
> Rowe: "He had a guy wrapped around his waist. He just grabbed hold of him and threw him into the ground like he was a piece of turf!"
>
> Bassett: "Unbelievable! Watch this and watch Wilder closely."
>
> Rowe: "Hey, folks, watch 32. Watch Bradley hand it off to 32. Now watch this. 'Get out of my way!'"

The game was first-year Mizzou coach Warren Powers's first showdown with his mentor Tom Osborne, whom he coached under at Nebraska. "Warren Powers wanted that game so badly," said former offensive lineman Howard Richards, who spent that cold November night clearing holes for Mizzou's 6'3", 225-pound sledgehammer. "He wanted to beat Nebraska so bad."

Thirty-seven years later, Bradley couldn't shake the images from his memory of No. 32 plowing through one Cornhusker after another. "He refused to go down," Bradley said. "I mean, he refused to go down time after time after time. They just could not get him on the ground."

Wilder set Mizzou's career rushing record with 2,357 yards from 1978 to 1980. Wilder's production—he had eight 100-yard games—could have been more prolific in another system, in another era. Powers's favored split-back veer offense was ideal for a dual-threat quarterback such as Bradley and helped develop receivers such as Leo Lewis and Kellen Winslow, but Wilder, a runner, might have been better suited for the power formations of Mizzou's past. "He's a guy I think [Missouri] underutilized," Richards said. "It was more of a balanced offense, but if James had run out of an I-formation, he could have been among the nation's rushing leaders throughout his time there. He was a brute."

Until midway through the 1978 season, Wilder shared most of the workload with other backs. He still managed to set the team rushing record despite getting fewer than 10 carries in 8 of the 36 games during his time on campus. Around the team, Wilder was quiet and kept to himself, teammates recalled. He lived off campus with his wife. "But what a player," Richards said.

In 1981 Tampa Bay made Wilder its second-round draft pick and he rewarded the franchise with 9,508 yards of offense and 47 touchdowns over nine seasons. He still stands as the Buccaneers' career rushing leader. "I've said it before, and I'll say it again: he's the best running back I've ever seen," Hall of Fame linebacker Lawrence Taylor said in 1985, when he was the best defensive player on the planet. "He's worse to run into than Eric Dickerson."

In 1994, four years after Wilder retired from football, he was inducted into Mizzou's Intercollegiate Athletics Hall of Fame. In 2008, 30 years after Wilder's indelible performance at Nebraska, the Tigers did something they hadn't done since his magical night: Mizzou finally won again on the Cornhuskers' home field, snapping a 15-game losing streak in Lincoln.

60 The Junkyard Dog

Years before Mizzou joined the Southeastern Conference, one of the greatest gifts to Tigers basketball came from the SEC. In 2006 the Tigers took in an SEC transfer who would help restore a lifeless program. Born and raised in Birmingham, Alabama, schooled at Vanderbilt in Nashville, DeMarre Carroll came to Missouri to play for Uncle Mike. That would be MU head basketball coach Mike Anderson. Carroll would leave as so much more than the coach's nephew—and years later was still embraced as one of the most beloved players of his generation, despite playing just two seasons in Black and Gold.

How is that possible? Three reasons: One, Carroll's teams won—a lot. His senior year, the Tigers won 31 games, captured the Big 12 tournament, and reached the Elite Eight of the NCAA tournament. Two, his passion, his hustle, and his relentless drive resonated with fans who came to watch him outmuscle opponents and embrace Anderson's ferocious style. Three, he did it all with a smile that lit up Mizzou Arena. "I'm a man on a mission," the 6'8" forward said in 2007 after sitting out the previous season per NCAA transfer rules. "My mission is to be the best basketball player I can be."

But first, an inauspicious start. In July 2007 a melee broke out in downtown Columbia, and while Carroll tried to pull teammates away from a fight, he was shot in the ankle. The Tigers were already suffering an image problem after a string of off-field problems—fans hadn't forgotten the troubling end of the Quin Snyder era, either—but Carroll's incident would soon become a footnote in a brilliant two-year run. As a junior, he helped instill a missing toughness within Anderson's team while adding some scoring punch (13 points per game) in the frontcourt. The Big 12's newcomer of the year led MU in rebounds, steals, and blocks.

Nicknamed the Junkyard Dog, Carroll was even better as a senior and—perhaps more important—taught a promising freshman class a master's course on how to play the game and win over a hungry fan base. Carroll led Mizzou in scoring (16.6) and rebounding (7.2), gave the Tigers tireless defense, and played most possessions like they were game points.

DeMarre Carroll looks past his defender in a 2009 game against Texas Tech.

A first-team All–Big 12 selection, Carroll was also MVP of the Big 12 tournament after leading Mizzou to three wins in three days in Oklahoma City. He had nine 20-point games during the season, including a career-high 31 in a victory at Iowa State. "Once I transferred here, everything started going wrong, and I was just like, 'Man, what did I get myself into?'" Carroll said after beating Baylor in the Big 12 Championship Game. "My uncle told me to keep having faith and the...sun [would] come up at the end."

The sun eventually set on Mizzou's season short of the Final Four, but Carroll ended his short career as a fan favorite. "That's what an Elite Eight and Big 12 championship will do for you, especially at a time when the fan base hadn't seen good basketball in a long time," said teammate Kim English, a freshman guard on the 2009 Elite Eight team. "He was such a worker," English said of Carroll, who averaged 14.9 points and 6.9 rebounds in two seasons at Mizzou. "He outworked people in the low block. He wasn't much of a shooter, but he was a grinder and battled."

The Memphis Grizzlies selected Carroll with the 27th pick in the 2009 NBA Draft, but it took several roster moves for him to find his footing in the NBA. Finally, with Atlanta, his fifth team in five years, Carroll morphed into a valuable and versatile small forward. Shedding 20 pounds from his 225-pound power forward body, Carroll became an elite perimeter defender and one of the league's better three-point shooters. During the 2014–15 NBA season, Carroll produced the third-best win shares metric by a Mizzou player in the NBA. Among former MU players, only Indiana's Steve Stipanovich (1986–87) and Kansas City's Larry Drew (1982–83) had better NBA seasons according to the advanced statistic. Carroll capitalized with a four-year, $60 million free-agent contract with Toronto.

Six years removed from his days at Mizzou, Carroll returned to Columbia in 2015 for his annual youth camp, hosting a gym full of players, some too young to remember his two-year ride with the

Tigers. But their parents remembered. "It just shows that winning changes everything," Carroll said. As promised, Carroll delivered on his mission.

61 High Cotton for Tony Temple

For Tony Temple, it was karma. After nearly setting the Sun Bowl rushing record with 194 yards, Temple trudged to the postgame stage in El Paso, Texas, to receive the game's MVP trophy, voted on by a panel of reporters in the fourth quarter. One problem: the votes were cast while Temple's Missouri Tigers had the lead. Oregon State erased a 14-point deficit in the fourth quarter and won the 2006 bowl game 39–38 on a gutsy walk-off two-point conversion on the final play of regulation. Bowl officials decided to veto the media's MVP selection. Upset enough about his team's collapse, Temple was kindly asked to go back to the locker room. The MVP honors went to someone else: Beavers quarterback Matt Moore. A year later, back in the state of Texas, Temple earned his trophy.

The Tigers were 11–2 after losing the 2007 Big 12 Championship Game but believed they deserved a place at the BCS table, namely an invitation to the Orange Bowl. Instead, the selection committee inexplicably chose 11–1 Kansas—the team Mizzou had just beaten a week earlier in the epic Armageddon at Arrowhead showdown in Kansas City. The Tigers were snubbed and settled for the Cotton Bowl, a matchup in Dallas against Arkansas from the mighty SEC. Mizzou had not only lost the Big 12 Championship Game but blew their chance to play for the national title. The consolation prize was the program's first New Year's Day bowl game since 1970.

Could the Tigers shake off their hangover and salvage a memorable season with one last victory? Could the Razorbacks handle Mizzou's prolific passing game? How would the Tigers slow down the game's best running back, Darren McFadden? These anticipated storylines would become sidebars to the day's headline.

It had been a tumultuous senior year for Temple, who posted three 100-yard rushing games during the regular season but missed two games (and most of a third) with an ankle injury. One of the most ballyhooed recruits to play for Mizzou during the Gary Pinkel years, the Kansas City native was probably playing his final college game in Dallas. Temple played just one game his freshman year in 2004 but suffered a season-ending injury. He petitioned the NCAA for an extra year of eligibility, but the odds were against him returning in 2008.

In Dallas, Temple showed the world how to make an exit. With Arkansas's defense focused on Mizzou's four- and five-receiver passing formations, the Tigers put the ball in Temple's hands…over and over again. He racked up 281 rushing yards—more than any back among the collection of stars to play in the Cotton Bowl had gained. More than Doak Walker, Jim Brown, Earl Campbell, Bo Jackson, Ricky Williams and, yes, even Dicky Maegle. Who's that? In 1954, Rice's Maegle set the Cotton Bowl rushing record with 265 yards on just 11 carries against Alabama. "Honestly, I thought if anyone would have a chance of breaking the record, I would have thought it would have been one of the Arkansas running backs," Maegle said when interviewed after Mizzou pounded the Razorbacks 38–7.

Needing 25 yards to break Maegle's record, Temple saved his most dazzling play for last. With his hamstring starting to tighten, Temple took a handoff, bounced to the right side of his line, spun out of a tackle and outran a pack of Hogs to the end zone for a 40-yard touchdown. Temple's hamstring gave out near the goal line, but quarterback Chase Daniel and offensive lineman Tyler Luellen carried him back to the sideline to begin the celebration.

"Arkansas, they came with a great plan to stop our passing game," Temple said after the game, which indeed proved to be his last with the Tigers. "I'm just doing my job, doing what I'm supposed to do."

Temple's single-game rushing total ranked third in school history and put him over the 1,000-yard mark for the season, making him Mizzou's first running back to rush for 1,000 yards in back-to-back seasons. And, yes, he was named the game's MVP. No veto this time.

62 D-Line Zou

Gary Pinkel's first recruiting mission at Missouri was a total bust. Justin Smith, an All-American defensive end as a junior in 2000, wanted to leave school for the NFL Draft. Pinkel, just hired to replace head coach Larry Smith, said Smith was his first and most important recruit. Justin Smith attended Pinkel's introductory press conference…but was soon off to the NFL, becoming the fourth overall pick in the 2001 draft. He split the next 14 seasons in Cincinnati and San Francisco, producing at a Hall of Fame level during his time with the 49ers.

Smith clearly made the right choice, but Mizzou's defensive line would carry on without him. Over the course of the next 15 years, the Tigers specialized in producing elite players across the defensive front, all under the watch of a college offensive lineman who over time earned nationwide acclaim as one of the game's best defensive line teachers.

Craig Kuligowski had to be talked into playing high school football in Southgate, Michigan—he played tuba in the marching band—and soon developed into a standout lineman on both sides of the ball. He earned a scholarship at Toledo, where he became an All-Conference offensive tackle. Kuligowski had a new head coach his senior year, a guy by the name of Nick Saban. A year later, after Kuligowski graduated, Saban left for the Cleveland Browns and recommended his old college teammate for the Toledo job: Gary Pinkel.

Pinkel inherited Saban's Toledo assistants for his first season but a year later rebuilt the staff with young, hungry coaches. One of them was Kuligowski, who moved up from recruiting coordinator to tight ends coach to the job where he'd find his calling: defensive line coach. Kuligowski kept the same title when he followed Pinkel to Missouri after the 2000 season.

From 2001 to 2015, he produced 22 defensive linemen who earned first- or second-team All-Conference honors, two All-Americans in Shane Ray and Michael Sam, and four first-round NFL Draft picks in Ziggy Hood, Aldon Smith, Sheldon Richardson, and Ray.

Over time, D-Line Zou was born. Part fraternity, part sales pitch, it was all about branding for the D-line factory that Kuligowski, a Detroit native, set up in Columbia, Missouri. "We sell the heck out of it," Kuligowski said after the 2014 season, when Ray became his fifth player since 2005 to leave school early to enter the draft. "We don't encourage these guys to leave early," he said, "but we tell these kids we've got a plan in place for them to graduate, we've got a plan in place to develop them, win games, and make them the best NFL prospects we can."

The factory came under new management after the 2015 season when Pinkel retired and the bulk of his staff scattered, including Kuligowski, who became the D-line coach at Miami. But the program left behind more stars along the front four, led by Charles Harris and Terry Beckner Jr., an East St. Louis product widely rated the nation's top defensive tackle recruit in 2015. Harris enjoyed an All-SEC season in 2016 and, like his predecessors from D-Line Zou, became a first-round draft pick, going to the Miami Dolphins with the No. 22 selection.

63 Retired but Not Forgotten

Six retired numbers of seven Mizzou football greats grace the bricks that surround Faurot Field. A bit much? Compared to other teams around the country, programs that have produced more championship teams and All-American players, well, yes it is. Mizzou got a bit intoxicated with retiring numbers in the 20th century, resulting in a revamped policy in the 2000s that will allow only the elite of the elite players of the future to receive the honor.

Shortly after they completed their playing careers, Missouri retired quarterback Paul Christman's 44, center Darold Jenkins's 42, and halfback Bob Steuber's 37. A half-century passed before the Tigers removed two more numbers from their inventory while honoring three all-time greats. In 1995 the Tigers retired No. 23, worn by running back / defensive back Johnny Roland and defensive back Roger Wehrli, and No. 83, worn by tight end Kellen Winslow. "I'm sure every player who's put on a uniform dreams of one day having his number retired," Winslow told the *Post-Dispatch*. "It's an honor. It's a bit overwhelming. It's taken a while."

That gave the Tigers five retired numbers—more than future SEC contemporaries Auburn (three), Georgia (four), LSU (two), Florida (zero), and Alabama (zero). And Mizzou wasn't done at six. Brock Olivo, who set MU's career rushing record as a senior in 1997, qualified for the honor when he became the first winner of the Mosi Tatupu Award, given to the nation's best special teams player. At the time, MU's retired-number policy stated that a player was automatically eligible if he won one of five national awards. The Mosi Tatupu was not among the five awards, but MU athletics director Joe Castiglione and Coach Larry Smith approved Olivo becoming the seventh player to receive the honor. Castiglione was gone within a year, off to become the AD at Oklahoma, while Smith was fired after the 2000 season.

On September 13, 2003, Olivo had his day as the Tigers permanently retired his No. 27. "My name on that wall is a representative of everyone who came through Missouri at that time," said Olivo, who wrote the foreword for this book. "And for that I'm very proud."

Between Christman and Olivo, Mizzou retired as many numbers (six) as they won conference championships. That led to changes in 2003. Approved by the Intercollegiate Athletics Committee, the school decided an athlete has to meet the following requirements to become a candidate for number retirement:

- Earn a bachelor's degree from MU
- Be of "unquestioned good character, reputation, and integrity"
- Represent the school well by "displaying the highest degree of sportsmanship"
- Participate as a member of an MU sports team more than five years prior to the number retirement

And here's the biggie:
- Achieve one of the following: win the Heisman Trophy in football or be named the National Player of the Year in men's or women's basketball, baseball, soccer, or softball, or in women's volleyball

That narrowed the future field quite a bit, which means a handful of Mizzou greats will never see their numbers hang alongside the others at Faurot, including Justin Smith's 96, Brad Smith's 16, Chase Daniel's 10, and Jeremy Maclin's 9.

Over at Mizzou Arena, six numbers of MU men's basketball greats hang in the rafters: Jon Sundvold's No. 20, Norm Stewart's 22, Willie Smith's No. 30, Doug Smith's 34, Steve Stipanovich's 40, and Bill Stauffer's 43. Mizzou has retired two women's basketball players' numbers: Joni Davis's No. 33 and Renee Kelly's No. 42.

64 West Is Best

The Kansas Jayhawks thought they had a solid game plan going into the second week of the 1998 season. Quarterback Corby Jones was the centerpiece to the Mizzou offense, and if you can stop Jones—as the Jayhawks did a year earlier in Lawrence—you can stop the Tigers. "[Kansas coach] Terry Allen said before the game that he wasn't going to let Corby Jones beat them," Jones recalled. "Well, Corby Jones didn't beat them."

On September 12, Kansas's defense and the college football world became acquainted with Devin West, MU's 6'2", 222-pound senior tailback from Moberly, Missouri. Missouri's logjam of running backs became a committee of one in 1998, and West spent the season shattering records. On a blistering 94-degree day, with Kansas focused on Jones, the fulcrum to Mizzou's option attack, West slashed the Jayhawks with quick-hitting runs up the middle or snagged the option pitch and found alleys on the outside. By game's end, West had plucked the Jayhawks for a single-game

Mizzou record of 319 yards on 33 carries. The Mizzou rushing record had stood since the days of Don Faurot's split T offense, when Harry Ice ran for 240 yards against Kansas in 1941. West's total was the third-highest in Big 12 history to date. "When we ran the option, Kansas made sure they had two people accounted for me, and when I pitched that thing out there, it was just open field," Jones said. "That—coupled with the way our offensive line was playing—made for a dangerous combination."

"I'm not taking anything away from Devin's effort today," Allen said after the game, "but we kind of allowed the middle to be exploited." Sure, but it took an elite back to punish the Jayhawks' strategy time after time.

As humble away from the game as he was dominant on the field, West rarely basked in the spotlight—not that day or any other during his record-breaking senior year. "When it comes down to it, when you know the game's on the line, there's just something inside of you that won't let you down," West said after the 319-yard performance. "No matter what happened, no matter how many yards I had or how tired I was, I was still going. I wasn't going to quit."

"I've coached for a lot of years and had a lot of great backs," Missouri coach Larry Smith said after the game, which fell on his 59th birthday, "but I swear I've never had one that gave that kind of effort. That was something special."

West had been a productive reserve his first three years at Mizzou, backing up Brock Olivo, who finished his career in 1997 as the school's career rushing leader. By West's senior year, the timeshare was over. While Jones hobbled around with a sprained toe, West became the Tigers' most prolific offensive player, finishing with eight 100-yard rushing games, including a 252-yard explosion against Iowa State later in the season.

"While Devin was very, very fast, he was smarter than he was fast," Jones said. "He understood where everything was going to open. He'd see the defensive front and know which way people were going to go. Lateral quickness was never Devin's strength, ever. It was our running joke. But to watch him read a block before the block happened and get through a hole and get through it quickly was something special."

By season's end, West owned the two biggest rushing performances in team history. He finished fifth among Division I rushers with 1,578 yards, another school record. But that would be it for West's football career. He suffered a stress fracture in his foot preparing for the Senior Bowl and went undrafted. Just a one-year starter at Mizzou, West finished his career as the school's No. 2 all-time rusher. Fittingly, the only player ahead of him on the list? Olivo.

65 "The Cats from Ol' Mizzou"

Yeah, those eight Big 8 championships were nice, but one of Norm Stewart's biggest hits happened nowhere near a basketball court. Looking for something original to spice up his TV show, Stewart and his team entered a Kansas City recording studio in late 1986 and made hip-hop history.

OK, maybe not exactly, but after Stewart, Derrick Chievous, Lynn Hardy, and the rest of the roster cut "The Cats from Ol' Mizzou," you could never accuse Stewart of being old-fashioned. The coach, 51 at the time, slipped on headphones and added his own verse to the 3:44 song—and showed considerably more chops in the studio than some of his players.

The Tigers recorded the song just after Christmas while in Kansas City for the BMA Holiday Classic and later shot dancing scenes at an aerobics studio in Columbia. The rap video made its national debut during halftime of the February 7, 1987, broadcast of Mizzou's game at Oklahoma.

The lyrics remain etched in the memory of Mizzou's most loyal fans. Eat your heart out, Kanye:

"The Cats from Ol' Mizzou"
Chorus: We are the Tigers, steeped in tradition. A Big 8 title is this year's mission. Young and hungry, we'll not fail. So we'll keep on rapping our Tiger tales.

(Funky beat. Funky beat. Funky beat.)

Hardy: My name is Lynn, I play to win. I run the court from end to end.

Side to side or in transition, we run right through our opposition.

One of the guys from the Motor City Crew, one of the Cats from Ol' Mizzou.

Nathan Buntin: The Breeze is in from the Motown City. When you see me slam my opponents show pity. I might be a freshman but watch out for 8. When you're reading Tiger tales you'll be playing Big Nate. We're really young but watch what we can do. An aggressive bunch, the Cats from Ol' Mizzou.

Chievous: My name's D.C. from the streets of Queens. I came to Mizzou on a precious dream. Striving and teasing as you can see, I'm real nice and one to please. I don't shoot, I don't score. I'm in the game making the crowd roar. You listen to me and here I go. My name's D.C., and I don't move slow. Just give me the ball and see what I can do. I'm just one of the Cats from Ol' Mizzou.

Mike Sandbothe: I'm Sandman Mike from Washington, Mo. My shooting and passing can make the team go. My defense is mean and I can stop you cold. My

Tiger tales are Black and Gold. Small-time boys, we can rap, too. Just another Cat from Ol' Mizzou.

Devon Rolf: They call me Devo. I'm down to brawl. My three-point jumper is really tall. I like to get down and play the D, take it to the hoop and get nasty. I work really hard the whole year through. I'm just another Cat from Ol' Mizzou.

[Chorus]

Michael Ingram: I'm Michael Ingram, master of the dunk. Throw it in the paint and opponents will get punked. I went to juco quicker than most so I can tell my Tiger tales coast to coast. I'm from the Windy City, just blowing through and through, just another Cat from Ol' Mizzou.

Lee Coward: I'm Cadillac Coward but the name is Lee. Coming in fresh I will take no mess. Just watch my shot, it's very hot. Just another Cat from Ol' Mizzou

Greg Church: I'm Greg Church from the Show-Me State. From inside or out the basket's my fate. Whether I sub or even start I come in the game and play real hard. Boy from Palmyra, telling Tiger tales, a hardworking Cat from Ol' Mizzou.

Gary Leonard. I'm Gary Leonard and anything but little. I'm Mizzou's hope for a big man in the middle. Whether slamming it home or playing in a crowd, I tell my Tiger tales loud and proud. I protect the hoop from the likes of you, just one of the Cats from Ol' Mizzou.

Norm Stewart: I'm Stormin' Norm. I don't speak jive. After coaching 20 years I'm glad I'm alive. I'm old and bald and down in the back. You would be too if you coached this pack. They work hard, you know it's true. I'm proud to be a Cat from Ol' Mizzou.

66 Sparky

Wilbur "Sparky" Stalcup didn't build Missouri basketball into a powerhouse, but he proved the Tigers could win at the conference level, and perhaps his greatest contribution was a player he recruited, coached, hired, and mentored: Norman Eugene Stewart.

But long before Stalcup and Stewart crossed paths, Sparky sprung like a sapling from one of college basketball's most fertile coaching trees. Hailing from Oregon, Missouri, Stalcup attended Maryville State Teachers College—later renamed Northwest Missouri State—where he played for one of the game's coaching titans, Henry Iba. Stalcup would replace Iba as the head coach in Maryville and win three conference titles in 10 years at the helm.

After serving in the navy, Stalcup resumed his coaching career at Missouri, where he replaced George Edwards, who in 1946 retired as the Tigers' all-time wins leader. Stalcup brought a different personality to the job, to say the least. "As a coach, he was a firebrand and hell-raiser, a rough-and-tumble son of a gun who relished trading barbs with officials, opposing coaches and unaccommodating fans," wrote Michael Atchison in *True Sons: A Century of Missouri Tigers Basketball.* "One friend in the press wrote that Stalcup 'hated losing worse than poison' and that he 'wouldn't let his mother drive the lane.' When he paced the sidelines, Sparky possessed a mean streak a mile wide and he expected his players to carry the same attitude onto the court. To play for Stalcup was to play for keeps."

The Tigers never won a conference title in Stalcup's 16 years on the sideline—the Big 6 expanded to the Big 7 and into the Big 8 during his tenure—but finished second six times and produced nine winning records the first 10 seasons. Some of the program's most prolific players starred on Stalcup's watch, including Thornton Jenkins, Dan Pippin, Bill Stauffer, Charles Henke, and, of course, Stewart, the pride of Shelbyville, Missouri. Stewart attended Mizzou on advice from Indiana coach Branch McCracken, who wasn't sure Stewart could last with the Hoosiers. Indiana's loss was Stalcup's gain as Stewart became an All-Conference player and two-time captain, and left as the program's career scoring leader. He'd later join the coaching staff, learning the game alongside the fiery Stalcup. "Stalcup influenced me defensively because he was an Iba man," Stewart said. "He had a good philosophy of offense but really had the techniques of defense. Spark's influence was he guided me as a player and as a coach and introduced me to everybody in the coaching world. If he was going somewhere, I was going with him."

Stalcup's teams were less competitive in the conference after Stewart's playing days, but in 1956 Stalcup made a landmark decision for the program and the university: Al Abrams, a 6'5" player from St. Louis, became MU's first African-American scholarship athlete and one of the program's best players. Abrams's arrival marked a milestone in Stalcup's career arc, though the Tigers continued to fade in the league standings. Stalcup retired from coaching after the 1961–62 season, leaving the court with more wins (195) than any previous coach. Only one man would eclipse him on that list: his protégé, Stewart.

Stalcup would go on to work in the athletics department, including two years as AD, and continued to work as the radio analyst for Mizzou football games. He died in 1972, too soon to see the unprecedented heights the program would reach under his apprentice.

67 To the Victor Go the Spoils

Not everyone in Williams-Brice Stadium might have realized there was such a thing as the Mayor's Cup on September 27, 2014, but that didn't keep Missouri teammates Maty Mauk and Evan Boehm from merrily parading into the visitor's locker room carrying the silver trophy.

Wait, Missouri and South Carolina play for a rivalry trophy? They sure do. Whether the game's in Columbia, Missouri, or Columbia, South Carolina, the SEC East foes claim the cup after a victory, just as the Gamecocks did after an overtime win on the Tigers' home field in 2013. As they continued to transition into the SEC, the Tigers had infinitely more rivalry trophy games (two) than they did genuine rivals (zero). Meeting for the first time as SEC opponents in 2014, Missouri and Arkansas played in the inaugural Battle Line Rivalry, complete with a corporate sponsor and shiny new trophy—even though the teams hadn't met in the regular season since 1963.

Perhaps the new rivalries will catch on with time and develop the kind of mutual vitriol that defines the SEC's best grudges. Until then, Mizzou fans only have memories of true rivalries that were forsaken with the 2011 decision to leave the Big 12 for the SEC. With the move, the Tigers bid farewell to three rivalry trophy games. Another was lost when Nebraska bolted from the Big 12 for the Big Ten. The Tigers and Cornhuskers played annually for the Missouri-Nebraska Bell, a bell that was stolen from a church in Seward, Nebraska, by fraternity members from the Lincoln campus. In 1927 the bell was awarded to the winner of the MU-NU football game, with an *M* engraved on one side and an *N* on the other. Mizzou won the first trophy game 7–6, but the Huskers mostly dominated the all-time series, which stood at 65–36–3 when Nebraska left for the Big Ten. Nebraska won 24 straight in the series from 1979 to 2002. Mizzou's longest winning streak in the series was six, from 1957 to 1962.

In 1929 Missouri and Oklahoma began a tradition as student organizations from both schools smoked a ceremonial peace pipe during halftime of their matchups. The winner took home the Tomahawk-shaped pipe, which allegedly belonged to Chief White Eagle of the Pawnee tribe. The pipe later went missing, and the halftime tradition with it. The peace, though, did not extend to

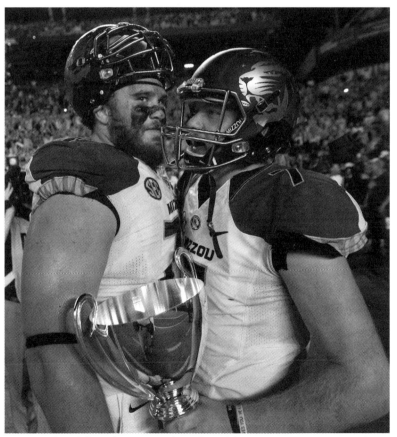

Evan Boehm (left) and Maty Mauk (right) celebrate a victory against South Carolina in 2014.

the field. The Sooners dominated the series, set at 67–24–5 when Mizzou joined the SEC. OU won 14 in a row from 1946 to 1959, while the Tigers never won more than two consecutive games in the series.

They had more success securing the Telephone Trophy, given to the winner of the Missouri–Iowa State game every year starting in 1959. That year, as the coaches took their spots in the Ames, Iowa, press box before the game, the phone wires somehow got crossed and the coaches could hear their counterparts from the other team chattering on their headsets. Northwestern Bell of Ames donated the trophy, made of—what else?—a telephone, painted in both teams' colors. Mizzou owned a 61–34–9 record in the series before conference realignment.

Missouri's most historic and embraced rivalry of its pre-SEC days adopted a game-day trophy in 1937, when the Tigers and Kansas Jayhawks began exchanging a tom-tom drum used by the Osage Indian tribe, a version of which now rests in the College Football Hall of Fame in Atlanta. The drum was replaced by later versions, taking the form of a bass drum with both teams' logos in the 1990s. The series stands at 57–54–9 in MU's favor, though that record reflects KU's forfeited victory in 1960 as a Mizzou win.

68 The Voice

The Mizzou radio booth has been home to some of the most well-known voices in American sports: Harry Caray, Jack Buck, Bob Costas, Joe Buck, Dan Dierdorf, Kevin Harlan, Jon Sundvold. But only one man takes it to the house. That would be Mike Kelly, the Voice of the Tigers in basketball since 1991 and football since

1994, a man who is unmistakable in person because of his shiny bald head you can spot from the upper deck at Mizzou Arena, and on the air because of his straight-shooting delivery of the action before his eyes. And when a Mizzou player heads for the end zone, you can count on his trademark catch phrase: "He takes it to the house!"

"I was at a football practice in 1996 and watching the defensive backs do their one-on-one drills," Kelly said. "I heard a couple of them say, 'Grab that baby and take it to the house!' I was just like, *Hmmm, I kind of like that.* So I started using it…. That's sort of become synonymous with me. Sometimes I look for other ways to describe [a touchdown], but I think I've used it longer than anyone else."

When the 2017 seasons began, Kelly had called more Tigers games than anyone since the days of Mahlon Aldridge, the primary radio voice for the Missouri Sports Network from 1947 to 1973. Aldridge, based out of Columbia's KFRU, teamed up with former Mizzou basketball coach Wilbur "Sparky" Stalcup through 1966, until legendary football coach Don Faurot took over as color analyst from 1967 to 1972. At that time, the Missouri Sports Network didn't hold exclusive rights to Mizzou games, so other stations around the state carried games too. During the same eras, Caray called the games for KMOX in St. Louis in the 1950s and '60s, followed by Jack Buck for a few years in the '70s. KMOX took over as the flagship station for the MSN in 1973 and replaced Aldridge with veteran sportscaster Bob Starr. Dan Kelly, better known for calling hockey games, later followed, along with Bill Wilkerson, whose time at the Mizzou microphone spanned three decades, from the late 1970s to the early 1990s.

Starr doubled as MU's basketball play-by-play voice, a job that bounced around among Costas and John Rooney during the 1970s and '80s. A mainstay behind the mic was Columbia's Rod Kelly, a versatile analyst who also broadcast Mizzou baseball and women's basketball games during his long career.

In 1988 KMOX hired a young local broadcaster who had paid his dues across the Mississippi River, calling games for the University of Illinois—mostly women's volleyball and women's basketball. Mike Kelly from Dupo, Illinois, joined the Midwest's premier news talk radio station, the place where young broadcasters from the region and beyond dreamed of hearing their voices broadcast across the airwaves. In 1989 KMOX general manager Robert Hyland made Kelly an offer. "He said, 'You're off on Monday and Tuesday,'" Kelly recalled. "You want to make a little extra money? Go to Columbia and do this show. It's called *Tiger Talk*.' That's how the relationship with Mizzou began."

Kelly took the job as the host of basketball coach Norm Stewart's weekly radio show. By the next season, Kelly filled in for a few basketball broadcasts alongside play-by-play announcer Tom Dore, a former MU player. The next season, Kelly took over as the play-by-play voice, with 22-year-old Joe Buck as his analyst. "Anybody who gets into sports broadcasting wants to do play-by-play," Kelly said. "So for that opportunity to present itself at 28 years old in a Division I program in the Big 8 Conference, working for a guy like Norm Stewart, it was a dream come true."

The sidekick job became a revolving door of former Mizzou players, from Sundvold to Jim Kennedy to Gary Link. No matter who sat nearby in the analyst chair, Kelly clearly defined the roles. "I've always tried to focus on calling the play and getting out of the way," Kelly said. "I've always thought the play-by-play guy was the headwaiter. Call the play and get out of the way and let the color analyst do his job. With analysts I've worked with, I've always told them the same thing: 'I'll do the who, the what, the when, the where. You tell me why. Why did it work? Why didn't it work?'"

"True professional," Link said of his longtime radio partner. "The guy is rock-solid. He prepares. His timing is terrific. He paints

Mizzou Radio Teams

Football
Mahlon Aldridge and Sparky Stalcup, 1947–66
Mahlon Aldridge and Don Faurot, 1967–72
Bob Starr and Dan Kelly, 1973–75
Dan Kelly and Bill Wilkerson, 1976–81
Bill Wilkerson and Pete Woods, 1982
Bill Wilkerson and John Rooney, 1983
John Rooney and Dan Dierdorf, 1984
Bill Wilkerson and Kevin Calabro, 1985
Bill Wilkerson and guest analysts, 1986
Bill Wilkerson and Kevin Harlan, 1987–88
Bill Wilkerson and Tom Dore, 1989–90
Bill Wilkerson and Kellen Winslow, 1991–93
Mike Kelly and Kellen Winslow, 1994
Mike Kelly and John Kadlec, 1995–96
Mike Kelly, John Kadlec, and Vic Faust, 1997–98
Mike Kelly and John Kadlec, 1999–2010
Mike Kelly and Howard Richards, 2011–present

Basketball
Bob Starr, 1973–74
Bob Starr and Rod Kelly, 1975
Bob Costas and Rod Kelly, 1976
John Rooney and Rod Kelly, 1977
Bob Costas and John Rooney, 1978
Bob Costas and Rod Kelly, 1979–80
John Rooney and Rod Kelly, 1981–84
Kevin Calabro and Rod Kelly, 1985
Kevin Harlan and Rod Kelly, 1986–89
Tom Dore and Rod Kelly, 1990
Mike Kelly and Joe Buck, 1991
Mike Kelly and Jon Sundvold, 1992–93
Mike Kelly and Jim Kennedy, 1994
Mike Kelly and Gary Link, 1995–2016
Mike Kelly and Chris Gervino, 2017–present

a picture. Some games I'll shut my eyes and just listen. The trick to radio is we have to give people what's going on without them seeing it. On TV, you don't have to talk. You really have to stay in the game, but we stay in the moment. And Mike is as good as there is."

In 1994 Kelly was entrenched as Mizzou's basketball voice when another opportunity unfolded. Wilkerson left the Mizzou booth to become the voice of the NFL's Arizona Cardinals. Athletics director Joe Castiglione and Roger Gardner of Learfield Communications called Kelly in St. Louis. "They said, 'Hey, we've decided to name you the voice of the Tigers for football,'" Kelly said. "That was a really interesting moment in my life. I [had] just lost my dad in '93. He was always proud of what I'd done in my career and was a lifetime KMOX listener. It was really a cool moment for all of us."

After calling games for a year with former Mizzou and NFL tight end Kellen Winslow, Kelly was paired with John Kadlec, a former MU player and longtime coach. Kadlec thought his new role would be for one game in 1995. "Sixteen years later…" Kelly said. Kelly and Kadlec became the sound of Mizzou football for a generation of radio listeners, chronicling the brief rise of the program under Larry Smith and the sustained ascent under Gary Pinkel.

Not long after Kadlec stepped away from the job in 2011—his replacement was former Mizzou offensive lineman Howard Richards—Mizzou began maneuvering out of the Big 12 and into the SEC, another sea change Kelly was there to observe. When the 2017–18 basketball season tipped off, Kelly had called games for four Mizzou head football coaches and six basketball coaches—in two arenas and three different conferences. Since 1996 143 different Mizzou players have taken it to the house under Kelly's watch and call.

"For a kid who grew up in Dupo, Illinois, from a family that could never really afford to go to a Big Red game or afford to go to many Cardinal baseball games, to be blessed to do what I've done for 25 years doing basketball and 27 years doing the coaches show, I could have never imagined it," Kelly said in 2016. "When you get into radio, you don't know what the future holds. You don't know how good or bad you are. Others judge. There are tangible measures that tell a businessman or salesman if he's successful or not. We don't have that luxury. It's someone's ear."

69 Mighty Joe Moore

One of the greatest running backs in Mizzou history had no intention of playing the position in college. Joe Moore came to MU from Beaumont High School in St. Louis hoping to play offensive guard or linebacker. He'd either block for Dan Devine's running backs or chase after them. Four years later he left Columbia as the school's most prolific runner. Devine's staff eventually convinced the six-foot, 200-pound Moore to play in the backfield, and he soon became the cornerstone to a record-breaking offense.

Moore set MU's single-season rushing record in 1969, leading the Big 8 champions with 1,312 yards, good for third place nationally and second in the Big 8, behind only Heisman Trophy winner Steve Owens of Oklahoma. Moore trampled over defenders with his punishing style. "Joe was 250 pounds of rocks stuck in a 200-pound sack," former teammate John "Nip" Weisenfels said. "We used to not like to play Nebraska because typically up there it was cold, and on top of that every one of their backs was six foot, 230 pounds, and hit like a ton of bricks. Joe hit like that except he was faster. He could take off and be gone in no time." Just ask Michigan. Moore had the quintessential play in MU's signature nonconference victory in 1969, a 62-yard touchdown on a draw play in the second half in Ann Arbor.

In 1970 Moore was on track for more records and perhaps national accolades. He ran for 604 yards and six touchdowns through the first four games. Of all placcs, though, Moore's college career ended for good in Nebraska, home of the game's hardest-hitting backs. Dave Waline, an All-American defensive tackle for the Cornhuskers, separated Moore's shoulder early in the game. He was already MU's career rushing leader, but he'd never play for the Tigers again. "I'm convinced he had a shot at the Heisman Trophy, and maybe [he'd have] been the front-runner, had he not gotten hurt," Weisenfels said.

"I thought my career was over," Moore told the *Post-Dispatch* years later. Not quite. The Chicago Bears chose Moore 11th overall in the 1971 draft, hoping they had selected the next Gale Sayers. Not exactly. Injuries limited Moore to just 281 yards in 23 games over two seasons. He was out of the league by 1973 and later played a few seasons in Canada. In 1980 James Wilder eclipsed Moore's Mizzou career rushing record, but Moore's 1969 single-season rushing record lasted until Devin West broke it in 1998.

Injury stole countless yards from Moore in college and the pros, but he left his mark on Mizzou. "I felt I represented everybody in the state of Missouri," Moore told the *Post-Dispatch*. "I really did take it personally that when people spent their money for that ticket, they would be satisfied that Joe Moore had earned that scholarship."

70 Truman the Tiger

In the 1860s there was no man more feared in Boone County, Missouri, than William "Bloody Bill" Anderson, the Confederate guerilla, the marauder, the butcher, the bushwhacker. Anderson didn't serve in the Confederate Army but earned his reputation terrorizing Federal soldiers and Union citizens throughout the Missouri countryside. He rode with famed outlaw William Quantrill on their savage attack on Lawrence, Kansas.

In 1864 roughly 120 citizens of Columbia banded together to protect the town from Anderson and his riders, who were under the command of Confederate general Sterling Price and rumored to be on their way to Columbia. Captained by Major James Sidney Rollins, a congressman later decreed as the "Pater Universitatis Missouriensis," or "Father of the University of Missouri," the citizens called themselves the Missouri Tigers. They built a blockhouse at Broadway and Eighth Street to protect the courthouse. Anderson never arrived. The town was saved.

Around the turn of the century, when Missouri launched its varsity football team, the school chose to honor the brave citizens who had assembled to protect the town. From the 1917 spring edition of the *Missouri Alumnus*: "At a mass meeting at which the organization was perfected and the team cheered on to its first game, an old graduate, remembering the fighting Tigers who defended the University in times less bright, suggested the name of Tigers for those who were to defend their school in the realm of athletics. The sobriquet was unanimously selected and has sunk deep into hearts of all Missouri's supporters, though now but few recall its origin."

Truman leads the charge at the 2014 Cotton Bowl.

In the 1940s students began dressing as a Tiger mascot during games, with the original editions made of yellow cloth with painted stripes and a papier-mâché head. Before long the school had both a female version, Lil Tiger—who wore an apron—and Big Tiger, her male counterpart. The two mascots were consolidated into one version in 1981, followed by a naming contest sponsored by the cheerleading team. Students voted for Truman, in homage to the 33rd U.S. President and Missouri native Harry Truman. Truman the Tiger made his debut at Mizzou's 1986 season opener against Utah State, a 24–10 victory.

Truman, played by six different students whose identities are kept private by the athletics department, was named the nation's best mascot in 2004 and 2014. The 2014 title came three years after one of Truman's lowest moments as Mizzou's mascot: at the 2011 Independence Bowl in Shreveport, Louisiana, Truman bobbled and dropped the game's crystal trophy, shattering the decorative bowl in countless pieces near the field just before kickoff. (Truman had no comment on the busted bowl.) After beating North Carolina that day, the Tigers later accepted a duplicate version, free of paw prints.

The 2016 season kicked off with a 30th birthday party for Truman as the mascot popped out of his own birthday cake at the team's season opener against Eastern Michigan.

71 Catch Some Rising Stars

Quarterback Chase Daniel used to say the Mizzou offense would go days without letting the ball touch the ground in practice. Hyperbole much, Chase? Was this just a Texas-sized myth from the Texas gunslinger? Was it possible Daniel's corps of pass catchers was that special? "That's really how it was," former All-American tight end Chase Coffman later said. "Just name off the guys we had." OK, we will.

As brilliantly as Daniel piloted the Missouri offense from 2006 to 2008, his college career coincided with the arrival of MU's greatest and deepest collection of talent at receiver and tight end. Seven players whose careers overlapped from 2004 to 2009 left MU ranked among the program's top nine for career receptions. Mizzou's no-huddle, pass-heavy philosophy helped produce those statistics, and Daniel's accurate right arm factored into the record-setting performances. But every great quarterback has great targets. Daniel had many.

First, the tight ends, who weren't prototypical tight ends. Martin Rucker and Coffman rarely put their hand on the ground in a three-point stance. Instead, they were tall slot receivers in MU's four- and five-wide formations. They blocked on the perimeter but rarely grappled with a defensive lineman along the line of scrimmage. But, man, could they catch. Rucker, an All-American in 2007, finished his career as the school's career receptions leader with 203. A year later, Coffman eclipsed him, finishing with 247 catches. Coffman, son of former NFL tight end Paul Coffman, spurned his father's alma mater (Kansas State) to play for the Tigers, and like Rucker, he earned All-America honors as a senior, plus the John Mackey Award as the nation's best tight end. While Rucker preferred to drag tacklers for extra yards, Coffman perfected the open-field hurdle, leaving many Big 12 defenders lunging for air with a clear view of his No. 45.

At wide receiver, Jeremy Maclin's career required a year on the sideline—he shredded his ACL during a preseason workout in 2006—but he erupted in 2007, his first of two consecutive All-American seasons as a receiver and return specialist. The St. Louis native played just two years in Columbia but produced more all-purpose yards (5,609) than any player in Mizzou history. An electric runner and receiver out of the slot, Maclin set MU records for receptions (102) and receiving yards (1,260) in 2008.

A year later, with Maclin off to the Philadelphia Eagles, Danario Alexander recovered from a season-ending knee injury and blew past Maclin's records, catching 113 balls for 1,781 yards and 14 touchdowns—all MU single-season records. His knees would eventually betray him in the NFL, but when healthy, the 6'5" Alexander was Mizzou's most lethal combination of size, speed, and explosiveness.

It wasn't just the superstars moving the chains. Will Franklin, Tommy Saunders, and Jared Perry, all outside receivers in MU's system, were reliable sidekicks, and each finished in MU's top nine for career catches.

Franklin, Rucker, Maclin, and Coffman were all drafted by NFL teams, while Alexander lasted a few years in the league as an undrafted free agent. Did the cast of playmakers appreciate their brilliance at the time? "I think I didn't really see it until after I was gone," Coffman said. "When we were here, we just kind of expected it. We expected, 'Hey, he's going to make this play, he's going to make that play.' We had five guys on the field who Chase could go to anytime he wanted that could make plays."

It wasn't just talent and depth that made the group unique. Egos and agendas didn't obstruct their path to the end zone. Receivers coach Andy Hill made sure of that. So did Mizzou's spread-the-wealth system. Daniel's favorite receiver was the open receiver. "That was extremely special because you see guys, not just today but in the past, and [egos] can kind of tear up a team," Coffman said. "The 'one bad apple' kind of thing."

"It was pretty cool, man," Maclin said. "Everybody wanted everybody to be successful. Obviously I was a younger guy. For Will and Tommy to accept me and bring me in there and not have any egos, not have any hard feelings toward the type of season I was having, was awesome.... It was really a pretty unique team."

72 Brewer Fieldhouse

From 1930 to 1972 Missouri basketball called Brewer Fieldhouse home. Or was it Brewer Field House? Documents and media reports over the last 80 years can't seem to agree, but the building's place in Mizzou history is undisputed.

Originally designed in 1929 as an extension of Rothwell Gymnasium on the south end of Mizzou's campus, the new building was named after former football coach and athletics director Chester Brewer, the man who conceived the tradition of homecoming and oversaw the field house's construction.

Rothwell was completed in 1905 for $69,000 and was home to the school's first varsity basketball team in 1906–07. Connected to Rothwell by a hallway, Brewer opened in 1930, a $300,000 building with a distinctive dirt floor, covered by an elevated hard surface for basketball games. Brewer, which also housed an indoor track, would eventually seat up to 6,000 fans.

Opening night came on January 13 against visiting Kansas State, a victory overshadowed by a near crisis when a set of bleachers collapsed and left 300 fans sprawled on the ground. Luckily, only a few minor injuries were reported. Otherwise, the new arena drew strong reviews. "The opening games of basketball have been a delight, with the splendid floor and beautiful lighting effect of the building, and what is more satisfactory, the ample seating capacity to take care not only of all the students but all of the public and friends who wish to see the team in action," Brewer wrote in the *Missouri Alumnus* in 1930. "The indoor track is one of the best in the country and without a doubt will give track athletics a stimulus that will soon be felt. In addition to these two sports, there is ample room for all of the athletic and recreative [sic] activities of the University. After the few weeks the building has been in use it is apparent that it will be the most used, best known and most conspicuous building on the campus."

Mizzou formally named the field house in Brewer's honor on February 21, 1930, as the Tigers welcomed the rival Jayhawks from Kansas, "which must necessarily gladden the hearts of all whom, under the beneficent reign of Missouri have learned to regard with antipathy the roar of 'Rock Chalk, Jay Hawk,' etc., which intermittently sweeps across the barren plains of Kansas," the *Columbia Daily Tribune*'s J.P. Hamel wrote in the *Missouri Alumnus* that year. "Once in the lead the Tigers took the ball down to their own barnyard and played catch until the Kansans decided something had to be done. When they went out to break up the Missouri tactics they disrupted their own defense and rapier-like Tiger thrusts under the basket ran up the Tiger score. At first the Kansans were dismayed. Then they were frantic. But always they were futile. Missouri won, 29 to 18."

The Tigers would play in Brewer for 43 seasons. Among the visitors were Kansas legends Wilt Chamberlain, Clyde Lovellette and Jo Jo White, Saint Louis U's Ed Macauley and Indiana's Walt Bellamy.

As Mizzou athletics grew, Brewer got too crowded. The track team competed there. Wrestling too. When bad weather hit town, the football team practiced inside Brewer. The baseball team had a batting cage in the fossil of a facility. In the late 1960s the school finally got its wish for a new arena, the cavernous Hearnes Multipurpose Building, finished in 1972 and named after Governor Warren Hearnes, who helped convince state lawmakers the flagship school needed a bigger, more modern home for hoops. Still, Brewer "retained a certain dog-eared charm," Michael Atchison wrote in *True Sons: A Century of Missouri Tigers Basketball*. "The austere, almost industrial, environment proved inhospitable to visiting teams. Players crossed a grimy track between the locker room and court, and navigated fences that surrounded the floor. And the crowds, when packed in tight, could be imposing."

The final men's basketball game at Brewer tipped off on March 11, 1972, against Oklahoma. Fittingly, the Tigers marked the end of an era with the start of another: Norm Stewart's team clinched an NIT invitation with a victory over the Sooners, the Tigers' first postseason berth since 1944. They would become a postseason fixture under Stewart for the next three decades.

Over time, Brewer got multiple facelifts and by the 21st century became part of the Student Rec Center, which later evolved into the 300,000-square-foot MU Student Recreation Complex, complete with the sparkling Mizzou Aquatic Center, spacious weight rooms, climbing wall, martial arts studio, and more.

Through all the changes, Brewer's place in the program's history is never lost on Mizzou's most faithful. "A stimulating, partisan crowd—cheering its Tiger heroes, breathing defiance to the visitors—had to be part of that 'home-court advantage,' often said to be worth five to seven points," longtime sports information director Bill Callahan wrote in the *Missouri Alumnus* in 1971. "For backup support, there was Mizzou's band—brassily blaring 'Dixie' in the earlier, less-sensitive days, and 'Fight Tiger' later on—to quicken the pulse-beat. How many thousands of shouts, cheers, and tears have been expended there? How many thousands of echoes—of applause, of boos, of bouncing basket balls, of running feet, of timers' guns, of whistles, of the crack of the bat—how many thousand have evaporated into the rafters of Brewer?"

73 Motown Tigers

The most important assistant coach in Mizzou basketball history spent 17 seasons alongside Norm Stewart on the sideline, but Rich Daly's best work came on the recruiting trail, mostly far away from Missouri—in Michigan.

There were six reasons to explain Daly's nickname, Dr. Detroit. They arrived at Mizzou between 1984 and 1989. In chronological order: Lynn Hardy, Nathan Buntin, Lee Coward, Doug Smith, John McIntyre, and Jeff Warren. Smith was the biggest star of the bunch, but together the "Detroit Tigers" helped form the core of teams that won two Big 8 regular-season championships, two Big 8 tournaments, and made five NCAA tournament appearances. The 1989–90 team that reached No. 1 in the national polls had four starters from the Motor City: Smith from Mackenize High School; Buntin and Coward from Murray-Wright High; and McIntyre from Catholic Central, plus a year at the University of Detroit.

A native of Moberly, Missouri, Daly coached at the high school level then moved to Moberly Area Community College, where he worked under future NBA coach Cotton Fitzsimmons. Daly later served as head coach at Pensacola Junior College in Florida, where he won 80 percent of his games over six seasons, then five years as an assistant at Tennessee-Chattanooga. In 1983 Daly joined Stewart's staff at Mizzou, replacing longtime aide Gene Jones. Daly's specialty soon became apparent. "He knows more about where players are than anybody I know," former Stewart assistant Gary Filbert once told the *Post-Dispatch*. "He knows how to recruit players. It doesn't matter where the players are…. He has a good feel for what makes a player choose a particular school—the coach, the family, a girlfriend, whatever. If you say no, he'll try to find a way to make you say yes."

It didn't take long for Daly to work his magic for a program that needed to reload its talent base after winning four straight Big 8 championships behind the tandem of Jon Sundvold and Steve Stipanovich. Detroit became Daly's favorite marketplace as he fostered relationships with the area's most influential coaches.

Stewart liked mining Detroit players because, one, they were plentiful, and, two, they brought an edge to the program, especially those who weren't heavily pursued by the top teams in the state. In Detroit, within the shadow of Big Ten powers Michigan and Michigan State, Daly built a pipeline, starting with Hardy, the playmaking point guard, then inside-and-out combo Buntin and Coward. Smith, the 6'10" scoring machine, would come next, along with McIntyre, the three-point specialist. Warren, a valuable 6'8" forward, arrived in 1989, along with Daniel Lyton, another inside player, though he'd leave the program before playing a game.

With Daly's friendships in Detroit came enemies—namely, the other college coaches trying to recruit the Motor City. Some were outspoken, criticizing Daly and his tactics far more harshly than coaches would dare in modern times. "We've heard [Mizzou] has a lot of help in the Detroit area," Michigan State coach Jud Heathcote told the *Post-Dispatch* in 1988. "What that means, I don't know. Boosters, friends of the programs, they aren't supposed to be involved in the recruiting process."

"I don't doubt that Jud tried to do whatever he could to keep us from recruiting in his territory," Stewart later wrote in his 1991 memoir. "Daly was embarrassing him."

In 1989, Mizzou turned to Daly and the Tigers—that's how Mizzou marketed the Detroit core on a VHS highlight tape they showed recruits—to salvage a season in turmoil. Stewart was diagnosed with colon cancer in February, putting Daly in charge for the rest of the season. He'd coach the Tigers to the Big 8 tournament championship and two more wins in the NCAA tournament.

Daly's Detroit ties would eventually lead NCAA investigators to snoop around Mizzou's program and take a special interest in his relationship with local hoops guru Vic Adams. After a lengthy investigation, the Tigers landed on probation for two years and absorbed a postseason ban for 1991. Daly lost his job, briefly, when the NCAA's Committee on Infractions charged him with unethical conduct. But Daly won his appeal and rejoined Mizzou's staff for the 1991–92 season and remained on Mizzou's staff until Stewart stepped down in 1999. But the Detroit pipeline went dry.

Daly's six Detroit Tigers combined to give Mizzou 6,170 points, 2,484 rebounds, 1,428 assists while playing a collective 603 games.

74 Winslow Calls for Action in Canton

Mizzou has produced its share of Hall of Famers beyond its in-house Intercollegiate Athletics Hall of Fame conceived in 1990.

In 2007 legendary basketball coach Norm Stewart was part of the second induction class for the National Collegiate Basketball Hall of Fame in Kansas City.

The gridiron edition is far more populated with Black and Gold. Seven Mizzou football players and two coaches have been enshrined in the College Football Hall of Fame in Atlanta, starting with quarterback Paul Christman in 1956 and followed by Coach Don Faurot (1961), running back Bob Steuber (1971), lineman Ed Travis (1974), lineman Darold Jenkins (1976), Coach Dan Devine (1985), running back / defensive back Johnny Roland (1998), tight end Kellen Winslow (2002), and defensive back / return specialist Roger Wehrli (2003).

Two Tigers have been enshrined in Canton, Ohio, home of the Pro Football Hall of Fame: Winslow and Wehrli. When Winslow became the first player from Missouri to receive the honor on July 29, 1995, he barely mentioned his college alma mater in his acceptance speech of more than 3,000 words. He thanked his family. He thanked his coaches and teammates from East St. Louis High School and the San Diego Chargers. He thanked only three people from Mizzou: Charles Schmitz from the College of Education, assistant coach Prentice Gautt, and Walter Daniel, the former vice chancellor who served as Winslow's mentor during his time in college.

It was an unconventional speech, to say the least. Rather than touch on past heroics and highlights on the football field, Winslow used his platform that day to address political and racial topics that transcended pro football and all of sport. He focused on affirmative action and challenged President Bill Clinton and the Supreme Court to push for better opportunities for minorities.

Here are parts of Winslow's speech:

> I call on the President of these United States to continue his support of affirmative action programs in a fashion that will continue to provide opportunities for minorities in both the private and public sector. That even if the program must change significantly to fit the restrictive

Kellen Winslow addresses the audience at the College Football Hall of Fame Gridiron luncheon in 2006.

guidelines set by the Supreme Court that that program be given the funding and the power to enforce those guidelines. In the long run, history will reward you, Mr. President, for taking the tough stance, for standing for what is right and for what is just.

* * *

For years we have been told to help our own. To rally our political forces and clout and work within the system to bring about change for our people like so many other ethnic groups have been able to do. For African Americans many social advances can be directly related to advancements in sports. It has also been said that sports is a microcosm of society, a mirror, reflecting the issues of a larger society. If so, maybe the progress made in sports can serve as a model for society. Therefore, due to our representation on the field of play this seems the most logical place to begin. The past, present and future African American athlete must come together with well-defined goals and methods for bringing about change in sports. While the African American athlete of yesteryear can speak of their experiences and realities of life after professional sports, the African American athlete of tomorrow can learn from those experiences and turn and face those realities. However, it is the African American athlete of today who must be the driving force, for they are the ones with the platform and the ability to bring about change.

* * *

In other words, tomorrow Kellen Winslow may no longer have a platform for which you address these issues. But a Michael Jordan, an Emmitt Smith, a Shaquille O'Neal will have such a platform for some time to come. We have been challenged time and time again by members of public and private sector both black and white to do something for our own, to stop being a burden on society, seeking handouts and special privileges. Today, I encourage the African American athlete to awaken and join me in accepting that challenge, to awaken and our rightful role in society as leaders. To awaken and accept the responsibility that comes with fame and fortune. To awaken to the realities of the uncertain plight of the African American condition even as we approach the twenty-first century. It is now with a great deal of humility and with the full appreciation for what the game has given to me. I am pleased to take my place among the greats of the National Football League. To God be the glory.

75 You Can Take the Cowboy out of Holts Summit...

In late January 1998 the telephone rang at the Smith home in Holts Summit, Missouri, a small town near Jefferson City and just south of Columbia. It was Florida coach Steve Spurrier on the line. David Smith's son, Justin, had pledged a verbal commitment to Missouri more than a year earlier. National signing day was a few days away.

Spurrier owned an SEC championship ring for each finger on one hand and a national championship ring for the other. But he needed something he hoped Holts Summit would deliver—a tight end. "I know we've never called you or contacted you," Spurrier said, David Smith recalled years later. "And we know you gave a verbal to Mizzou. And we know you've got like 23 relatives who graduated from Mizzou and that it's only 29 miles away from home. We don't want to harass you on your decision, but our All-American tight end just went down with a torn ACL, and we think you can come in here and play."

Was this a prank call?

"He knew stuff we didn't know about us," Smith said. "And we didn't even have a clue he knew who we were or who Justin was.... It really dawned on us that [Justin] might be pretty good."

Spurrier thought so, though the phone call was a short one. Smith stuck with his commitment to Missouri and became one of the program's greatest defensive players. But he didn't stop in Mid-Missouri. The kid from Holts Summit would go on to have one of the longest and most productive NFL careers of any player from Mizzou.

A hulking specimen as a freshman, the 6'5", 255-pound rookie made an immediate impression the first day he stepped on campus. Even Missouri's veteran offensive linemen couldn't help but marvel at the newcomer. "Wow," offensive guard Craig Heimburger, a senior when Smith arrived, said years later. "He came in and was lifting the same amount of weights as the veterans right away. He was growing and getting stronger each day. It was unheard of."

It didn't take more than a few practices for the coaches to realize what Highway 63 had delivered. "He came in and just dominated," defensive line coach Dave Toub remembered. "He was so fast. Coming from the backside on the edge as a defensive end, he would chase everything down. And we knew right there he was special."

"He was huge. He was fit. He was ripped," quarterback Corby Jones said. "We knew he could make an impact. We weren't sure how much of an impact he could make as a freshman. It was a matter of picking things up. But you put him on the edge and say, 'Go get the football.' That's basically what we did."

Smith earned a starting job as a freshman and made fools of Big 12 offensive tackles, finishing with 86 tackles, including 13 behind the line of scrimmage. The first Mizzou true freshman to start every game since 1986, Smith was named the league's best freshman. For an encore, Smith tallied eight sacks as a sophomore then set single-season Mizzou records as a junior with 11 sacks and 24 tackles for loss. The Tigers were otherwise inept—head coach Larry Smith was fired after the season—but against a convoy of double and triple teams, Smith emerged as one of the nation's elite players. "To watch him develop and see what he became was absurd," Jones said. "He knew he was gifted and we knew he had the potential to be very good."

Smith left school after his junior year—though he attended Gary Pinkel's introductory press conference to hear out the new coach—and became the No. 4 pick in the 2001 NFL Draft, heading to Cincinnati. Smith had seven strong but unspectacular seasons with the Bengals then enjoyed a career renaissance after hitting the free-agent market. He became the game's preeminent 3-4 defensive end in San Francisco, where he made five straight Pro Bowls from 2009 to 2013.

Not unlike his time at Mizzou, Smith took no interest in the spotlight while starring in the Bay Area. He declined endorsement deals. He turned down *Sports Illustrated* when the magazine wanted him for a cover story. He had no use for the national attention or self-promotion. "His favorite thing to do," David Smith said during the 2011 season, when Justin finished third for NFL Defensive Player of the Year, "is go to Costco, buy a bunch of hamburgers and pork steaks, bring those home, and grill them and have people over. That's his way of being big-time. If he can sit on the back of a pickup's tailgate, it makes it that much better."

In college, Smith never warmed up to his media-bequeathed Godzilla nickname. Friends called him Smitty. In San Francisco he was Cowboy—a nod to his roots on the farm back home. In Holts

Summit, Smith bought Railwood Golf Club and charged patrons a modest $25 for a round.

Smith's muscles worked in the Bay Area, but his heart always belonged to Central Missouri. After the 2014 season, Cowboy took his last ride, calling it quits when a shoulder injury forced him to retire at 35. A possible dark horse for the Pro Football Hall of Fame, Smith produced at a rate that stacks up against any NFL player to come through Mizzou: 1,370 tackles, 87 sacks, 16 forced fumbles, 3 interceptions, and 30 passes defended. Smith's 87 sacks ranked 10th among active players when the 2014 season ended, while only two current players at the time of his retirement started more games than Smith's 217: future Hall of Famers Peyton Manning and Charles Woodson. Naturally, Smith moved back to Missouri when he retired from the NFL—back home, to the place he knows best. "You come in, you go out, everything moves on," Smith said. "It was a good ride."

76 Super Bowl Champions

An NFL rookie in 2014, Seattle Seahawks right tackle Justin Britt joined an exclusive fraternity, becoming only the eighth Super Bowl starter who finished his college eligibility at Missouri. "That's a small number," Britt told the *Post-Dispatch* before Super Bowl XLIX in Phoenix. "It's definitely something to be proud of. I'm happy with my time at Mizzou, and everything I've learned there. It's a great program, a great place to go to school, and a great place to mature as a man. To represent Mizzou in the Super Bowl is an honor. I want to be a good example of someone who comes from Mizzou."

The Seahawks couldn't outlast New England, leaving Britt without the elusive Super Bowl ring. Heading into the 2015 NFL season, only four players who finished their college careers at MU have started and won a Super Bowl: Steelers linebacker Andy Russell (Super Bowl IX, X), 49ers defensive back Eric Wright (XVI, XIX, XXIII, XXIV), Rams linebacker Mike Jones (XXXIV), and Patriots defensive back Otis Smith (XXXVI). Of those four, Wright was the only one to earn All-Conference honors at Mizzou.

Seven other former Tigers have won Super Bowl rings as backup players: Dolphins defensive back Henry Stuckey (Super Bowl VII), Giants running back Tony Galbreath and defensive lineman Jerome Sally (XXI), Redskins offensive guard Phil Pettey (XXII), Patriots defensive lineman Rick Lyle (XXXVIII), Saints quarterback Chase Daniel (XLIV), and Broncos linebacker Shane Ray (L). The 1986 Giants are the only Super Bowl–winning team to feature multiple MU players in Sally and Galbreath.

A handful of other former Tigers played on Super Bowl–losing teams, most recently Panthers defensive end Kony Ealy (Super Bowl L), 49ers teammates Justin Smith and Aldon Smith (XLVII), and Steelers defensive lineman Ziggy Hood (XLV).

Another two former Tigers started for Super Bowl winners only after finishing their college careers at other schools: Oakland defensive lineman John Matuszak (Super Bowl XI, XV) and Denver tight end Byron Chamberlain (XXXII, XXXIII). Chamberlain transferred to Wayne State and later emerged as one of John Elway's weapons in Denver.

Matuszak, one of the NFL's most colorful characters in the 1970s, was the draft's No. 1 overall pick in 1973. He bounced between franchises before finally finding a home with the Raiders, starting in Super Bowl XI and XV.

Long before that, Matuszak came to Mizzou to play tight end for Dan Devine—until a fateful night altered the course of his career during his sophomore year in 1970. A drunken air force cadet flirted with Matuszak's girlfriend at a Mizzou fraternity party, Matuszak told the *New York Times*, and soon became acquainted with both of the football player's fists. "They said afterward I broke most of the bones in his face," he told the newspaper in 1973. "He was in the hospital eight weeks and I was charged with felonious assault." Matuszak later pleaded guilty to a reduced charge and Devine suspended him for the rest of the season, with the promise he could return for the 1971 season. Except Devine wasn't Missouri's coach in 1971. He had left for the Green Bay Packers, and his successor, Al Onofrio, told Matuszak he should transfer. He moved on to the University of Tampa and became a star player—and played his final college game against Kent State, featuring future Missouri coach Gary Pinkel, in the 1972 Tangerine Bowl.

Before he died in 1989 of an accidental overdose of a narcotic painkiller, Matuszak starred in several movies and TV shows, most famously the football classic *North Dallas Forty* and the 1980s cult hit *The Goonies*, in which he played Sloth.

77 The Comeback Kid

One of the most important plays in Missouri football's modern history seemed so improbable two years before Henry Josey launched himself past the Texas A&M Aggies and into instant Mizzou lore. On November 30, 2013, the Tigers handed Josey the ball on third-and-1 in Missouri territory, hoping to maintain possession in an evenly matched tie game between the SEC's two newest members. With 3:34 left, Josey needed only a yard. He gave the Tigers so much more. Fifty-seven yards later, Missouri led the Aggies 28–21 and had all but clinched its first SEC East Division championship. One last defensive stop and the unlikely champions were crowned. A year earlier, the Tigers won just five games as SEC rookies and routinely looked overmatched against their new conference peers, especially against the Aggies, who clobbered Mizzou 59–29 in the season finale.

Then again, the 2012 Tigers were missing their explosive tailback. Josey suffered a season-ending and career-threatening knee injury in the 10th game of the 2011 season. Josey shredded multiple ligaments, his meniscus, and his patellar tendon in an injury Mizzou's medical staff likened to a violent car crash. His football career was in serious jeopardy, but doctors and trainers never let that thought slip past their lips. "We never said to Henry Josey, 'You'll never play again,'" team surgeon Pat Smith said. "I'm a positive person, and I always feel I can fix most things."

Josey missed the entire 2012 season while going through a grueling rehab process. By the spring of 2013, though, Josey began to run—and run fast. One day during a spring practice, Coach Gary Pinkel noticed a blur along the sideline. It was Josey. "I had tears in my eyes," Pinkel said. "To think where he was and how he got there…"

On August 31, 658 days since he last played a game, Josey's comeback came full circle. He ran for 113 yards in the season opener against Murray State, including a 68-yard touchdown run of vintage Josey speed down the sideline. He dashed right over the exact spot on Faurot Field where his knee had combusted 22 months earlier. "It looked like he stomped right on that spot [on the field], like he was reclaiming it," former Mizzou linebacker and Josey's close friend Will Ebner said after the game. "It was really moving."

Three months later, Josey had already clinched a 1,000-yard campaign in one of the great comeback seasons in Mizzou history. With his third-down dash against the Aggies, Josey made his memorable season one for the ages for the Tigers, sending MU to

Atlanta for the SEC Championship Game against Auburn. He'd finish the season with 1,166 rushing yards, two short of his 2011 total but good for sixth place on the team's single-season list. "That was fitting—fitting for Henry Josey and the kind of year he's had, who he is, and what he's about," Pinkel said of Josey's game-clinching touchdown. "He's sacred to Mizzou fans."

After the season Josey surprised the coaching staff when he entered the 2014 NFL Draft and passed on his final year of eligibility. He left school 428 yards short of passing Brock Olivo as Mizzou's career rushing leader among running backs. Josey went undrafted and later resurfaced in the Canadian Football League. His Mizzou legacy, though, was already in place, topped by his game-winning touchdown run against Oklahoma State in the Cotton Bowl—on his final college carry, no less. "Just being able to have a game like I did and play the way I did," he said, "there's no other way I'd rather leave my mark at Mizzou."

78 A Pioneer on the Hardwood

His No. 50 doesn't hang from the rafters at Mizzou. He didn't set scoring records or lead the Tigers to championships. But Alfred Abrams Jr. contributed to the program's history—the university's history—unlike any student who came before or after him. In January 1956 Abrams became the school's first African American scholarship athlete. The 6'5" St. Louis native from Sumner High made his varsity debut a year later against Oklahoma on February 5, 1957. He came to Mizzou to make baskets not history, but his arrival and survival meant far more than the 706 points he scored for the Tigers.

At the time, though, Abrams's presence wasn't groundbreaking with those around him. Norm Stewart, a star player for the Tigers in the 1950s and later the program's greatest coach, was a senior when Abrams joined the team. "Small-town person that I am," Stewart later told the *Post-Dispatch*, "you know it never really entered into my thinking: 'Well, here's history.' I was busy trying to pass English, probably." Stewart added, "He was another guy; he was on the ballclub. Now that you look back, sure, you can see what it meant. But then? He was not a difficult fit."

Abrams's career peaked in his junior year, 1958–59, when he led Wilbur "Sparky" Stalcup's Tigers with 16.2 points and 9.3 rebounds per game. Though there were barely 100 black students on campus at the time, Abrams was treated well in Columbia during his career. The Brewer Fieldhouse crowd gave him standing ovations for his first and last games.

Away from home, Abrams felt the generation's ugliness of discrimination in other towns. Coaches and teammates told stories of Abrams being turned away at hotels and restaurants, including a scene in Houston when Abrams was forced to stay in a dorm room at nearby Texas Southern when the Tigers were in town to play Rice. Abrams slept well enough to lead Mizzou with 23 points in a victory the next day.

After a brief professional career in Seattle, Abrams returned to St. Louis and finished his business degree at Washington University, followed by a master's degree at St. Louis University. A heart condition took Abrams far too early in 1982. He was just 44.

Twenty-three years later, Missouri posthumously inducted Abrams into its Intercollegiate Athletics Hall of Fame. "He did what he had to and didn't expect any type of recognition, that kind of thing," his widow, Glenda Abrams, told the *Columbia Daily Tribune* in 2005. "I think he would have been, of course, very excited about it, but at the same time, a little humbled."

79 Gage Pulls Double Duty

The image is forever burned in the memory of Mizzou diehards: Justin Gage sprawled out on the Compaq Center floor in San Jose, California, diving headfirst after the ball as it trickled out of bounds in the 2002 NCAA tournament. Gage, a record-breaking superstar on the football field, played a different role on the basketball court. He hustled, he rebounded, he crashed onto the floor to chase after loose balls he had no chance of recovering. That's exactly what he did in that NCAA Regional Semifinal victory over UCLA. "That was the best play of the season," Missouri coach Quin Snyder said after the win. "It just said everything."

Gage came to Mizzou in 1999 as a 6'4" quarterback from Jefferson City but left as the school's most prolific pass-catcher. That was only half the story. Gage played on four losing football teams while the Tigers worked through a head coaching transition, but he also gave the basketball team valuable minutes on three NCAA tournament teams. He left as one of the school's most accomplished two-sport athletes. Mizzou football coach Gary Pinkel was willing to share Gage with Snyder and appreciated the player every bit as his hoops counterpart. "We'd like to have a locker room full of that type of competitor," Pinkel said.

Gage lost his football redshirt nine games into his freshman season when Larry Smith's staff impulsively pushed him into the lineup to salvage a sorry season. He played quarterback the final three games of the season and barely completed a third of his passes. The next spring, he shifted to wide receiver. If Smith's staff blundered by wasting Gage's year of eligibility, it deserved credit for moving him to wideout. "At the time I was thinking, *I'm a quarterback*," Gage later said of the move. "But just going out to practice and running a few routes and seeing how much easier the receiver spot was and how fun it was, it was something I thought I could do. I was really glad that they thought about doing that."

At receiver, Gage gave the offense an instant jolt. He would leave Mizzou holding all four major school receiving records: career receptions (200), career yards (2,704), single-game receptions (16), and single-game yards (236, set twice).

One career goal eluded Gage, as he never played in a bowl game—his dad, Al Gage, was Indiana's starting tight end in the 1968 Rose Bowl—but he was part of three NCAA tournament basketball teams, playing a valuable role as a defender and rebounder.

At the start of the 2000–01 season, Gage joined the basketball team shortly after leading the football team with 44 catches. As the Tigers traveled to the Great Alaska Shootout, radio analyst Gary Link remembered Gage telling him, "I feel like my body's been hit by a train."

But he found a way to hit back on the hardwood. Everyone noticed. "He did exactly what Quin wanted him to do," Link said. "All of a sudden those skill guys got a little toughness in them. They've got a guy who's diving on the floor and doing all the dirty work and loving it. His numbers were nothing, but he guarded people and he rebounded."

Gage passed on playing basketball his senior year so he could focus on preparing for the NFL Draft. He became a fifth-round pick by Chicago and over eight seasons with the Bears and Titans caught 201 passes—one more than he caught in three seasons at Mizzou.

80 A Golden Age along the Offensive Line

For years at Mizzou the offensive line meeting room was more like the witness protection program. The Tigers produced some outstanding offenses in the 1990s and 2000s, but the blockers along the line of scrimmage had trouble gaining notoriety for a quarter century—especially at the pro level. From 1988 to 2013, just four Mizzou offensive linemen were selected in the NFL Draft, and none higher than the fifth round. The trend buckled in 2014 when Seattle chose All-SEC tackle Justin Britt in the second round. In 2015 tackle Mitch Morse went to Kansas City, also in the second round. Two more were drafted in 2016, Evan Boehm and Connor McGovern. Perhaps an O-line renaissance was under way.

Among the 33 first-team Mizzou All-Americans from Ed Lindenmeyer in 1925 to Shane Ray in 2015, a dozen played along the offensive line, starting with tackle Lindenmeyer, an anchor up front under Coach Gwinn Henry. Later in the 20th century, the Tigers produced nine All-American offensive linemen from 1962 to 1987, including five first-round selections in the NFL draft, all of whom were offensive tackles: Francis Peay (1965), Russ Washington (1967), Morris Towns (1976), Brad Edelman (1981), and John Clay (1986). Among the five, Washington enjoyed the longest pro career, playing 15 seasons for the San Diego Chargers that included five Pro Bowl selections.

That golden era of Mizzou offensive lines produced another four second-round picks, including one player who led one of MU's most fascinating post-football careers. Ed Blaine gave four years of his life to Mizzou football, rarely leaving the varsity's line of scrimmage between 1959 and 1961. Recruited out of Farmington, Missouri, by assistant coach John Kadlec to power the

Tigers' power running offense, Blaine earned All-America honors as a senior in 1961. He played five seasons in the NFL, winning a championship with Vince Lombardi's Green Bay Packers in 1962, as a rookie. Blaine joined Philadelphia the next year but after the 1966 season made the unlikeliest of decisions for an NFL star: he walked away from football.

Blaine spent the next half-century studying, teaching, and practicing medicine. Few players in Mizzou history did more with their careers after leaving the game. Over a cup of coffee in downtown Columbia in 2015, shortly before retiring at 75, Blaine told the story of his decision to leave football:

Playing professional football was beyond my fondest dream. Then I get drafted by a world-champion team, so I was like, "Screw medicine! I'm going to be a hero, a football star." I dropped out of the medical program at Missouri, but a guy named Clint Conoway, a professor in the zoology department—we don't even have a zoology department anymore—he was my mentor. He said, "Look, if you agree to just play five years, I'll bring you back every spring to work on your master's degree and then you can decide what you want to do." That's what we did. I'd come back every spring. Cliff was one of the most important people in my life because he kept me on track. I could have stayed and played 10 or 12 years in the NFL and had been a lot more mentally deficient. But five years was a great time for me to end my career. I had accomplished what I could have accomplished. I played in the Pro Bowl. I played for the world champions. I was satisfied.

I knew the rest of my life was going to be very different. Science and sports don't mix very well, so they were always a separate thing for me. Every day I spent on the football field I was risking a concussion or serious injury that might influence the other parts of my life. Five years was a good stopping point because it made me eligible for a pension. Leaving football was the biggest challenge of my life. I was in Philadelphia and doing well. The coaches really wanted me to stay. I was bombarded by people, from the fans to businesspeople in Philadelphia who could help me, telling me not to retire. Boy, I came close, because it would have been really lucrative for me to go back. I think my top salary was $18,000 a year. That was a good salary back then. I think they were offering me $25,000, which would have been one of the highest salaries on the team, even more than the quarterback.

But I managed to say no. It was the most important and best decision I made in my life. Not to diminish the role football played in my life. It played a very positive role. I'd benefited from it, but if I played it out until the end, I would have been at risk to not be where I am today. I look at a lot of my old buddies, and before they retired, they were in ordinary jobs. I don't know of anyone else who was a university professor, so I was really proud of my achievements.

Blaine earned his PhD in physiology and later completed postdoctoral work at the University of Melbourne. He later returned to Mizzou's medical school and served as director of the Cardiovascular Research Center, specializing his research in hypertension and heart failure. Heady stuff for an old offensive lineman.

81 The Point Guard from Moss Point

Thank goodness for Litterial Green. If not for Georgia's three-time All-SEC basketball standout, Mizzou never would have discovered one of its all-time greats.

MU assistant coach Rich Daly struck out while trying to recruit Green, but he couldn't help but notice his younger teammate in Moss Point, Mississippi. Melvin Booker was hardly a blue-chip prospect. His only Division I scholarship offers were from Central Florida and South Alabama. And the three major in-state programs—Ole Miss, Mississippi State, and Southern Miss—weren't interested.

Landing elite recruits wasn't easy for the Tigers in the final years of the 1980s, not with the NCAA breathing down Daly's neck for violations tied to his Detroit pipeline. The investigation sent Daly to all corners of the map looking for unheralded prospects. He didn't land Green, but he never forgot about Booker.

The 6'1" guard arrived at Mizzou in 1990 with little fanfare. He left as one of the school's most decorated players, a second-team All-American, and Mizzou's fourth Big 8 Player of the Year in five years. "I'm not the type of player who will go out and score 30 or 40 points every night," he said when the accolades piled up in 1994. "I'm more of a team concept player who does many things to help the team out. I need my teammates out there with me."

Booker was selling himself short. He finished his career as MU's No. 5 scorer of all time—and No. 1 among players shorter than 6'4"—and No. 2 on the career assists list. His 183 career three-pointers stood as the school record for three years. Booker scored at least 10 points in all but three games his junior and senior years. He averaged 20 points in seven NCAA tournament games, including a career-best 35 against Wisconsin in 1994. By all accounts he's one of the best offensive players ever to suit up for the Tigers, and among the program's three greatest point guards.

Booker's emergence at Mizzou was baptism by fire: after Booker signed with Mizzou, veteran point guard Travis Ford transferred to Kentucky and backcourt star Anthony Peeler was ruled

Melvin Booker makes a fast break against Syracuse in the NCAA West Semifinals in 1994.

academically ineligible for the first semester of the 1990–91 season. Booker played heavy minutes immediately and scored in double figures in his second and third games.

The rookie guard endeared himself to Stewart and Mizzou fans before the season's opening tip when he lost three teeth in a bizarre mishap during a military science class that also injured freshman teammates Jevon Crudup and Lamont Frazier. Booker underwent a five-hour oral surgery two weeks before the first regular-season game. "You get your teeth knocked out, then have an oral surgeon put them back in," Stewart said at the time. "Then you come back out there and play. He's a small guy. You go running through the lane. You're taking charges. You're bopping around. That takes some courage. That kid's gutty."

By the end of his four-year career, Booker had helped lead Mizzou to two Big 8 tournament championships and the 1994 regular-season title. The crowning moment for a tight-knit senior class that included Crudup, Frazier, and Reggie Smith came on March 5, 1994, when the Tigers edged Nebraska to complete a perfect 14–0 Big 8 regular season—at home on senior day, no less. Fittingly, Booker's three-point play in the final seconds clinched the victory. "It's a great way to go out," Booker said. "The way we won, 14–0. My parents are here to see me play. Game-winning shot. It's like a dream come true."

Booker went undrafted that summer but made the Houston Rockets roster a year later then resurfaced with Denver and Golden State for a total of 32 career NBA games, averaging 5.2 points per game. He'd continue his career overseas, including several years in Italy.

In 2013 Booker was back in the local headlines when the Tigers recruited his son, Devin, who, like his dad, starred at Moss Point High but unlike Melvin was highly pursued by some of the nation's top programs. Cleverly, Mizzou staged a turn-back-the-clock exhibition game that fall, welcoming the 1993–94 team back to Columbia for a pregame ceremony at the Hearnes Center. MU rolled out the red carpet for the former Mizzou players, including the one whose son just happened to be deciding between Missouri, Kentucky, Michigan, and Michigan State. The sweet-shooting 6'6" Devin—five inches taller than Dad—filmed the ceremony from behind the Mizzou bench and sat alongside Stewart and other dignitaries, including Missouri governor Jay Nixon. But a week later, Devin settled on NBA factory Kentucky over Melvin's alma mater, much to his dad's initial disappointment.

"It was really, really tough on me," Melvin said at the time. "It would have been a dream come true to not only see my son play at my old high school but play at my college. But I have to support him 100 percent. He made the best decision for himself, and I'm proud of him for that."

In his only appearance at Mizzou Arena, Devin scored nine points against the Tigers in 2015, his one and only college season. Melvin watched from the front row wearing a homemade T-shirt that read A House Divided and featured both teams' logos.

TVZ

Few players inspired more promise than Tony VanZant. Few delivered more tragedy. He was the 1985 Parade Magazine National Player of the Year and was supposed to become the superstar running back who would rescue Mizzou football from the depths of the Big 8. As a senior at Hazelwood Central in St. Louis, VanZant ran for a mesmerizing 2,736 yards and 36 touchdowns. He was destined for stardom in college and beyond.

But three weeks before his first scheduled practice at MU, VanZant played in the fateful Missouri Lions Club All-Star Game in Jefferson City. The star running back from St. Louis blew out his knee on his second carry of the exhibition. He missed his entire freshman season and was never the same player again. "I don't regret it," VanZant said in 2013 from his office at Lincoln University in Jefferson City. "People ask me all the time, 'Would you play in the all-star game again?' I say, 'Yeah. So what?' They say, 'Why? If you're the top player in the country, why would you risk yourself getting hurt?' But I could trip over a curb and get hurt. I don't regret it at all."

In 2011 VanZant joined the football coaching staff at Lincoln, where the home games are played at Dwight T. Reed Stadium, the same field where VanZant tore up his knee a generation earlier. Years later, he could still find the spot on the field where he got hurt. He suffered a torn ligament and cartilage damage and didn't play again until 1987. He'd never recapture the burst that made him a high school legend in St. Louis. For his college career, VanZant carried the ball just 51 times for 203 yards and one touchdown.

VanZant battled depression after the injury but later found solace in coaching at the high school and small college level. He didn't hesitate to join the Lincoln staff to work under head coach Mike Jones, a Mizzou teammate and former St. Louis Rams linebacker. Naturally, VanZant would coach the Lincoln running backs.

Yes, he'd have to work near the spot that changed his life forever, but VanZant still loved the game. "I don't know if anyone else sees it," Lincoln assistant coach and former MU teammate Damon Frenchers said in 2013. "On game days, everybody's hooting and hollering trying to fire the kids up, and I look over there and he's kind of walking a little slow. That's him thinking, *Gosh almighty*."

83 Braggin' in the Lou

Some Mizzou freshmen just don't know better. They see the Illinois basketball game on the schedule and assume it's just another non-conference contest. It's a neutral-site matchup against a Big Ten opponent staged around the holidays in St. Louis. Is that all? "Not being from the area, you never know how big something is," said former Tigers guard Kim English, who came to Mizzou in 2008 from Baltimore.

He figured it out quickly, as they all do when they step on the court for their first Braggin' Rights game and witness the capacity crowd split down the middle, full-throated Illini fans in Orange and Blue, their Mizzou counterparts in Black and Gold.

The holiday tradition is one of the few annual rites Mizzou has left that remains pure and untouched. With MU still new to the Southeastern Conference and severed from its Big 12 (and Big 8) rivals in the conference realignment divorce of 2011, Braggin' Rights might stand as the Tigers' only genuine living grudge match. "We were 10–1 my freshman year and ranked No. 25," English remembered. "We were slated to win that game but just got whipped. It ruined Christmas. That feeling stays with you. I didn't even fly back to Baltimore. I stayed in my room all of Christmas Eve and Christmas Day. I knew that I never wanted to lose that game again."

Missouri and Illinois hadn't always met in St. Louis. The flagship schools from bordering states met 11 times between 1932 and 1979 on their respective campuses, with the Fighting Illini holding a 7–4 edge. When the schools agreed to move the game to the St. Louis Arena—the Checkerdome, as it's fondly remembered—Lou Henson's Illini dominated Norm Stewart's Tigers in the early years, winning 9 of the first 10 games, including eight straight from 1983 to 1990. Stewart proved he could capture Big 8 titles. He could outfox his Big 8 peers and pluck the feathers of the rival Kansas Jayhawks. But he was no match for the Illini.

"Border War? Try Border Bore," *St. Louis Post-Dispatch* columnist Bernie Miklasz wrote after the 1989 game, No. 5 Illinois's eight-point win over No. 4 Mizzou. "The action may be thrilling, but the result is anticlimactic. We know what will happen. They should print on the ticket, ahead of time: Illinois wins; no refund. Illinois wins; drive home safely. Illinois wins; be kind to Norm Stewart.... Yes, the Arena was still home of the blues Wednesday. Mizzou's blues. But this annual skirmish, which pits two eccentric country-boy coaches and their nationally ranked teams, was grand theater for 18,398 spectators. And that's why we love it, regardless of which side of the Mississippi you pay taxes. Once a year, Missouri and Illinois give our sleepy sports town a case of the fever."

Stewart's Tigers finally snapped the streak in 1991, their first of four straight wins over Illinois, including the epic triple-overtime win in 1993. Stewart joked after ending the streak he wasn't aware the winner took home a trophy—a towering trophy at that. "Oh, golly, there are no hills left to climb," he joked after the breakthrough win.

After Stewart retired, Mizzou's St. Louis blues continued in the form of another extensive losing streak, this one nine straight from 2000 to 2008. On the morning of the 2009 game, English woke up in the team hotel with text messages from Mizzou football players Blaine Gabbert and Wes Kemp. Both grew up in St. Louis. "I know it doesn't mean much to you, but this game means so much to us in St. Louis," English said their texts read. "I told him we'd win."

They did. English and his classmates, who'd go on to win more games than any four-year class in team history, finished their careers with three straight wins over the Illini. "It was an amazing feeling," English said. "It gives the entire state of Missouri a merry Christmas."

In 2002 the schools brought the rivalry to St. Louis on the football field. Dubbed Arch Madness, the game was set at the Edward Jones Dome, former home of the St. Louis Rams before they returned to Los Angeles in 2016. The football series was all Mizzou once it returned to the Gateway City, with the Tigers sweeping all six games in 2002, 2003, and from 2007 to 2010, including brilliant breakout performances by Brad Smith (2002) and Jeremy Maclin (2007) in their college debuts.

84 Larry Drew: Floor Leader

Before Jon Sundvold, before Lee Coward, before Melvin Booker and Phil Pressey, there was Larry Drew, the first prolific Mizzou point guard of the modern era. One of the great floor leaders of Norm Stewart's 32 years coaching the Tigers, Drew was the consummate coach on the floor, plus a dynamic scorer and playmaker.

Drew joined Stewart's rotation immediately after arriving from Wyandotte, Kansas. He butted heads with Stewart early in his career and almost quit the team, but as a sophomore he led the Tigers to a surprise championship in the Big 8 tournament. By his junior year, Drew was among the league's top guards, leading the Tigers in scoring (15.2 points per game) and assists (4.3). As a senior, Drew showed the ropes to underclassmen Sundvold and Steve Stipanovich and guided Mizzou to its first of four straight Big 8 regular-season championships. "You have to understand, no one else offered him a scholarship," former teammate Tom Dore said. "He had this huge chip on his shoulder. And he loved Norm.

Larry had a Norm impersonation that was really good.... But when you played with Larry, you always knew the ball could come your way at any point in time. And Larry could score. He worked and worked and worked. That was, to me, that was just huge. He was a guy you wanted to be on the floor with."

Drew averaged 12 points per game for his college career and 3.7 assists while nearly shooting 50 percent from the floor. He finished his career No. 2 on the team's career scoring list and with more assists than any player in team history.

But Drew's career was just getting started when he left college. The 17th overall pick in the 1980 NBA Draft by Detroit, Drew played 10 seasons in the league with the Pistons, Kings, Clippers, and Lakers. In Kansas City he enjoyed his best season in 1982–83, averaging 20.1 points and 8.1 assists, and 2.8 rebounds, one of the finest NBA seasons by a former Missouri player. He closed his career with the Lakers, coming off the bench to play alongside NBA greats Magic Johnson and Byron Scott. Drew stayed with the Lakers as an assistant coach once his playing days were over and spent the next two decades on five different NBA staffs.

In 2010 Drew landed his first head coaching job, leading the Atlanta Hawks to three straight winning seasons and three playoff appearances. He had less success in Milwaukee, where he lasted just one season. From there, Drew joined the coaching staff in Cleveland, where he experienced his career highlight. Led by LeBron James, the Cavaliers erased a 3–1 deficit in the 2016 NBA Finals and beat Golden State to bring home the city's first professional sports championship since 1964. Drew coached Michael Jordan in Washington and Shaquille O'Neal and Kobe Bryant in L.A., but nothing compared to winning a championship with James.

Weeks after the Cavs celebrated the championship, Drew credited his old college coach for sending him along his long path. "I wanted to be a coach that could deliver the right level of discipline,"

Drew said. "I wanted to be a coach that was going to be successful and deal with different issues both on and off the floor. With Coach Stewart, I had never played for a coach with his style, so it was tough for me to make adjustments. Thank God I hung in there."

85 Keyon and Clarence

Keyon and Clarence. Clarence and Keyon. Always together—until they weren't. Keyon Dooling and Clarence Gilbert joined the Missouri basketball team in 1998, both from the same high school in Fort Lauderdale, Florida, not so much as a package deal but best friends and backcourt partners nonetheless. Dooling was the dazzling athlete, a skinny 6'3" ball-handling wizard whose jumping ability defied gravity. (An Allen Fieldhouse rim would attest to that.) Gilbert was the gunner, a 6'2" shooter whose jump shot had no conscience.

They met in a youth recreation game at age nine and went on to attend the same summer camps and played on the same AAU teams. They split up in high school—Gilbert to Dillard, the local public school, and Dooling to Cardinal Gibbons, a private Catholic school—but reunited their senior year at Dillard. They combined to average 47 points, 10 assists, and 11 steals. Both chose Mizzou, a program on the decline, as Norm Stewart's team had missed three straight NCAA tournaments. Dooling chose the Tigers over Clemson and Maryland. Gilbert's other top options were Georgia and Michigan State.

Their impact would be subtle initially, but the freshmen helped the Tigers back to the NCAA tournament in what turned out to be Stewart's last season. The longtime coach and Dooling had a heated exchange in a 19-point loss at Colorado. Dooling later said he embarrassed himself and his family that day by disrespecting Stewart. Dooling redeemed himself the next four games—all victories—and averaged 19.3 points.

When Stewart stepped down, both players denied rumors they played a role—they insisted they didn't threaten to transfer if Stewart returned for a 33rd season—but both were quick to embrace new coach Quin Snyder, who promised a more up-tempo style. "He's my type of coach," Gilbert said. "He likes to run-and-gun and get after people."

The Fort Lauderdale tandem thrived in Snyder's system: Dooling became MU's leading scorer (15.3 points per game) and Gilbert emerged from role player to three-point sniper (13.7). Dooling's most memorable basket never officially counted: he delivered a vicious one-handed dunk at Kansas on March 5, 2000, soaring over KU's Ashante Johnson. But official Bob Sitov called Dooling for charging. The Tigers lost by one. "It was the best play I've seen in college basketball this year," Snyder marveled.

Two weeks later, Mizzou's first-round loss to North Carolina in the NCAA tournament was Dooling and Gilbert's last game together. Dooling entered the 2000 NBA Draft and became the 10th pick by Orlando, which quickly shipped him to the Los Angeles Clippers. In the NBA, he was never a star but lasted 13 seasons and played for seven teams. He peaked in 2008–09 with New Jersey, averaging 9.7 points and 3.5 assists per game. Dooling played for the Clippers, Heat, Magic, Nets, Bucks, Celtics, and Grizzlies. He spent time as a representative for the players union and worked for a while in Boston's front office. He made more than $30 million in NBA salary, reached the playoffs five times, and played alongside superstars Shaquille O'Neal, Dwyane Wade, Grant Hill, Dwight Howard, and Kevin Garnett. "It was fulfilling for me," Dooling said of his pro career. "I got the full NBA experience."

Meanwhile, Gilbert stuck around in Columbia and produced one of the most prolific careers in Mizzou history. Gilbert's scoring average climbed each season, and by his senior year, he evolved into Snyder's most complete player: a tenacious defender, dangerous shooter, and the team's primary ball handler. Midway through the season, Snyder made Gilbert his point guard, and he helped lead the Tigers to the Elite Eight as a 12 seed in the 2002 NCAA tournament, averaging 17 points and 3.2 assists. Gilbert finished his career ranked seventh on MU's all-time scoring list. His 43 points against Iowa State in 2001—a quadruple-overtime classic—has been eclipsed just three times in team history. He went undrafted but had several productive seasons overseas.

His childhood friend's career reached a second arc at the twilight of his time in the NBA. In 2012, shortly before he was about to rejoin the Celtics for a second season, Dooling suffered a breakdown and was hospitalized in a mental-health facility. For years he had repressed being sexually molested as a child. After undergoing therapy, Dooling found a new purpose. He retired from basketball in 2013 and became a motivational speaker and certified life coach. In 2014 he shared his experiences in his first book, *What's Driving You?: How I Overcame Abuse and Learned to Lead in the NBA*.

"I felt like with my fame and my platform, I thought God was putting me in position to be an advocate to fight for what I believe in," Dooling said. "My primary reason was to raise awareness for sexual abuse and tell my story and how I became a leader in the NBA."

86 Knock, Knock…It's Mizzou

You can pinpoint several milestone moments as the turning point of Mizzou football under Dan Devine. One of those came on September 26, 1959, perhaps more a moment of rich symbolism than great consequence. After the Tigers defeated Big Ten powerhouse Michigan 20–15 in Ann Arbor, Michigan, Devine's team headed to the visitors' locker room at Michigan Stadium, the famed "Big House" of college football. The Tigers discovered something surprising: the door was locked. "Devine just steps up and says, 'Hit it,'" former offensive lineman Ed Blaine remembered.

Half a century later, the image is still crystal clear in Blaine's mind. Teammates Bucky Wegener and Mike Magac followed their coach's orders. "Bucky lowered his shoulder," Blaine said, "and knocked the door in." The Tigers had arrived—and they weren't asking permission or making apologies.

In his memoirs, Devine described a gentler scene, saying his players "took the door off its hinges and laid it on the floor." Either way, the Tigers made their entrance and poured into the locker room to celebrate an important win over the Big Ten school. It was Mizzou's first win over Michigan and first win at a Big Ten stadium since 1953. For years, budgets in the red had forced Mizzou to schedule games like this to help balance the department bank account. This wasn't a particularly great Michigan team, but for a Mizzou program that had scheduled upcoming nonconference games at Penn State, Minnesota, Arkansas, Illinois, and UCLA, to beat the Wolverines on their home field was a statement. To take down their locker room door was another.

Devine, a former assistant coach at Michigan State, the Wolverines' archrival, took extra pleasure in the win. "Fritz

Chrysler was the athletic director at Michigan, and he was really ticked off about the door," Devine wrote. "I was so happy…but I couldn't care less [about the door]. It was his fault nobody had been there to open it for us or we wouldn't have had to take it down."

Blaine said players wondered for years how the door got locked. "Were they trying to frustrate us?" he asked. If so, the ploy didn't work. In Devine's second season in charge, the Tigers gained some credibility with the win and launched into the program's most successful decade.

87 Gary Link: The Ambassador

For years, Gary Link was easy to spot at a Mizzou basketball game. Like he was conducting an orchestra, Link kept his hands in constant motion along the sideline. The longtime radio analyst talked with his hands as much as his mouth. He pointed. He slashed. He dribbled. Sometimes, inadvertently, he smacked.

Sitting courtside at the Kiel Center in St. Louis, Link got especially animated during his first Mizzou-Illinois Braggin' Rights game in 1996. "I'm calling the play, and Link gets excited and his hands go flying," play-by-play voice Mike Kelly recalled. "He hits the corner of my microphone and it flips up and knocks my glasses off my head. I look up at him and he got a little sheepish. We go to break and I say, 'Hey, man, this is a noncontact sport.'"

The Mizzou lifer must be excused. Link's passion for Tigers basketball could barely be contained. A high-scoring 6'5" guard from Lindbergh High in St. Louis, Link arrived at Mizzou in 1970 and became a valuable role player alongside stars John Brown and Al Eberhard. Brown and Eberhard are two of four players in team history to average double-digit rebounds for their career—a statistic Link proudly credits to...Link. "Somebody had to miss a hell of a lot of shots for those guys to get all those rebounds," he joked.

With Brown off to the NBA, Link had his best season in 1973–74 as Norm Stewart's senior cocaptain, averaging a career-best 17.3 points per game. But the Tigers tumbled in the Big 8

Link prepares for action in 2006.

standings, finishing 12–14. "I scored a lot of points, but you know what? I had a lot more fun my sophomore and junior year," Link said. "Basketball's a team sport. What made it harder was guys were quitting. Al and I were the captains, and my God, we were trying to keep the team together. It was an emotional year. My stomach hurt the whole year. I really felt like I let the whole team down. Coach, Al, and myself." The season bothered Link so much, he skipped out on the postseason team banquet, leading to a brief falling out with Stewart. "I was young, dumb, and mad," he said.

Link returned to St. Louis, where for years he helped run his family's commercial construction business. Eventually, his alma mater pulled him back. In 1996 Missouri needed a new radio analyst to work with Kelly. Former Tigers players Jon Sundvold and Jim Kennedy had served as analysts in past seasons, and Stewart wanted another former player to take the job. He reached out to Link. "I told him, 'Nothing against Jon or Jimmy, but you've got that good journalism school. Maybe you should have a professional call the game,'" Link said. "Coach Stewart would say, 'That's a great idea, Gary. As soon as one of your J-school students plays for me, he can do it.'" Link took the job, forming a partnership with Kelly that listeners would hear for the next 20 years. Link was Kelly's radio partner through the 2016–17 season, until he parted ways with his alma mater after an administration regime change.

Before Link's first game on the broadcast, a home win over Chicago State, Kelly handed him a tape recorder and told him to interview the visiting coach for the pregame show. "I said, 'OK,'" Link recalled. "Then I went back to Mike. 'Show me how to turn it on.'" He continued, "I listen back to some of those early games, and wow, I was brutal. I'm not sure my mom would listen to some of those games. It was just baptism under fire."

After a dreadful loss at Kansas State in 1998, Link approached his former coach for the postgame interview. Link chose his words…poorly. "They just hammered us," he said. "So after the game, I go to ask my two or three questions to Coach Stewart. He comes walking over to me. He was ashen. I said, 'Coach, when you've been around as long as you have, you're going to have games like this.'" Oops. "He goes, 'No, Gary, you shouldn't,'" Link said. "And he just turned and walked away." Radio silence. "Back to you, Mike!"

Over time, Link found his voice on the airwaves and played the impassioned Xs and Os expert alongside the straight-shooting Kelly. In 2000 Link joined the athletics department as special advisor to the AD and became an integral ambassador for his cherished program.

On the air, Link nurtured a unique chemistry with his long-time partner. They could finish each other's thoughts. "We see things the same way," Kelly said. "We both spent so much time around Coach Stewart that we both learned the game through his eyes. From a play-by-play standpoint, the thing you want your color analyst to do is be prepared. I've never, ever had to worry about Gary Link being unprepared for a game. First of all, he lives the game. He's thinking about it all the time. He's got volumes of information in his mind or that he's written down. The bigger challenge for me is staying out of his way, making sure I'm calling the play and not trying to add anything that would take away from what he might say."

"It's been a blast," Link said. "It keeps you close to the game. I've worked with five coaches, and each one is unique in their own way. They know I'm a Mizzou homer and I'm proud of it."

No different than his senior year at Mizzou, the losses crushed Link's basketball soul, and the wins stretched a smile across his face. The ambassador lived and died with each possession, each game, each season. "Oh my gosh, absolutely," he said. "We're down eight with two minutes to go, I believe we can get three stops and win the game. I'm still into it until the very end. I hurt after those games as much now [as] when I played. I really do."

88 Phil Pressey: The Playmaker

Nobody in Missouri basketball history set up his teammates for more baskets than point guard Phil Pressey. Remarkably, he set the school assists record in just three seasons. Perhaps more remarkably, the 5'11" playmaker from Texas might have been his era's least appreciated player.

Pressey entered his junior year in 2012 as the preseason SEC Player of the Year after leading the Big 12 with 6.4 assists per game as a sophomore. A point guard, though, is only as good as the talent around him, and as the Tigers entered the second season of Coach Frank Haith's regime, Pressey was the lone player to return from a nucleus that had won 30 games the previous season. Gone were seniors Marcus Denmon, Kim English, and Ricardo Ratliffe, the team's three leading scorers in 2011–12. Michael Dixon was back but never played a game as a junior and later transferred to Memphis. Key backup Matt Pressey, Phil's older brother, had departed, along with reserve forward Steve Moore.

As a junior, Pressey became more of a scorer, by necessity at times. He took more shots and his shooting percentages slipped, but he remained an elite playmaker, leading the SEC in assists (7.1) while feeding a revamped cast of teammates. Without an established clutch scorer on the roster, Pressey tried taking on that role. Mixed results ensued during an uneven season. His defense took off some nights too.

Still, as an offensive playmaker, he's peerless in Mizzou history. He led the Tigers in scoring seven times as a junior and had six games with 10 or more assists, including a school-record 19 in a loss at UCLA. He finished his career with school records for assists (580) and steals (196). "I say he was the best point guard in Missouri history," English said. "I know Larry Drew and Doc Hardy and all the great point guards that we had, but Phil Pressey was the best. He was just a dynamic guard."

English added, "For what he was dealt [his junior year], the kid had to play with literally zero returners his next year. And he still broke the Missouri assist record in three years and led them to the NCAA tournament with some key losses."

Everyone remembers the UCLA game in 2012, but Pressey had a signature performance six days earlier against Illinois in a game that illustrated his value to the Tigers. As the Tigers were still trying to identify their core scorers, Pressey shot just 3-of-19 from the floor but handed out 11 assists, pulled down seven rebounds, and scored eight of MU's final 12 points in a nine-point win over No. 10 Illinois.

Mizzou was one-and-done in the NCAA tournament during Pressey's sophomore and junior seasons, but he was hardly at fault. In the stunning first-round upset to No. 15 seed Norfolk State in 2012, Pressey scored 20 points and handed out eight assists. A year later, in a loss to Colorado State, he led the Tigers with 20 points and seven assists. He played a combined 72 minutes in the two games and turned the ball over just four times.

"Phil is one of the best passers I've ever been around," Haith said after the 2012–13 season, which proved to be Pressey's last in a college uniform. "He sees things happening that others don't see. That's his biggest strength, and that will be his calling card when given a chance to play in the NBA."

Pressey got that chance, but not the easy way. He entered the 2013 NBA Draft as a junior but wasn't selected. He signed with the Boston Celtics that summer, then made the roster as a backup point guard. After two seasons with the organization, he joined Portland as a free agent in 2015 then bounced around the league with several franchises—with his Mizzou records safe and sound and nobody close to matching his career marks.

89 We're No. 1

As he strolled into Spanky's Sports Zone for his weekly radio show, Gary Pinkel soaked in the standing ovation and cracked a smile. The fans roared, "We're No. 1! We're No. 1!" It was Sunday, November 26, 2007. Hangovers across the state had just started to subside.

Less than 48 hours had passed since Saturday's epic 36–28 victory over Kansas at Arrowhead Stadium. As expected, the Tigers were rewarded in the national polls. For the first time in nearly half a century, Missouri was the No. 1 team in the land. Only a few fans in the audience that night were old enough to remember the last time Mizzou had held the No. 1 ranking, a one-week stay on top of the Associated Press and UPI coaches polls in 1960. "Obviously, the fans and players that played here over the years and the loyal fans that we have, and alumni, everybody gets a piece of that, and they enjoy it," Pinkel said of the No. 1 ranking.

In 1960 the second-ranked Tigers had climbed to No. 1 after improving to 9–0 with a 41–19 win at Oklahoma. Also that weekend, No. 1 Minnesota fell to Purdue, clearing a spot at the top for the Tigers. It was a short stay. Mizzou's perfect season ended a week later with a 23–7 loss to Kansas, a victory the Jayhawks later forfeited for using ineligible player Bert Coan.

There was a sense of symmetry with the Tigers' next poll take-over. In 2007 the victory over No. 2 Kansas, coupled with No. 1 LSU's loss to Arkansas, pushed one-loss Mizzou to No. 1 in the AP poll and the Bowl Championship Series standings. In 1960 the Tigers earned the top ranking by beating Oklahoma, then lost it by losing to Kansas. In 2007 Mizzou followed the win over Kansas… with a loss to Oklahoma. The Big 12 Championship Game defeat eliminated the Tigers from the national championship picture. But for a week, the Tigers had captured the nation's attention. Quarterback Chase Daniel adorned the cover of *Sports Illustrated.*

Eight years separated the Missouri basketball team's two appearances at the top of the polls. In 1982 Norm Stewart's Tigers beat Oklahoma by 20 points on January 23 to reach 16–0 and climb to No. 1 for the first time in team history. North Carolina had been No. 1 but lost to Wake Forest. The Tigers took over the top spot on January 25, becoming the first Big 8 team in 23 years to lead the poll. "On one hand, I could take it or leave it and not worry about it," Stewart said at the time. "But on the other hand, why shouldn't we have it? Our players work as hard as any, and we're 16–0, so why not?"

The fun lasted two weeks. Nebraska came into the Hearnes Center on February 6 and stunned the Tigers by 16 points. Mizzou's star-studded team of Ricky Frazier, Jon Sundvold, and Steve Stipanovich had won 19 in a row but struggled against a Huskers team that would finish fourth in the Big 8. "I read in the paper this morning that Missouri was bigger than us and that we didn't have anyone to contain Stipanovich," Nebraska forward Ray Collins told reporters after the game. "They said the game wouldn't be as close as it was in Lincoln. It wasn't." The Tigers would capture their third of four straight Big 8 championships but lose in the NCAA tournament regional semifinals.

In 1990 Stewart's fourth-ranked team toppled No. 1 Kansas on January 20 to improve to 14–1, and when the rest of the top seven AP teams lost, Mizzou vaulted to No. 1. Stewart took the ranking in stride. "This is a college town, and we've got a lot of things that are No. 1 at Missouri," he said. "The basketball team is one of them, so it's great to get the recognition."

The Tigers stayed on top until a seven-point loss at Kansas State but reclaimed the No. 1 ranking after taking down top-ranked Kansas in a No. 1 vs. No. 2 showdown—in Lawrence,

Kansas, no less—and No. 11 Oklahoma in a five-day span. As of 2018, the win at Kansas was one of only four times Missouri had beaten the nation's No. 1 team—and the only time on the road. Missouri quickly slipped to No. 3 after losing at Oklahoma, then imploded down the stretch, losing four of its final five games.

90 The Warhorse

Mizzou's Detroit connection in the 1980s delivered some of the era's best players, including Lynn Hardy, Doug Smith, and Nathan Buntin. Then there was Jeff Warren, a lanky 6'8" post player whose game was anything but flashy, and far from dynamic. He wasn't a particularly prolific offensive player, but Warren found ways to contribute to winning basketball and in some ways embodied the classic Norm Stewart player: tough, smart, selfless. He was tall and skilled, no doubt, but the other qualities made him a favorite among coaches, teammates, fans and, yes, opponents. Stewart's best teams always seemed to have at least one Jeff Warren. From 1989 to 1993, Stewart had the original.

"The Antlers had a nickname for Jeff," said former MU teammate John Burns, referring to the famous student fan group. "They called him the Warhorse. Because that's what he was. He wouldn't quit as a player."

There was no quit in Warren in 2014 when lymphoma attacked his body, but the disease was too much to overcome. He died in May 2015 at 44. Warren's death was jarring for those who watched him play and admired his relentless approach on the court. "He was at peace with [the disease]," Burns said. "But he said, 'I'm not going to quit,' even though he knew his time was coming."

"He was loyal as could be as a friend," Burns added. "He could keep going on and on and it wouldn't matter what was going on with him. That was remarkable about him. He was very kind-hearted and very spiritual throughout this fight."

Warren, who averaged 6.7 points and 4.4 rebounds per game during his four-year career, was among Stewart's favorite players. "It's a long list of wonderful guys that I had," Stewart told the *Kansas City Star*. "If he's not at the top, he's close."

Warren, from Litchfield, Michigan, had his best season at Mizzou as a junior in 1991–92, averaging 9.6 points and 6.0 rebounds. That season, he set the team record for consecutive field goals made, 24, set over four games, one short of the NCAA record. He ended his career as the program's most accurate shooter of all time at 61.4 percent (since eclipsed by Ricardo Ratliffe in 2011–12) and still holds two of the team's top 10 single-season field goal percentages, 67.6 in 1990–91 and 62.8 in 1991–92. He didn't let opponents have it easy, either: his 345 career fouls rank sixth all-time.

"He did all the dirty work," Burns said. "He would rebound. He played defense. I always gave him trouble about fouling all the time.… He just did everything. He made us better. That's the type of guy he was personality-wise. He wasn't, 'Hey, look at me.' It was more like, 'What can I do to get better?'"

Warren, also a three-time Academic All–Big 8 selection, closed his career leading the Tigers to the 1993 Big 8 tournament in Kansas City, where he'd ultimately make his home with his wife and two sons. He left a beloved winner in more ways than one.

91 Coach Izzy and the Hoops Pioneers

Their names don't resonate with modern fans. Their jerseys don't hang from the Mizzou Arena rafters. But long before the Stewarts and Stipos and Sundvolds and Peelers defined the modern era of Missouri basketball, the program took shape in the early 20th century, built on the backs of pioneer players and coaches.

The first Mizzou head basketball coach? That would be Dr. Axel Isadore Anderson. His claim to fame? He only coached one season consisting of 16 games but scored two victories against the man who invented the sport—on consecutive March days.

March 11, 1907: Missouri 34, Kansas 31
March 12, 1907: Missouri 34, Kansas 12
Dr. Isadore Anderson 2, Dr. James Naismith 0

Before he coached the Tigers, Anderson was a football star at Mizzou and later served as an assistant coach. When the school looked to launch a basketball program, he landed the assignment—and was an instant success.

The *Missouri Alumnus* reported in 1924:

'Izzy,' as he was popularly known by the entire student body, was one of the greatest football players Missouri had ever had. Although he had never played basketball he was a keen student of the game and the results he obtained vindicated their choice of him as Missouri's first coach. Missouri's big squad practiced for about one month before the first game, but long before the end of that time the general make-up of the team had been determined by Coach Anderson.

When Central College, the first team to call on Missouri, came to Rothwell Gymnasium the night of January 11, 1907, an enthusiastic crowd of students was on hand to greet the first game and the new team. Missouri started off by giving Central a terrible drubbing to the tune of 65 to 5.

Anderson spent just one year coaching the team. He'd later work as a college football referee but made his mark as an anesthesiologist for nearly 50 years before his death in 1961.

What about Mizzou's first All-American? That would be Fred Williams. Doubling as a high jumper on the track team, the center was described as a "long distance goal-shooter" by the *Savitar* and was widely considered the best player in the Missouri Valley Conference. Sadly, Williams didn't live to see past 40. He was killed in a car crash in 1937.

Who was Missouri's first great coach? That was undoubtedly Walter Meanwell, an innovative Englishman from Leeds, England, whose reputation preceded his arrival in 1917. In six years at Wisconsin, Meanwell claimed first place in the Big Ten (then the Western Conference) four times and won 101 of 110 games overall. He coached just two seasons at Missouri, going 17–1 both years, both ending with Missouri Valley championships, the first league titles in the young program's history. Known for a highly structured offense based on short, crisp passes, Meanwell also believed in tight zone defenses. He doubled as Missouri's athletics director.

"Several new features of playing introduced by Dr. W. E. Meanwell did much to strengthen the Tigers in their offensive," the *Missouri Alumnus* reported in 1918 after his coaching debut, a 40-point win over Tulsa. "The short pass with both hands was used throughout the game, enabling the Tigers to work the ball around their opponents in bewildering fashion."

The article continued: "Another change introduced by Doctor Meanwell is a new long-distance toss for the basket. The success the Tigers forwards attained in this new style of goal throwing was proof of its efficiency. A new method of passing the ball by bouncing it on the floor was also introduced in the game."

Meanwell returned to Wisconsin after his brief stay at Missouri and won another four league titles in 14 years. Largely recognized for his work at Wisconsin, the 5'6" coach some called the Wizard or Little Doctor was inducted into the Naismith Memorial Basketball Hall of Fame in 1959.

92 "Fight, Tiger"

Missouri's student body needed a jolt in the 1940s. Around campus, students believed that World War II had stripped away a sense of school spirit. In 1946, the first season of Don Faurot's second venture as football coach, the school had a solution: MU held a contest to come up with a new school fight song. The tune would make its debut in time for the homecoming game against Kansas.

The Friday night before the season finale, students gathered at Brewer Fieldhouse to hear the winner. Fifty-two songs were submitted. "Over a radio program halfway through the rally, it was announced that 'Fight, Tiger' was the winner," campus humor magazine *Missouri Showme* wrote. "Copies of the words were distributed to the students, and as the band swung into the music, the song was sung hesitatingly through the first verse, but with gusto and enthusiasm as the words became familiar."

Robert Karsch, a doctoral candidate and the organist at First Presbyterian Church, composed the music. He'd go on to become a political science professor at MU. Donald MacKay, an undergraduate, wrote the lyrics, just 55 words in total:

Fight, Tiger, fight for old Mizzou.
Right behind you, everyone is with you.
Break the line and follow down the field.
And you'll be on the top, upon the top.
Fight, Tiger, you will always win.
Proudly keep the colors flying skyward.
In the end, we'll win the victory.
So Tiger, fight for Old Mizzou!

"I sat down at the piano and worked out the tune in about two hours," Karsch later told the *Missouri Alumnus*. "I wrote the music in E-flat because horns play most easily in that key. I also kept the range narrow so no part would be too high or too low for any voice."

"He told me he had some music he thought was good enough to win the fight song contest and asked me to try putting words to it," MacKay told the magazine. "I was pretty excited when I got the call telling me that our song had been chosen. The prize was a combination radio-phonograph."

There was just one problem with the prize. "I guess it never occurred to the contest planners that two persons would collaborate," MacKay said. "It cost me $35 to win the contest, because I bought Bob's half of the prize."

Their collaboration edged "Roar On, Missouri" and "Fight On for Old Mizzou," and became a staple at every Mizzou football and basketball game for decades to come.

93 Marching Mizzou

Their drumbeats and brassy notes provide the soundtrack to fall Saturdays in Columbia. They are the members of Marching Mizzou, the school's 300-strong marching band, the largest student organization on campus and one of the oldest.

For more than a century, they've kicked off each and every home football game with a meticulously orchestrated routine that Mizzou loyalists know by heart. The game-day staples are there every week: "The Missouri Waltz," "Tiger Rag," "Old Missouri," "Every True Son/Fight, Tiger," and "Eye of the Tiger," Marching Mizzou's unmistakable interpretation of Survivor's cut from the *Rocky* movies.

In 1885 the military assigned Major General Enoch Crowder to commission a military-style university band, thus launching the University Cadet Band, one of the first of its kind on a college campus. The band, playing mostly classical tunes by Beethoven, Mozart, and other prominent composers, became more popular and soon made its debut on a football field. Under the watch of directors George Venable and later George Wilson, the Cadet Band evolved from its military roots and toward its modern form.

In the 1950s women were allowed to join the band, by then known as the Big M of the Midwest. In 1957 the group enlisted female baton twirlers, the first rendition of the now-famous Golden Girls, who by the 1970s dropped their batons for sequins and choreographed dance routines.

Under Director Charles Emmons, Flip Tigers became the band's signature pregame tradition, debuting at the 1960 Orange Bowl. Members form the word *Mizzou* while playing the fight song, then morph into the word *Tigers*.

The full band typically travels to one road football game each year and sends its skeleton pep band, Mini Mizzou, to other games. Every so often, the band makes a major trip, most recently to Dublin, Ireland, for the 2012 St. Patrick's Day Parade.

But every fall, you can count on Marching Mizzou for at least six Saturday performances on their home stage, blasting their most familiar tunes. In 2016 Erin Cooper became the first female director of Marching Mizzou in the band's history, the only female director in the SEC, and Marching Mizzou's 16th director overall in its 131st year of playing tunes for the university.

Members of the esteemed Marching Mizzou enter Faurot Field with fanfare.

94 Barry Odom: From Train Wreck to Conductor

Ricky Hunley knew there was something special about Barry Odom when he coached him at Mizzou in the 1990s. Odom wasn't the biggest or fastest linebacker on the team. Staying healthy was always a challenge for the Oklahoman. "We threw his little ass in there, and he'd just go full speed, no matter how big the other guy was," Hunley said years later. "He was just a train wreck."

Torn ligaments in both knees couldn't stop Odom from finishing his career fourth on Mizzou's all-time tackles list. Neither could a handful of other injuries. Like the time in 1999 when he slipped on the locker room tile floor at Memphis and busted his eye open. He needed four stitches shortly before kickoff. He still managed to make the game's first tackle—and shredded all the ligaments in his left thumb on the play.

"He was the epitome of a middle linebacker," former MU defensive lineman Steve Erickson said. "He was tough. Wrist, knee, shoulder, ankle. It didn't matter. He was going to be out there playing, whether he was exhausted or sick. With that mental toughness, he led us by example. He was on the field for every practice, every play that he physically could [be]."

"He was the constant leader," Hunley said. "I just wish he had the size so he could have made it to the next level."

Fifteen years later, Hunley learned even more about Odom: the guy could coach too. After the 2011 season, Odom gambled on his career when he left the safety and comfort of serving on Gary Pinkel's defensive staff at Mizzou for a more rewarding but riskier position: defensive coordinator at Memphis. He helped transform the downtrodden program into a top 25, 10-win team by 2014, with Hunley on his staff coaching the defensive linemen. Like so many peers who worked alongside Odom or against him, Hunley figured it was only a matter of time before Odom landed his first head coaching job.

That happened sooner than most imagined—in the SEC, no less. After a season back on Pinkel's staff as defensive coordinator, Odom was announced as Pinkel's successor on December 4, 2015, becoming the 32nd head coach in Mizzou history. At 39, Odom became MU's youngest head coach since Warren Powers, who was 37 when his debut season kicked off in 1978.

Odom's only previous head coaching experience came at Columbia's Rock Bridge High School—more than a decade before Missouri athletics director Mack Rhoades picked Odom over more seasoned candidates. "He is the right person," Rhoades said. "This is the right time. This is the perfect fit to lead our program to that next level."

When hired, Odom became the ninth-youngest head coach among the 128 teams at the Football Bowl Subdivision level. Odom's defense was outstanding in 2015 despite Mizzou's 5–7 record. The Tigers allowed no more than two touchdowns in eight of 12 games. In the SEC, only Alabama allowed fewer points per game during the regular season.

But it wasn't just his on-field credentials that landed Odom the top job at his alma mater. Widely admired by players and peers, Odom had spent years preparing for the opportunity, collecting stacks of notes he'd taken during countless staff and department meetings over a decade at Mizzou. From the time he joined Mizzou's staff as a lowly administrative assistant in 2003, he worked closely under Pinkel, one meticulous no-nonsense coach learning from the master of the minutia. To hear Odom explain his rise from the bottom of Mizzou's staff to his place as Pinkel's successor, it was a lifetime in the making. Destiny, perhaps.

When the 2016 kicked off, Odom became the fourth Missouri graduate to serve as MU's head coach since the 20th century began.

The first was a legend: Don Faurot. The second was a footnote: Chauncey Simpson. The third was a disaster: Woody Widenhofer.

"At the end of the day, the place you graduate college from is going to have a special place in your heart," said Odom, who played for the Tigers from 1996 to 1999. "Missouri's an unbelievable, tremendous state. The people of Missouri are the best. I look forward to representing them.... This is where I wanted to be, without question."

Odom's first season was loaded with learning experiences for the first-time college head coach. The Tigers led the SEC in total offense, but the defense struggled to embrace a new scheme and had bigger problems tackling ball carriers. Mizzou allowed the most yards in the conference and finished 4–8. Odom's Tigers opened 2017 picked to finish last in the SEC East, but his expectations never dimmed. "When you win four games, guys, believe me, it hurts your soul," he said before the season. "And that's where I was at. So you figure out how to fix it, whether you inherited the problems or you had the problems on your watch. That's the job of a coach. That's why they call you 'Coach.' Go fix it."

In 2017 Odom's Tigers began the year 1–5 and appeared overmatched in troubling home losses to Purdue and Auburn. After five straight losses, Odom lit a fire to inspire his team—literally. During a team meeting, Odom used a can of lighter fluid to torch a stack of papers that included scouting reports and other remnants of the team's ugly start, a symbolic gesture that became the season's crossroads. The Tigers finished the regular season with six consecutive wins and earned their first bowl invitation in three years, a spot in the Texas Bowl against Texas. The Longhorns were the better team in Houston, winning 33–16, but Odom earned some validity—and a contract extension—with his team's turnaround. His 11 wins were the most for a Missouri coach through his first two seasons since Powers in 1978–79.

95 Corey Tate Beats Buzzer, Crushes Kansas

One of the most famous shots ever to leave the hands of a Mizzou basketball player came in a losing season by a role player who will forever be remembered for his game-winning basket on February 4, 1997: Corey Tate.

Few could have expected a thriller on this Tuesday night in Columbia, much less a Mizzou victory against Kansas. Norm Stewart's team was just 11–10, short on high-profile talent and winless in four games against ranked opponents, albeit by only 13 points collectively. Kansas, meanwhile, was 22–0, ranked No. 1 and teeming with star power, led by center Raef LaFrentz, point guard Jacque Vaughn, and small forward Paul Pierce. It was Mizzou's first of three games in a nine-day span against top-six opponents.

But a classic Border War showdown soon unfolded. Stewart's Tigers traded leads and scraps with Roy Williams's cast of future NBA millionaires, taking the Jayhawks to double overtime. Once there, with time running out and the score locked at 94–94, magic ensued.

Mizzou leading scorers Kelly Thames and Derek Grimm had fouled out, leaving Stewart with a lineup of Dibi Ray, Jason Sutherland, Tyron Lee, L. Dee Murdock, and Tate, the 6'4" senior swingman whose star-crossed career had been defined by injuries— until that night.

As the seconds ticked away, the Tigers labored to find an open shot in the halfcourt. Lee held the ball on the wing and tried to make a move to the basket, but Vaughn reached in and picked his pocket. Vaughn poked the ball loose but couldn't secure it.

St. Louis native Bob Carpenter had the assignment for the TV broadcast that night, sitting alongside analyst and former

Mizzou All-American Jon Sundvold. "Tyron Lee, dribble penetration," Carpenter said, his voice rising as the seconds disappeared. "Vaughn had it…"

The ball trickled across the floor for a few bounces and found its way into Tate's hands. Tate was coming off a career-best 22-point game against Kansas State. To that point, he had 12 points against the Jayhawks.

"Missouri gets it…"

Tate scooped up the ball and, as he fell back to his left, flicked a 16-foot jumper from just behind the foul line.

"*Corey Tate! Corey Tate!*"

The shot rattled home with 5.6 seconds left. Barring a meltdown on the defensive end—UCLA's Tyus Edney had shattered Mizzou's dreams with less time on the clock just three years earlier—Tate would have a new moment to define his career. Indeed. LaFrentz couldn't get off a shot as time expired. Missouri 96. Kansas 94. Corey Tate, Border War icon. His teammates mobbed him on the court.

"I'm going to cherish this," he later said. "That's why you go to college: to do something everyone will remember you by." He added, "It was a dream come true, a playground dream."

It was easily the greatest highlight during an otherwise forgettable Mizzou season. The Tigers finished with a losing record (16–17) for the first time since 1979. Kansas wouldn't lose again until the NCAA tournament regional semifinals.

The magnitude of the upset wasn't lost on Stewart minutes after it happened. "I've seen all the [Kansas] teams since 1952—and I wasn't an expert analyst in '52 like I am now," he told reporters. "And this team ranks with any of them. That's a great team."

Eighteen years later, Tate came back to the place where he made his magical shot and joined the Mizzou coaching staff under head coach Kim Anderson, who was an assistant under Stewart during Tate's playing career. Tate's game-winner against the Jayhawks was mentioned in the first sentence in his introductory news release—a shot never forgotten. "He talks about it a lot," Anderson said in 2015, shortly after hiring Tate. "Actually, [his wife] Nicole was here the other day; I think he's probably talked about it quite a bit around their house. You're always going to remember him for that shot. That was history. If you ask him about it, he'll tell you all about it. And he should. I don't blame him."

"Did it change my life? My legacy? You can say that," said Tate, who lasted only a year on Mizzou's staff before leaving for Saint Louis University. "I took it in stride and tried to make the best out of it when people still talk to me about it. But I always say that play was never drawn up for me."

A few years ago Tate ran into Vaughn, who became a coach in the NBA. Did Tate's shot come up? Of course. "He acknowledged me," Tate said, "and told me, 'Man, you ruined our perfect season.'"

96 Columbia's Downtown Dining Treasures

There are dozens of Columbia restaurants to satisfy your game-day appetite on a Saturday in the fall or a wintry evening after a Mizzou basketball game. But there are only a few that qualify as CoMo institutions. Perhaps just two: Booches and Shakespeare's, two local landmarks smothered with their own personality and, more important, home to the town's signature dishes.

No trip to Columbia is complete without a cheeseburger at Booches Billiard Hall, at 110 S. Ninth Street, a local treasure founded during the Chester A. Arthur administration. Paul Blucher Venable opened Booches in 1884 on Broadway—his nickname was

Booch—before new ownership moved the business to its current Ninth Street location in 1928.

Just remember to bring cash—no frills and no credit cards at Booches—and don't expect any of those modern extravagances like plates or silverware. The greasy burgers are served on wax paper and nothing else. No french fries, either, bub. Just stick to Booches' holy trinity and you'll survive: burgers, beer, and billiards. And don't ignore the wall decor, either. Absolutely "no sniveling," as the sign reads. Instead, feel free to engage in the rules of the house: "Feasting, imbibing and debauchery."

Less ancient but no less popular is Booches' Ninth Street neighbor, Shakespeare's Pizza, founded in 1973 and across the street from Mizzou's famed School of Journalism. Thick, crunchy crust, oozy mozzarella, and fresh meat and veggie toppings define the cherished slices of goodness. Shakespeare's opened two roomier locations in the 2000s, one on the south edge of town, another on the west side, but the downtown original remained the most authentic edition—until it was demolished in 2015. Owners temporarily moved the local favorite a block west on Eighth Street, then rebuilt the original as the ground floor in a multifloor building for offices and housing. The new store at the old location opened in 2016. Ninth Street, Eighth Street, it doesn't matter where the pies are cooked for Mizzou fans. As the store's slogan goes, "It's the pizza, stupid."

Booches and Shakespeare's, like the Tigers, are part of Mizzou culture—without the disappointment and heartache. Heartburn? Possibly.

97 The Columns

It's a great place to sit and study or take a nap on a sunny afternoon. It's the ideal backdrop for a family photo on homecoming weekend. Need a meeting place on campus? The Columns on Francis Quadrangle on the Missouri campus no longer serve their original purpose, but they're far from useless.

They're pillars—literally—of a campus that's grown through three centuries but hasn't lost touch with its past self. The six columns originally supported Academic Hall, home of the campus's administrative offices, completed in 1843. Built from limestone secured from the Hinkson Creek Valley, the Columns were the last thing standing when a fire raged through Academic Hall on a snowy Saturday evening on January 9, 1892. The university's curators initially voted to remove the Columns, but a local backlash saved the six towering structures. They live on and make for a picturesque setting overlooking the rest of the quad. Over time, they've come to be the most identifiable image of the campus.

At the beginning of every fall semester, the school hosts Tiger Walk, inviting the freshmen to take part in the ritual of walking south through the Columns to signify their entrance into college.

"Never will we forget the opposing dignity and solemnity of those six tall, grim gray sentinels, the columns," the *Savitar* reported in 1905. "How silently, yet faithfully, they seem to stand and watch over their charges, the surrounding buildings. When will their vigil cease? Not until they have crumbled away and been forgotten let us earnestly hope that such whenever be the case let them live forever!"

98 Rock M

It's among the simplest, most unique sights in college football: the grassy hill behind the north end zone of Faurot Field, adorned with sharp, white rocks in the shape of a capital *M*. The Rock M.

Those jagged chunks of whitewashed rock are literally pains in the butt for a three-hour football game, but they give the stadium its distinct look, shaped in a trademark insignia that's gone unspoiled by modern marketing or Nike branding. The Rock M remains the rare commercial-free billboard, a link to Mizzou's past when letters were good enough for logos and didn't require fancy fonts or modern imagery.

Made from leftover rocks from the stadium's original construction in the 1920s, the *M* is 95 feet tall and 90 feet wide. Every August, freshmen gather for the traditional painting of the rocks, applying a fresh coat of shimmer for the upcoming season.

The Rock M made its debut for the 1927 season opener on October 1 of that year, against Kansas State. The Tigers won 13–6 and went on to capture the Missouri Valley Conference championship. "Five hundred freshmen joined hands and encircled the cinder track in a single line while the band played 'Ole Missouri' in the center of the field," the *Savitar* reported in 1928. "The pennants of all the Missouri Valley fluttered and danced above the stadium on the long line at the open end of the gridiron. A huge stone M—the work of the Frosh the night before—loomed up white and threatening against the embankment."

For several years, senior players marched to the hill at the conclusion of the home finale and picked out a rock for a souvenir, then climbed on their teammates' shoulders for a celebratory charity ride into the locker room, hoisting the rock high.

99The Antlers

Love them or hate them, they're not going anywhere. They'll get to the arena before you and outlast your stay. Formed in 1976, the Antlers have been attending Mizzou basketball games longer than Norm Stewart coached the team. Think about that for a moment. Stewart coached the Tigers for 32 years. The 2017–18 season marked 42 years since Antlers founders Jeff Gordon and Rob Banning turned cheering and jeering into an art form. That's what you call longevity.

Of course, membership in the all-male student fan group turns over from year to year. Their seating location changes too. But their calling remains true from one decade to the next. The Antlers, named after Lily Tomlin's "Antler Dance" from a *Saturday Night Live* sketch, grew in membership over the years as more than 20 hecklers filled the seats in Section 16-A at the Hearnes Center. "We're tougher than the Duke fans," former Antler Paul Stoecklin told the *St. Louis Post-Dispatch* in a lengthy 1987 profile. "They may outnumber us, but nobody plays more mind games than we do. That's what we're all about."

The Antlers' most infamous antics have been well-documented:

In 1987 they sent well-traveled Kansas Coach Larry Brown a shirt with VAGABOND emblazoned on the front. A good sport, the head Jayhawk wore it on the Hearnes floor during pregame warmups. The Antlers serenaded Brown to the tune of the "Battle Hymn of the Republic": "Glory, glory Hallelujah. Don't let Larry Brown fool ya. He says he'll stay but then he'll go. That we know for sure. The coach is moving on."

In 1988 Iowa State's Jeff Grayer went into the stands to confront the Antlers before tip-off after they taunted him, calling the

Big 8's top scorer "Mama's boy." That earned the Antlers a scolding from AD Jack Lengyel.

In 1990 Arkansas coach Nolan Richardson called out the Antlers for taunting Oliver Miller, the Razorbacks' well-fed center. "We've got great fans, but these people are crazy," Richardson said. "I've never seen anything like this in the country." Richardson took umbrage with the Antlers sprinkling the Razorbacks with ice and water, saying they might have damaged his "$900 suit."

When Arkansas revisited Hearnes two years later, the Antlers made nice with Richardson and presented the Head Hog with a cheap knockoff suit. "The Antlers are great for basketball—inside the building," Richardson later said. "Outside of the building where teams are coming in, I'm afraid of that." Alas, Mizzou suspended two Antlers after the game for waving a decapitated hog's head too close to Arkansas players.

In 1995 Mizzou's administration had had enough of the antics and suspended the Antlers, booting them from their courtside seats—only to allow them to return to 16-A the next season.

Tension lingered between the Antlers and AD Mike Alden, and in 2014 the group was kicked out of consecutive games for language deemed inappropriate. "When we see people that don't reflect the values of what we do as an institution, certainly those things are disappointing to us as a university," Alden said after the second ejection. "We just want to make sure folks represent the university with class."

Eventually the Antlers returned to their seats amongst the thinning crowd of students as the program struggled in the early years of the SEC. In 2017, as new coach Cuonzo Martin collected one blue-chip recruit after another—led by the Porter brothers, Michael and Jontay—the Antlers needled long-lost students who were sure to repopulate Mizzou Arena that fall, posting a cheat sheet on social media, including the signature cheers and location of the scoreboard.

100 We're Going to Harpo's!

The warning came from the public address announcer urging fans to stay off Faurot Field. Fat chance. It was October 23, 2010, also known as the Last Day the Goal Post Died. The celebration at Memorial Stadium began as the seconds ticked away and Mizzou had—finally—defeated Oklahoma, ranked No. 1 in the Bowl Championship Series standings. Fans headed for the goal post, yanked it to the turf, and exercised the ritual performed occasionally over the past four decades. There was only one destination for that goal post: 29 S. Tenth Street, also known as the home of Harpo's.

Opened in 1971 by recent Mizzou grad Dennis Harper, the cherished watering hole somehow became the deconstruction site for toppled goal posts, one of the great time-honored traditions—maybe the greatest—for a football program and a fan base known mostly for their Saturdays ruined by fifth downs and kicked passes. But every few years, something magical unfolded on Faurot Field, and that towering goal post became the casualty. It came down when the Tigers upset Texas in 1997, when they beat rival Kansas in 2002, and when they snapped a 24-game losing streak to Nebraska in 2003. Stadium officials got smart after the 2010 Oklahoma game and installed collapsible goal posts that now survive the occasional field storm.

But where did it all begin? A generation earlier, the goal post first found its way to Harpo's in 1972 after a 20–17 victory over No. 7 Colorado when fans lugged their victim 17 blocks (roughly 1.2 miles) to the downtown bar for the postgame party. Soon enough, Harper figured out a strategy to help the process go smoothly without wrecking his bar. "I started handing out hacksaws," Harper once told *Mizzou*, the alumni association magazine. "They would parade downtown and say, 'Let's go to Harpo's!' They'd want to bring the goal posts inside, which would be a disaster. You could give them 10 hacksaws, and they'd just hack away out in the street."

Harper sold the bar in 2010 to a couple Mizzou grads, and when the goal post showed up later that fall after the homecoming victory over Oklahoma, the new owners were prepared. *St. Louis Post-Dispatch* columnist Bryan Burwell, tickled by the postgame ritual, followed the horde to Harpo's to chronicle the scene for the newspaper. A few days later, Burwell returned to Harpo's and visited with bar manager Stephen Savage for the complete play-by-play. "So they stationed the largest bouncers they could find at the door on 10th Street, hauled away the lovely female employees who were originally stationed at the door and made a valiant stand that made the owner and his insurance adjuster very, very happy," wrote Burwell, who treasured his Saturday visits to Memorial Stadium until cancer robbed readers of his prose in 2014.

After a brief standoff at the door that saw the kids who had hauled the goal post down to Harpo's peacefully turned away by the bouncers, things got even more interesting. They dropped the Day-Glo green post in the middle of the street, one piece in front of Harpo's and another a half-block down in front of the Japanese restaurant Sake's, and began turning them into souvenirs.

Burwell wrote in his article: "'All these students started coming out with buzz saws and circular saws and hacked off pieces of the goal posts,' Savage said. 'By the time I left here about 4 in the morning, they were still out here cutting away, passing out pieces of goal posts to anyone who wanted one.'" The goal posts were sliced into souvenirs that night that now reside on desks, mantels, and bookshelves around the state.

Selected Bibliography

For generations, Missouri fans have been blessed to read from talented and prolific writers on the beat. To supplement dozens of firsthand interviews for this project, many published stories provided rich context and quotes for various chapters of this book. From the *Post-Dispatch*, the work of Hall of Famer Bob Broeg, Dave Dorr, Jeff Gordon, Vahe Gregorian, Bernie Miklasz, and Jim Thomas were handy in shaping the stories you'll read in these pages. From the *Columbia Tribune*, the work of colleagues and great friends Joe Walljasper and Steve Walentik were helpful as well.

A special mention here, too, for former *Post-Dispatch* columnists and colleagues Bryan Burwell and Joe Strauss, both taken by cancer much too soon. For both, their final writing assignments were on Mizzou's campus. They were gifted writers and treasured friends.

Mizzou historian and statistics whiz Tom Orf is an ally to everyone in the press box. His vast and meticulous collection of stats and box scores were invaluable for this undertaking.

Two books were by my side throughout this project: Broeg's iconic *Ol' Mizzou: A Century of Tiger Football*, and its hardwood peer, Michael Atchison's *True Sons: A Century of Missouri Tigers Basketball*. Any Mizzou collection is incomplete without them. Norm Stewart and Dan Devine's memoirs were also excellent sources. John McGuire's 2004 dissertation on the history of Mizzou radio broadcasters was a gold mine of information. A special thanks to the staff at the State Historical Society of Missouri for their assistance. Any day digging through the Society's Norm Stewart collection is a day well spent.

In addition to the *St. Louis Post-Dispatch* and *Columbia Daily Tribune*, the following publications and their archives were helpful: the *New York Times, Sports Illustrated, The Savitar,* and *The Missouri Alumnus*, along with websites pro-football-reference .com, basketball-reference.com, and the Pro Football Hall of Fame's online archive.

The following books titles were especially valuable resources:

Atchison, Michael. *True Sons: A Century of Missouri Tigers Basketball.* Virginia Beach, VA: The Donning Company Publishers, 2006.

Broeg, Bob. *Memories of a Hall of Fame Sportswriter.* Champaign, IL: Sagamore Publishing, 1995.

———. *Ol' Mizzou: A Century of Tiger Football.* Columbia, MD: Walsworth Publishing Company, 1990.

Devine, Dan and Michael Steele. *Simply Devine: Memoirs of a Hall of Fame Coach.* Champaign, IL: Sports Publishing Inc., 2000.

Godich, Mark. *Tigers vs. Jayhawks: From the Civil War to the Battle for No. 1.* Olathe. KS: Ascend Books, 2013.

Stewart, Norm and John Dewey. *Stormin' Back: Norm Stewart's Battles On and Off the Court.* Champaign, IL: Walsworth Publishing Company, 1991.